THE SUCCESSORS

Henry Irving – The Antique

THE SUCCESSORS

by Laurence Irving

RUPERT-HART DAVIS
London
1967

Printed in Great Britain by
C. Tinling & Co. Ltd
Liverpool, London and Prescot

'Emperors don't have sons,
they have successors'

Peter the Great
by Laurence Irving (1871-1914)

After seeing this play at the Lyceum,
the Prince of Wales, later King
Edward VII, quoted this line when
the author, having played the name
part in his father's absence, was
presented to him as 'Henry Irving's
Son'.

ACKNOWLEDGEMENTS

THE STORY of my mother's childhood and adolescence has been pieced together from many sources, notably from the letters and publications of her sister and brother-in-law Mr (later Sir Edward) and Mrs E. T. Cook. I am, therefore, much indebted to Mr Douglas Duff for his permission to quote from these sources and for his kindness in sending me relative extracts from my uncle's diaries. From my cousin, Lady Hartley, I gained in our lively conversations an insight into the characters and accomplishments of the Baird family, particularly of my grandfather John Forster Baird and of his four elder daughters, and with her kind permission I am able to include two of Gertrude Baird's drawings among the illustrations.

For the revelation of the boyhood and the early youth of my father Henry Brodribb Irving and of his brother Laurence, I am wholly indebted to my cousin, Miss Irene Stoney, who gave me all the letters they had written to their mother Florence (later Lady) Irving, and by so doing made it possible for me to appreciate the psychological stresses of their upbringing.

My father's wooing of my mother, and the testing time between their betrothal and their marriage are recollected very largely from the letters he wrote to her at that time. In quoting those letters I have not, I believe, betrayed my parents' confidence or intruded upon the reticence that they and their generation preferred. For, after my father died, my mother herself edited them with a view to publication. I am very grateful to my sister, Lady Brunner, for putting at my disposal all the family records in her possession. I am much obliged to Mr H. G. Dixey for his recollections of the Dragon School and to Mr J. Lynam for his permission to publish the letter from his uncle, the famous 'Skipper', to my mother; and to Mr Reginald Jennings of Marlborough College for his kindly search through his records for traces of two eccentric Marlburians. My thanks are due to the executors of Sir Max Beerbohm for allowing me to include his letter to me and the text of his broadcast on my father as an appendix, and to the

Society of Authors for permission to quote from the Dramatic Criticisms of George Bernard Shaw.

As in times past, my warmest thanks are due to Mr A. P. Ryan for reading my manuscript, and for his sound advice which emboldened me to persevere in my presumptuous venture. All who have been lucky enough to have an enthusiastic and capable secretary will know how grateful I am to Mrs Philip Hayesmore for her continuing patience and industry. And to the affectionate perception of my friend the late Harold Child I owe the discovery of the semblance of my mother in the dedicatory lines from Spenser.

Above all, it is to my wife's steadfast care and faith through a time of stress that I owe the will and capacity to resume an undertaking that both of us have very much at heart.

CONTENTS

ILLUSTRATIONS

To

D. F. I.

1873-1933

So euery spirit, as it is most pure,
And hath in it the more of heauenly light,
So it the fairer bodie doth procure
To habit in, and it more fairely dight
With chearefull grace and amiable sight.
For of the soule the bodie forme doth take:
For soule is forme, and doth the bodie make.

Edmund Spenser

FOREWORD

Autobiography is inevitably a presumption. The subject must presume that his life has been of such matter as to call for an apology, and should therefore apologise for his presumption in making it. He may presume his unique achievement, his impulse to interpret his experience for the benefit of others, or the appetite of the public for a peep through the keyholes of forbidden chambers that he has been privileged to frequent. He may presume a duty to express his gratitude for blessings received or his grievance for misfortunes he has suffered. And the presumptuousness of the autobiographer becomes grosser as the years go by and the evidence of this presumption grows more and more voluminous.

What excuse, therefore, can I make for my own presumption? Conceivably anyone of my generation, that has spanned an epoch of violent social and aesthetic upheaval, imperilling and bewildering mankind, can boast mere survival as something of an accomplishment. Nevertheless I think my presumption would have lain dormant had not goads of circumstance pricked me into an awareness that in the face of autobiographical challenge I must take positive or evasive action; and, having spent too many years in situations where evasion was culpable and even merited death at dawn, I have taken the positive line of least resistance.

If I am found guilty of vain presumption I must inculpate the late Geoffrey Faber as accessory before the fact. But for his patience and persistent prodding I should never have written the life of Henry Irving. His kindly importuning began in 1938 during the celebration of the centenary of my grandfather's birth. The war spared me from committing myself to a task that I felt was beyond my capacity. The uncertain peace was for me further troubled by Faber's renewed instigations. A windfall of documentation and the confidence that he had instilled in me set me to work. He scarcely winced when I submitted the 300,000 words he had conjured out of me. He and our friend, T. S. Eliot, exonerated me from abbreviations. The mere size of the book convinced me that my duty to my progenitor and to my prompter had been fulfilled. But the hang-over of research and, no doubt, Faber's gentle haunting promoted in me an uneasy conviction that I had not, after all, fully discharged my liabilities.

It had often occurred to me that the significant centuries of the English theatre are out of step with the calendar by fifty years, in so far that each has its outstanding player and dramatist—names that immediately spring to mind at the mention of their particular period. Together Shakespeare and Burbage were the acme of the 1550–1650's, Betterton and Congreve of the 1650–1750's, Garrick and Sheridan of the 1750-1850's. As long as the recorded history of the English theatre runs Irving and Shaw will be the most memorable figures of the theatrical century that ended in 1960 and was remarkable for unprecedented reforms and innovations in stage practice. Irving died in 1905; his sons, Harry and Laurence, followed in his tradition until too early death spared them from witnessing the disintegration of a system that he had largely created and they had sustained. And here was I in 1960 at the end of a theatrical career that, though in no way comparable to theirs, had involved me deeply in the vicissitudes of an art that now they would scarcely recognise as the one they had served.

Thus I found myself in a position to view in continuity and at close quarters this latest century of the English theatre through the eyes of one family that, one way or another, had run the course and in some degree had ordered its direction. Encouraged by the realisation that, in effect, my life of my grandfather could constitute the first of such volumes as would be necessary to encompass such a project, I herewith offer up the second. It is to some extent concurrent with the first in that it recounts the childhood and adolescence of Irving's sons as they grew to maturity in the shadow or the radiance (as one may choose to regard it) of their father's lustre. It begins and ends with my birth and that, for the time being, is the measure of my autobiographical presumption.   L. H. I.

PART I

THE ROARIN' GAL

'Thou art thy mother's glass and she in thee
Calls back the lovely April of her prime.'

WILLIAM SHAKESPEARE
Sonnets

I

I WAS BORN in the early hours of April 11th, 1897. It was Easter Day. My delivery, a difficult one, at the hands of the pioneer woman doctor, Mary Scharlieb, had been *avant garde*. Yet within a few hours of my birth liquorice effigies of me were being sold by street vendors to atavistic members of the public with an instinctive urge to absorb something of the beauty and fertility of their goddess by consuming Trilby's baby.

For my mother, when she was but twenty-one years old, had won fame and the hearts of London playgoers by the innocence and charm of her performance as du Maurier's heroine in Tree's production of the play at the Haymarket Theatre. Her feet, upon which Praxiteles might have set his Artemis, were for their classic beauty and daring bareness the toast and talk of the town. Scarcely a year ago the road from Southampton Row, where we now lay together in Russell Mansions, to St Pancras Church had been thronged with crowds eager to see her wedded to the eldest son of their long-established theatrical idol, Henry Irving. Now, in a haze of fatigue and contentment, she heard the bells which rang in her married life ringing for matins. In a little while the Vicar, that dear, ugly saint Luke Paget, would be climbing up to his crow's-nest pulpit of Fairlop oak to preach his sermon, affectionately embracing his congregation in a roguish glance of wide-eyed wonder as though it was always a pleasant surprise to find anyone had come to hear him. Perhaps Mrs Paget would be allowed to see her for a few minutes later in the day. She certainly had prior claim as a visitor. For without her amused help and practical foresight the wedding day would have been even more chaotic than it was—with Harry so absent-minded and his brother Laurence, the best man, distracted by Tolstoyan misgivings recently acquired in St Petersburg.

How pretty her room was. She had planned it for this very moment. It was as cheerful and up to date as crackling chintzes and gay wallpaper and white paint over the mahogany fixtures of Russell Mansions could make it—very up to date with its *papier-mâché* baby's bath, gold and white, portable and raised to a convenient height on four elegantly turned and fluted legs. The sun would soon be over the meridian of Southampton Row and flooding through the lace curtained windows. The house seemed quiet.

Had anyone given Harry his breakfast? Perhaps he was still asleep; probably, after two performances on Saturday followed by an anxious and sleepless night. How lucky they had been during these last months to get an engagement together at the St James's Theatre with Alexander in *As You Like It*—she had not given up her part as Phoebe until someone in the audience had called the attention of the management to certain indications of the shepherdess's loss of innocence. And how had things gone last night at the Lyceum? The pains were beginning to be bad just about the time the curtain was rising on the first night of *Madame Sans-Gêne*. It would, of course, be Ellen Terry's evening. It was daring of her to challenge comparison with Réjane, who had made the part her own. It would be amusing to see how the lanky Antique (as Irving's sons nicknamed their father) could button himself into the part of a round-about Napoleon. They were all anxious for his success after the disastrous season following his accident on the first night of *Richard III*. But when she saw him last he seemed well enough and, as usual, supremely confident. At first in awe of him as a father-in-law, she had come to love this strange lonely man for the affection and kindness he had shown to her ever since her engagement to Harry.

How time had flown since Mr du Maurier had, after their first meeting, called her approvingly a 'roarin' gal'. What had she done to deserve the success and happiness that had crowded the years since she left school? She had to confess that in her desire for independence she had forced the pace a bit; but she had only tried to make the most of the opportunities that came her way. And looking back on it, all the paths she had followed led to Harry—though even he had hesitated to be bowled along at the spanking pace her guardian angel set her. Yet here she was, a bit battered but gloriously fulfilled, in her pretty room full of flowers, with friendly telegrams fluttering through the letter-box like autumn leaves—and with Harry's child, their son, in her arms. What strands of heredity, of circumstance in time and place, of random occasions and chance encounters had been woven into the fabric of this sunlit Easter morning?

The wide white sands of the Northumbrian coast between Lindisfarne and Dunstanburgh are pierced here and there by outcrops of black volcanic rock, great bastions of basalt masonry holding the ceaseless charge of the North Sea upon the low sandstone shore. The most massive of these obstacles lies athwart a gap in the dunes opposite the outlying reef of the Farne Islands; it is also the most grotesque—a primeval reptile stranded by some cataclysmic ebb, its horned tail trailing northward, its head half turned in blind bewilderment towards the breakers fringing its armoured sides. Its shoulder stands a hundred feet high.

Saxon defender and Danish invader in turn held this natural fortress, improvising with wood and stone strong points where natural features could be turned to their advantage. When Norman engineers and masons were set to work to mould the steep escarpment into a masterpiece of military architecture, they linked the dorsal notches of the rock with curtain walls, towers and baileys enclosing eight acres on the summit where they set a turreted keep, its corners orientated to deflect prevailing gales. And through the hundred and fifty feet of embattled rock they drove a shaft to the sweet clear water cupped in the sandstone springs.

Bamburgh Castle had only one gateway, portcullised and flanked by circular towers barring the steep ascent from the south-east. It looked and was impregnable. For never in its long history had its garrison yielded to force of arms until Edward III wrested it from the supporters of the Scottish king, by which time it was sadly in need of repair. Soon it ceased to have any military significance. But it became the background for this present story when Queen Elizabeth appointed Sir John Forster, warden of the marches, governor of the crumbling fortress. The Forsters were native to the place. Their manor to the westward of the castle, until the suppression, had been the house and oratory of the Friar Preachers since the reign of Henry III. Later Sir Claudius Forster received a grant of the castle and manor from James I. By the end of the seventeenth century the title and manorial land had passed to Sir William Forster and the castle to his great-nephew Thomas Forster of Etherstone, whose mismanagement of the estate led to its forfeiture to the Crown at the turn of the century.

Thomas Forster was evidently a feckless fellow. At the time of the Jacobite rising he had the misfortune to be chosen, owing to his local influence and social position, to command a ragged army of retainers and friends stiffened by a detachment of Highlanders. The fact that he was a Protestant with Jacobite sympathies led Lord Derwentwater to hope that he would overcome local anti-papist prejudices. On finding himself confronted by the King's army at Preston, with great common-sense but with disregard of the passions of his officers (one of whom tried later to assassinate him) he immediately surrendered and was soon reflecting on his inglorious career as a general in Newgate prison. Elsewhere some seventy-five Northumbrian noblemen and gentlemen were cooling their Caroline fervour in lock-ups and prisons as a result of his military inadequacy. Thanks to the courage and enterprise of his sister Dorothy, he made a serio-comic escape from Newgate and fled to France, where he died at the age of thirty-two and so would have passed into oblivion had not Sir Walter Besant celebrated his sister's exploit in a novel named after her. To cover his tracks after his escape a mock burial was held in St Aidan's Church, Bamburgh, with a coffin appropriately stuffed with sawdust. After a decent interval his remains were brought from France to be laid beside those of his devoted sister in the family vault.

Sir William Forster had died in 1701. Three children survived him —Dorothea, Ferdinand who succeeded his father as M.P. for Northumberland, and John. Five months later in Newcastle Ferdinand was enjoying a convivial gathering of the members of the grand jury of Northumberland when there entered to them Mr John Fenwick of Rock singing a popular local ballad—'Sir John Fenwick's the flower of them all!' Sir John had, like Ferdinand, been an ardent Jacobite, and four years earlier for his boldness had lost his head on Tower Hill. The fact that the more discreet Ferdinand still had his head on his shoulders, and that Fenwick's song implied criticism of his survival may have provoked them to attack each other; but their friends separated them and regarded the affair as settled. Next morning, however, by ill chance Fenwick and Forster met near White Cross. The altercation was renewed, swords were drawn and Forster was killed. Fenwick was hastily condemned and as speedily hanged upon a piece of timber between the gaol and the gaoler's house, the gates of the town having been shut for fear that colliers from his mines at Kenton might attempt a rescue.[1] The surviving John seems very naturally to have been all

---

[1] Earlier annalists of the Forster family attributed this murder to Sir John Fenwick. The authority for the above account was Mr Edward Collingwood, Recorder of Newcastle at the end of the eighteenth century whose father had been an eyewitness of these events. For this I, of Forster descent, am much indebted to Mr Hugh Pagan of Fenwick descent. In return I am ready to concede that Sir John was indeed the flower among our irascible ancestors.

for a quiet life—content, according to his epitaph, in his 'true affection to the church, the monarchy, his country and his sister'. For our present purpose he is memorable for having left a descendant, Matthew Forster, who was buried in Bamburgh churchyard in 1780.

Dorothea, after all these misfortunes, enjoyed a brief spell of happiness. Shortly before her father's death, she was wooed and won by the recently widowed Nathaniel Crewe, baron and bishop of Durham. She had been his first choice when, at the age of fifty-eight, he sought what he no doubt would have called domestic felicity. But she had refused him and he had consoled himself by marrying Penelope, Lady Tynne. It cannot be said that he was an attractive character. Soon after he was ordained he had gained the patronage of the Duke of York at whose Romish practices he was ready to connive, becoming in turn Dean of Chichester and Bishop of Oxford. Trimming his way through the turbulent reign of James II, he assisted at the degradation of Bishop Compton of Durham and was rewarded for his services with the vacant See. He left discreetly for Holland when James abdicated, returning to London the day before the period expired for taking the oath of loyalty to King William and Queen Mary. This and a handsome down payment to the Crown restored him to his See.

When he married Dorothea Forster he was sixty-seven. She was twenty-four and it would seem that there must have been some inducement to set off the disparity of age and the unenviable reputation he had rightly earned. Perhaps Dorothea changed her mind because her future husband had, since she first refused him, purchased from the Crown the castle and tenements of Bamburgh, so that her affections were shared between the Bishop and the *genius loci*. Throughout the fifteen years of their married life she helped him to redeem his past by restoring the castle (his gains, if ill-gotten, had been considerable) and making it the home of charitable institutions which later were nourished and perpetuated by the energy of his trustees.

The descendants of Matthew Forster, forsaking their unrewarding responsibilities as landed gentry, moved first to Alnwick and then to Newcastle, where wider and now respectable opportunities were to be found in the professions. By 1800 one of them, my great-grandfather John Forster, had taken his medical degree. Forster was a common enough name in Northumberland and there were many of them in Newcastle. Though there is no evidence of their close relationship, another John Forster grew up in Newcastle about the same time—the friend and biographer of Dickens. This would be of little significance did it not suggest that a taste for the arts persisted in these Northumbrians even if it only found expression when they moved south to a warmer climate of appreciation. My great-grandfather stood his ground in Newcastle, where he became a distinguished and honoured surgeon. The Forsters had always been a good-looking lot; by marrying Miss Potts, renowned in Newcastle for her beauty, my great-grandfather endowed his progeny with a dominant tendency to eyes as blue as the periwinkles on the dunes at Bamburgh and to fair complexions tough enough to be enhanced by exposure to the harsh Northumbrian winds. He left an enduring memorial in the shape of the first freestone house to be built in the town for a hundred years, anticipating and perhaps inspiring Grainger's rebuilding of the city in stone in 1835. This he did shortly after inheriting from his brother-in-law, William Baird, properties near Alnwick and at Yetholm on the banks of Bowmont River in the Border country. To comply with conditions of entail he undertook to assume the name of Baird, thus exchanging the proven and romantic ancestry of the Forsters for the shadowy claims of his Uncle William that the Bairds were the descendants of the Chevalier Bayard. But he did it with a flourish, obtaining by Royal Licence a grant of Arms and Crest 'exemplified to him and his descendants by Patent' displaying the bugle horns of the For(re)sters and the Boar of the Bairds—the latter having been granted to an earlier Baird by William the Lion whom, while out hunting, he rescued from the onslaught of a wild one. Happily these latest Bairds were of a generation too previous to be called upon to live up to their combative motto—*vi et virtute*.

He continued in practice, though it became increasingly evident that his skill was not matched by the robust health and nervous stamina needed to operate on half-conscious patients, probably in a frock coat kept for the purpose, stained with blood and pus and host to septic agents too often claiming the life that his surgery had saved. Sometimes after major operations he was himself in a state of collapse. The strain became more than he could stand. He died a comparatively young man in the early 1840s.

At that time his eldest son, John, was in his second year at Trinity College, Cambridge; his school days had been spent inconspicuously at Rugby under Dr Arnold. A place had been sought for him at Balliol College, Oxford. Evidently Thomas Arnold and John Forster Baird were on friendly terms. In 1838 Baird had invited his son's headmaster to stay with him in Newcastle for the meeting of the British Institution. Arnold replied that he could not accept this invitation.

...even if the time would allow of my absence from here. Yet I am so little of a scientific Man that I have always felt that I should be out of my Place at such a meeting, while, on the other hand, my Time in Westmorland is so important to me for my own writings that I scarcely allow myself to spend any Part of our Vacation elsewhere... but I shall not easily forget your kindness in giving it.

Your son is quite well and getting on well, I think, in his Form... I would myself have applied to the Master of Balliol on his behalf, but I have made it an invariable Rule never to apply for any Boy at this School except on public Grounds—that is, when a Boy is doing so well that I can really recommend him for admission at a good College, Honoris causa. Even this however would be useless at Balliol, for the Master told me some Time since that he was engaged for so long a Period that he did not like to enter any new Names on his List; this was his Answer when I applied to him in Behalf of my own eldest son.

In the event, though he could not in the public interest recommend young Baird to the Master, he was able to find enough honourable reasons for his son Matthew to jump the queue and land safely in the college of his choice. Although the Master's crowded list and the headmaster's scruples deflected my grandfather's course from Oxford to Cambridge, it was fated that Balliol should play its part in shaping the destinies of later Bairds.

Finding himself solely responsible for the management of the family estate, and realising that his mother, two sisters and a younger brother would be dependent upon him, John Baird left Cambridge and read for the Bar with the intention of practising in Newcastle. In due course he was called, though too faintly for him to shut his ears to more delightful occupations that life seemed to offer him. For by then he must have been as conscious of his talents as others were aware of his wit and charm. Thanks to the well-conducted theatres in Newcastle and Sunderland, with their excellent stock companies and visiting stars, he had become an enthusiastic playgoer. The burlesque, which invariably made up the double bills, awakened in him ambitions as a librettist. For all this, he found plenty of time to train as a rifleman in the Northumberland militia and to take part in its military and social exercises —the latter traditionally more rigorous than the limited evolutions of the parade ground.

But painting was his true bent. His natural facility as a draughtsman had been stimulated and refined by his friendship with the young landscape painter, Alfred Hunt. He must have met Hunt first when the latter was travelling in the Border country to fulfil a commission for John Wyatt, the Oxford print-seller. The two young men were equally undecided on their futures. For Hunt, a scholar, a winner of the Newdigate Prize and a fellow of Corpus Christi College, it was not easy to reject the security of an academic career in favour of the hazardous life of an artist. His friend, for whom the law had little attraction, had less difficulty in persuading himself of his true *métier*, assured as he was of the means to follow in some comfort the footsteps of Turner and Ruskin in search of the picturesque. Under the eye of Hunt he developed rapidly as a draughtsman, using his pencil accurately and sensitively in the style which Ruskin was to epitomise in his *Elements of Drawing*. He could not have had a better master. Hunt, who later became closely associated with the pre-Raphaelites, used colour with fastidious purity and lively effect. His pupil, though he soon learnt to forswear the use of body colour except as a tonal accent when sketching and to master the luminous, crummy technique of what Delacroix called the 'dry' English school, expressed himself with a more limited palette. He would no doubt have made his mark among Victorian painters had not private means and a natural modesty enervated his ambition. He became content to fill his sketch books with graphic studies, and was not easily persuaded to carry them further. He never acquired the professional competence to organise a picture in oils, which he found unsympathetic as a medium. His strength lay in composition and drawing; his weakness in a reluctance to commit himself to the arts. I remember very well a sombre study hanging in my grandmother's bedroom of Edinburgh Castle taken from the road running beneath it to the south; it was dramatic in its unusual and well-realised perspective and authentic in its atmosphere.

Thus committed at least to seeking a wider field of activity than Newcastle, in 1854 he married Emily Jane Brinton, the daughter of Henry Brinton of Kidderminster. Her sister, Martha, had already married Frank Crossley, thereby uniting the interests of two families who were carpeting the rapidly expanding empire not imperially red but with those dark encarnadined arabesques which were to warm the feet and confirm the well-being of their customers for the next hundred years. Emily Brinton was a deeply religious woman; in the home she made for her husband no day would begin without family prayers.

Yet he seemed to have no difficulty in persuading her to share his artistic interests or to approve his taste for the theatre.

They had not long been married when Baird was invited by Mr E. D. Davis, the actor and impresario, to write a burlesque for the occasion of the opening of the new Lyceum Theatre, Sunderland, recently risen from the ashes of the old Lyceum, which had been burnt down the previous year. The main piece in the bill would be Lytton's *Richelieu* in which Mr Davis's brother Alfred would play the Cardinal. The young librettist rose to the occasion and produced, as the day bills announced:

> *...a highly successful New Piece of Oriental Sentimentality or Sentimental Orientality, extracted from Dreams of Arabian Nights by the indefatigable Visionary* HOO-ZURE-ATAR *and which to be appreciated must be seen, as the most extravagantly laudatory encomiums must fall immeasurably short of the gigantic merit of*

THE ENCHANTED LAKE!
or
THE FISHERMAN AND THE GENIE

The author's style conformed to the comic convention of the period exemplified in the pages of *Punch*—his rhymed couplets appropriately laced with puns and extravagant archaisms. Most of the fun was derived from the impact of the magic on the mundane—a theme which, unredeemed by boisterous comedy, would be the mainstay of classic ballet and acceptable to its most sophisticated patrons. Further north, in Edinburgh, Mr Wyndham of the Theatre Royal could rely on similar *libretti* by a young journalist, William Archer, the latter's last fling before he assumed the gravity of the dedicated dramatic critic and the champion of Ibsen.

Baird and his young wife attended the first performance. With the rest of the audience they were eager to applaud the courage of Mr E. D. Davis in rebuilding his theatre, for he was a popular and respected local figure, having for many years furnished Northumbrian playgoers with the finest talents the English theatre had to offer. Tonight his hands would be as full as his heart was charged with emotion, personally responsible as he had been (and now proudly advertised) for the direction of the architects, masons, decorators, joiners, gas fitters and upholsterers who had lavished their art and skill on the new building. No less would be the demands made upon his brother Alfred. Not only as Richelieu would he challenge comparison with the great Macready, who had played the part in Newcastle shortly before his recent retirement, but as stage manager he would have to be alert for teething troubles that a new theatre and an untried company would be natural heirs to.

The curtain rose on *Richelieu*. The opening line 'Here's to our enterprise!' was spoken without much assurance by a young actor (habitués marked him as a newcomer) whose elaborate dress and properties were of a quality that his position in the company would scarcely warrant. In fact, though entirely dependent on Mr Davis's approval and his meagre salary as a probationer, he had spent a small legacy in equipping himself as best he could for this occasion. Had the Bairds consulted their programme they would have identified him as Mr Henry Irving, making his first appearance on the professional stage. In the second piece he would hardly be noticed among the Sultan's cooks (*Song:* 'Here you see a wretched crew!') riotously broiling a magic fish caught in the enchanted lake. No doubt the librettist was impatient for the end of *Richelieu*. Mr Davis had spared no expense in the mounting of the extravaganza. For the dances he had engaged the Viennoise Sisters; the orchestra was 'numerous and efficient', worthy to accompany his versatile brother Alfred as he wrung the hearts and stirred the local patriotism of the audience by singing ' 'Tis a place of beauty rare' and 'The Keel Row'.

All in all, it was a memorable evening for my two grandfathers so briefly and unwittingly in conjunction. Baird returned to Newcastle already determined to move to London; Irving, equally determined on London, had barely set foot on the long and rough road that eventually would lead him thither.

Shortly after this Baird's mother died. His sisters and his brother William, who was still at Oxford, were sent off on reconnaissance to London. Before long the whole family, including my grandparents' first infant daughter, were settled uncomfortably in a house in Belgrave Road—uncomfortably because my grandmother and her sisters-in-law were wholly incompatible. In due course, however, William Baird took orders, and his sisters left to keep house for him in the East End parishes he served. This made things easier in Belgrave Road for the time being and eased the strain that was never wholly relaxed between the restless father and a mother who soon found herself with five daughters of markedly different character and temperament. All shared their parents' good looks; the round head, golden hair and blue eyes of the Forsters tending to dominate the sharper modelling and dark colouring of the Brintons. Mary, the first child, was from the start robust and forceful, sharpening the edge of her natural imperativeness by having to take a hand in the bringing up of her younger sisters. The second, Emily, was as a child inclined to be morbid and delicate. As she grew up she threw off her physical frailty and masked her morbidity with an ironical sense of humour; only those close to her, and they were few, were aware that she was afflicted with an obstinate jealousy ever at war with her amiable nature and bedevilling the affectionate relationships with her family and friends she so much desired. There followed Gertrude, a child haunted by a mystical genius, secretly expressed in drawings of intimidating round-headed wide-eyed children, unnaturally mature, composing themselves in sinister detachment against elaborate architectural backgrounds as reminiscent of Brueghel as her macabre studies of gaunt princes attended by wizened familiars were of Hieronymus Bosch. So successfully did she conceal her strange gift from her sisters that they were surprised and not a little awed by the quantity and eccentricity of the drawings they found hidden away after her death. Nevertheless her haunted piety was as much a joy to her mother as her gaiety and invention were to her sisters, for she was the mainstay of the entertainments that they created for themselves—writing plays when called for and poems for the exercise of her own tenebrous imagination. Evie and Lilian were in a simpler mould; the latter was her father's favourite, quiet, good and companionable, but with that vulnerable gentleness which invites affliction.

John Baird soon arranged his life in a pattern that suited his nomadic tastes. Home was to be no more than a temporary base for foreign excursions. The Garrick Club provided the congenial male company he enjoyed; a rifle club in Wimbledon helped him to feel that, in the nation's hour of need, he would be a credit to the militia. Most of his time and resources were spent travelling abroad with his family in train, the children in the stern but devoted charge of their nurse 'Atty' Johnson, ever on guard to protect them from foreigners whom she regarded with distaste and suspicion. He led them through Switzerland and Northern Italy, even to the Tyrol, where the first two babies were carried over the Tête Noire in panniers slung on donkeys. Here, for the first and last time, he used his gifts with pen and pencil to some profit, preparing the first edition of Bradshaw's *Guide to the Tyrol*. His love of sketching never cooled, but as the years went by he became less and less inclined to elaborate his sensitive and promising studies.

The home bases were shifted frequently for reasons of convenience or economy. After moving to Richmond and a bleak wintering in Lowestoft the Bairds settled in Teddington, where, following a prolonged lull in child-bearing, my grandmother gave birth to her sixth daughter, Dorothea Frances.

II

'**D**A, GIVE ME YOUR BIG BROWN HAND!' Dorothea remembered very clearly demanding this of her father; less clearly she remembered him as a golden, handsome man, curly-haired, lightly whiskered and deeply preoccupied. Probably she never knew that her father's golden curls were attached to a wig; as a boy he had lost his hair following an attack of typhoid fever. Too soon the freckled hand, pale and wasted, would lie in hers for the last time before it was withdrawn forever.

Until her birth nothing had ever occurred to disturb the integration of a family self-sufficient in the nomadic life they led and content with the transient social backgrounds this entailed. The elder girls, the youngest of whom was now twelve, had as infants thrived in the care of their nurse Atty and had made the most of a broad, if haphazard, education by fifteen successive governesses, by sporadic spells in Swiss and German schools, by their mother's concern for good handwriting and religious observance and by the casual and cosmopolitan friends and acquaintances their gregarious and vivacious parents attracted wherever they went. The first cloud on their wide horizen had been some recent anxiety about their mother's health, for which a cure at Schwalbach was prescribed. While the parents were away Mary was left in charge of her sisters. A year of Sunday-school teaching in Teddington had developed her bent for managing children and winning their affection; contrarily, her mother, having inculcated the religious fervour which had quickened Mary's sense of social obligation, had discouraged the expression of it in good works, fearing perhaps they might induce in her an earnestness forbidding to eligible suitors. Now, no doubt, she was glad enough to be able to leave her children in such capable hands.

Mary's task was not made easier by having to cope with the 'vulgar and injudicious' nurse engaged to look after the baby. But it had been arranged that she should take them all to her beloved aunt Martha Crossley at Somerleyton Hall. There her only domestic cares would be the correction of the nurse and the restraint of her kindly and indulgent aunt, so prone to spoil her own or her sister's children. At Somerleyton Hall, a large Victorian mansion set in acres of inviting shooting, Frank Crossley had established an outpost for his social and political activities beyond the confines of the carpet factories of Halifax—ambitions which the Kidderminster Brintons seemed to lack. As a Liberal he represented Halifax in the House of Commons, and in due course his many benefactions to the town earned him a baronetcy. This passed, all too soon, to his only son, Savile, then a boy at Eton; his widow was left to manage his estates and to see to the upbringing of his high-spirited heir. This present visit was to have far-reaching consequences on the destinies of the Baird girls, not least on that of the infant of the party.

It looked as though Dolly Baird, with five transitory sisters, one of them old enough to be her mother, was in for a lonely childhood. When she was a year old, Gertrude withdrew into the Elysian shadows from which she had never wholly emerged. Her legacy of weird drawings and rapt rhymes left her sisters wondering at her brief and detached sojourn among them. Almost immediately her place was filled by the arrival of a seventh girl, Margaret, and Dolly was assured of a nursery companion.

Another and happier disruption followed two years later. At Somerleyton Mary had met a young Oxford undergraduate, Arthur Lionel Smith. Smith's mother had been widowed when he was a boy. His father was a civil engineer of considerable inventive genius, lacking, unfortunately, the capacity to attract money for the development of his projects. His family were left in poor circumstances. To the relief of his widow, some of his friends obtained a nomination to Christ's Hospital for one of his four boys. As luck would have it Arthur, at the age of six, was thought to be the most likely to benefit from the preparatory and public schooling the Bluecoat School had to offer. While he was there, his mother married again. Her husband, an American, carried her off to Chicago, where she became a Swedenborgian, one of a sect given, as Mary wrote later, to a 'vague and mystic optimism'. In her case vagueness amounted to forgetfulness of her children and optimism to a careless disregard of Arthur's material needs. Fortunately she had been a close girlhood friend of Martha Brinton who later, as Lady Crossley, did what she could to remedy this. The great promise that Arthur showed at Christ's Hospital encouraged her to see that financially he was able to follow up the school and college exhibitions he had won by

Daniel O'Callaghan.

John Forster Baird.

Drawings by Gertrude Baird as a child. *Top*, 'The Pied Piper' (six of the children are believed to be portraits of the artist's sisters). *Bottom*, 'Fantasy'.

entering Balliol College in 1869. Thereafter Somerleyton became his home and his money worries were relieved by his employment as a tutor to supplement the efforts of Eton to educate his benefactress's son Savile.

Lady Crossley was a woman of dominating personality. The Brintons were inclined to seriousness of mind often leavened by a gaiety of disposition; the Crossleys to physical exuberance curbed by a solemn regard for social proprieties. Evidently Savile was going to take after his father. His mother regarded sport as frivolous, if not downright mischievous, and found it hard to reconcile her love for her son with her instinctive disapproval of his aptitude and enthusiasm for games at the expense of scholarship. It fell to Arthur Smith to persuade her that sport in moderation engendered character, and the boy that Balliol was a desirable goal if he was to discharge the obligations that his father's early death had imposed upon him. Thus, the debt he owed Lady Crossley could be repaid by winning the confidence and affection of her son. For this task he was perfectly qualified; the measure of his success would be in retaining their life-long friendship and regard.

When Mary first met her aunt's protégé her hands had been overfull with the cares of a foster-mother—but not too full to be off now and again with her high-spirited cousin and his energetic young tutor. Arthur's job was no sinecure. By day he thrashed about the Broads in his pupil's yacht or rattled with him in tandem or coach-and-four along the road to Lowestoft; only at night could he persuade the reluctant scholar to attend to the amount of bookwork needed to get him through Responsions.

Further meetings at Somerleyton made clear to Arthur and Mary their affection and admiration for each other. Only some uncertainty as to how he was to earn a living delayed their engagement. After a creditable but not remarkable career at Balliol he was elected to an open Fellowship at Trinity College. But as there appeared to be no future for him in Oxford, where he would have found the life and work most congenial, he began to read for the Bar—not half-heartedly, for it was not in A. L. Smith's nature to do anything by halves, but perhaps without much enthusiasm.

I am sorry to leave Oxford [he wrote to his disinterested mother], *where the work is so congenial, and if I had £200 a year of my own would spend a year in study abroad and then come back to teach here, instead of involving myself in the 'nice sharp quillets of the Law' in*

B

London. But a Fellowship that is stopped, and with it one's definite career, by the comparatively innocent process of marrying, is not a fair thing to depend upon.

When Mary's father was told of their betrothal he, not unreasonably, was cool at the idea of the first of his quiverful of daughters marrying a man with no certain means of supporting her—a graduate, moreover, of a university and particularly of a college which Cambridge men had come to regard as a hot-bed of atheism, and a youth with evident gifts as a raconteur that threatened to rival his own in the so far undisputed preserves of his own dining-room. At first he insisted on a period of probation. Then, when perhaps some inner voice warned him that time was short, he agreed to their engagement in 1877, his practical objections having been overcome in part by the offer to Arthur of a lectureship in modern history at Balliol. In 1879 Mary was married from her home in Teddington. After an unconventional honeymoon— Arthur rowing his bride in a skiff (her hands ominously on the tiller ropes) down river from Oxford—they returned thither to set up house in Crick Row. By establishing this bridgehead over the frontiers of learning, Mary unconsciously was realigning the axis of her sisters' lives. This may have crossed the minds of the elder ones, since their sister's marriage had made them aware of their own eligibility. But Dorothea, as she came to earth after the first heady flight of her own gregarious spirit at the close of that wedding-day, had no idea that the departing bride and bridegroom had among their sparse luggage the Pandora's box of her predestination.

My grandmother, already harassed by trying to implement her husband's unrealistic ideas of economy, and, perhaps, by a sense of inadequacy in having failed to give him an heir, now suffered two grievous blows. Her youngest child, Margaret, was found to have a tubercular infection of the bone in her upper arm. After a successful operation all appeared to be well with her. Not long afterwards, she and her nurse, while out in the neighbouring country, were caught in a heavy rainstorm. She was brought home drenched but apparently none the worse. A few hours later she ran a temperature; what was at first thought to be a severe chill was diagnosed as rheumatic fever; more probably it was poliomyelitis. For a time her condition was critical. When the fever abated it was all too evident that she would be crippled for life. My grandfather, easily persuaded that the child might benefit by the change, moved his family to Hampstead. Scarcely had they settled in their new home when he himself sickened and six months later died.

The sudden loss of this warm-hearted, accomplished, pleasantly eccentric and always unaccountable father must have left the children dazed and bewildered. Here was too early an end of continental wandering, of the charm of making fleeting friendships in foreign lodgings, of moving restlessly from place to place, yet secure in his confident direction. My grandmother, much bereaved, left as she was with none too large an income, with three daughters of marriageable age and two infants—one of them to need perpetually the kind of care so hard to provide—was so stricken that her gaiety and wit, though charted indelibly in the wrinkles round her troubled eyes, were submerged in her lasting grief. She would find consolation only in her religion and to this she turned with increasing devotion.

There would be no more Bairds in that line. The legal contrivances to ensure their continuity had failed, nor do any other Forsters appear to have sought their ancestry in Bamburgh. All that remained of the elaborate lineal arrangements were the arms granted to old John Forster displayed upon the back of his son's now empty dining-room chair.

Dolly Baird was a child of the transition. Cradled in a family with firmly established social and moral values, in her childhood she would feel the tremors of impending upheavals; in her adolescence she would begin to question the validity of the codes and conventions that had sufficed her elder sisters. Nature had, however, endowed her handsomely with the capacity to meet the challenge of the years of change that lay ahead. Temperamentally and physically she was well equipped to take her coming emancipation in her stride.

Her nursery life was illumined rather than overshadowed by sharing it with her crippled sister. Already Margaret, with a disposition as radiant and zestful as her own, was coming to terms with her cruel handicaps, now recognised as likely to be lifelong. Gradually, as one by one the older girls left their home to be married, the pattern of the life of these two young children and their bereft mother began to take shape. The key to this pattern lay in the robust daughter of a Worcestershire farmer, Anne Baynton, who had been engaged as Margaret's nurse. From the moment she arrived at their Hampstead home, this young untrained girl, with tender compassion and a readiness to bring her gentle humour to bear on situations in themselves well-nigh unbearable, grappled successfully with physical and psychological problems that might have daunted a more skilled but less courageous attendant. For, orthopaedic treatment being in its infancy, the alleviation of spinal curvature and extensive paralysis was a matter of experiment as painful to administer as to bear. By trial and error methods and appliances had to be contrived to lift the prostrate child from her bed to a chair where she could be supported in a position that would enable her to develop and to exercise such very limited muscular activity as was left to her. For some time to come each day would have its prologue and epilogue of suffering made endurable only by the patient participation and rallying exhortation of a devoted nurse. Margaret could never be left to sleep alone; throughout her lifetime Anne Baynton was ever at her side. Soon the love of her two charges was expressed in the nickname 'Duck'. As soon she regarded and spoke of Margaret as 'my child'; and as 'her child', by providential survival, Margaret died sixty years later in her arms.

Dolly's extrovert and pitiful affections were deepened by constant care and consideration for her sister—a task made easier by the growing evidence of Margaret's bright intelligence and determination to overcome her disabilities. Before long their physical disparity was forgotten in their absorption in interests and amusements shared. If now and again they were parted, when Dolly went to visit Mary at Oxford, nothing was lost in the description of these excursions in such contrast to their secluded and preoccupied life in Hampstead.

She was four years old when she made the first of these visits. Already Mary remarked that she was 'a very active, long-legged and ambitious child'. Once when she met some rather aggressive boys of her own age in the Parks she challenged one of them to a race and won it. The boy, whose parents were friends of the Smiths, in the bitterness of his defeat burst into tears. He lived to become Deputy Master of the Mint; perhaps this early humiliation deprived him of that self-assurance which makes men Masters. Before she reached her teens it was apparent that she had inherited the physical characteristics of her ancestor, Dorothea Forster—'the delicate features, blue eyes, light hair, a complexion beautifully fair and the sweet, good-tempered countenance' that an antiquary had detected in a portrait of Bishop Crewe's wife in Bamburgh Castle. Yet for all her good nature she was developing an independence of mind bewildering to her mother and not a little disconcerting to her sister Mary. While staying with the Smiths on holiday at Sea View, she returned one day from the beach to tell Mary that she had made friends with a very nice little girl whose father sold hats. Realising that she had shocked her sister's sense of propriety, she added: 'But you see, he doesn't sell one hat or a few, he sells hundreds.' Mary was at a loss to understand how wholesale could be 'more honourable' than retail trade. She, like so many other women enjoying the fruits of the industrial revolution, had already forgotten that her social and material advantages were derived from the carpet mills of Halifax and Kidderminster, insulating herself in protective gentility against the realities of commerce. Though carpets were made to be sold, the selling of them was thought to be the concern of a lower caste. Only in the phenomenal sellers' market of the time could such attitudes have been afforded. When world competition became keener, such deeply ingrained prejudices delayed the awakening of English manufacturers to the fact that salesmanship was not only 'honourable' but vital to their survival. Nearly a hundred years would pass before the elegant members of our Embassies would recognise the commercial attaché as an acceptable and indispensable member of their communion. Dolly's acceptance of the hatter's daughter as an eligible friend was a straw in the rising wind.

In the middle eighties, when the Baird girls were frequent visitors to their married sister, the Oxford scene in which the Smiths were now playing an active part had changed very little since what Sir Geoffrey Faber has called 'the ecclesiastical civil wars of 1836'. Today a student peering into that society, so much more remote from his own than can be measured by the passage of years, cannot but marvel at the innocence and unworldliness of the sheltered life enjoyed by fellows and undergraduates alike. Though the outside world had begun to array itself for cataclysmic collisions barely thirty years distant, the minds of those entrusted with preparing that generation of young men for the political and administrative duties they would naturally assume were largely preoccupied with dreams of Utopias, with the imminence of a millennium or with controversies over Christian dogma that now seem artificial and almost frivolous. Few had heeded the distant minatory rumbling of the guns of Sedan; fewer were aware of the approaching death of Karl Marx or of his disruptive legacy that earnest disciples were already propagating in troubled corners of the world beyond the long shadows of their dreaming spires. Certainly no such uncomfortable realities had been allowed to intrude upon Oxford's grave contemplation of doctrinal intricacies and the ceaseless analysis of Plato.

At that time the small introspective world of the University was predominantly male. Mary Smith was but the twenty-first female to be included in the circle of 'University ladies'. On the other hand, almost every member of the academic staff was a man of marked and often eccentric individuality. Dusty though the scene may have become, each actor in it appeared to be under an obligation to assert his characterisation, and in most cases to enhance his *persona* with elaborate and often impressive make-up. Within their jealously defended enclave, they could develop and parade their mental and physical idiosyncrasies, confident that they would never have to discard them by forced conformity to the herd, or to impair their integrity by submission to the rough disciplines that would be the common lot of succeeding generations.

Almost the only sign of impatience with this complacent and stultifying orthodoxy was to be found in Balliol. There an effort was being made to encourage the English ruling class to break out of what was later described as 'the closed circle of their island minds'. Benjamin Jowett had exerted his influence on this College for forty years; for ten he had been its autocratic Master; his recent election as Vice-Chancellor of the University would enable him to sow the seeds of his enlightenment over a wider field. However parochial his outlook may now seem, he had every justification for believing that in Balliol he had created a dynamo to generate the powers necessary to administer an expanding empire. His college was already spoken of as 'a nursery for public men'. If the infant proconsuls were persuaded by their stern but animating nurse that mankind was, on the whole, well intentioned and biddable, it was because he and his disciples were convinced that the world was bound ultimately to recognise the wisdom and benevolence of their authority. If their lessons had now and again to be enforced by chastisement, the dirty work would be done by others. That the dirtiest work was afoot in almost every corner of the politically conscious world seems not to have entered Jowett's innocent head. He was intent that British affairs, domestic and foreign, should be politely administered. For better or worse his doctrine prevailed until 1916 when the electorate, recognising in the nick of time the harsh realities of the outside world, dismissed the quintessence of his persuasion, Asquith, and put its faith in the ruthless, capable but impolite hands of Lloyd George.

Even so Jowett had long ago learned to curb his enthusiasm for reform. He was still smarting from his conviction in 1855 by the Chancellor of the University for heresy following the publication of his speculation on the nature of the Atonement, and from the humiliation of having to endorse the Thirty-Nine Articles under the eyes of his accusers. Among other things, he was determined to liberate the University and the town from the puritanical bonds that restricted their full participation in the Arts. Fifteenth on the list he drew up of the aims he hoped to achieve as Vice-Chancellor was the encouragement of undergraduates to perform Greek and Shakespearean plays and, no doubt, at the back of his mind, the provision of a reputable theatre in the town where the best plays and the most accomplished players of the time could be seen. Support for this cause came immediately from a, perhaps, not entirely unexpected quarter, the Rev. Charles Dodgson of Christ Church. Writing to the University Press recommending the prospectus of a proposed 'dramatic school' the author of *Alice in Wonderland* insisted that:

> ...the stage, as every playgoer can testify, is an engine of incalculable power for influencing society; and every effort to purify and ennoble its aims seems to me to deserve all the countenance that the great and all the material help that the wealthy can give it; and even those that are neither great nor wealthy may yet do their part.

The letter was also published in the *St James's Gazette*. If it caught the eye of Henry Irving, now in the full flight of his endeavour to promote the theatre to the public esteem accorded to the other Arts, it may have directed his attention to Oxford as an academic centre ripe for conversion, and to the planning of a demonstration there which, with Jowett's support, proved to be so successful.

The Vice-Chancellor's efforts in this direction were helped undoubtedly by the enthusiasm of the response to Ruskin's lectures in Oxford, appealing, as they did, to the lethargic to recognise the relevance of art to the good life; less helpful were the aesthetic extravagances of Pater, in whom his opponents were only too ready to detect a subversive decadence. Ruskin's term as Slade Professor was drawing to a close; only his contemporaries were embarrassed by the eccentricity of his concluding utterances. The light of his vision had fallen impartially on the recently graduated Cecil Rhodes, Oscar Wilde and Arnold Toynbee, and would soon be reflected in their diverse decoding of his cryptic message. Things in Oxford were on the move, but in a direction mercifully concealed from those who had set them in motion.

The Smiths scarcely had settled in their house in Crick Road before the almighty Jowett revealed to them the part they were to play in his creation. The successful matriculation of Savile Crossley had not escaped his notice, fleeting though this sprint of scholarship had been.

In the scheme of things it seemed desirable that no son, however back-
ward, of a noble house or of any distinguished Englishman should be
denied the benefits that he and his college had to offer. It would be hard
if, because the public schools had failed to awaken in them a capacity
for passing examinations, they should lose the chance of developing
their latent powers by 'steady work', and waste their time in idle folly
they could too well afford. Reading parties of undergraduates, which
Jowett regarded as his invention, had proved that recreation and study
were not incompatible. Could not something of the kind be devised to
provide skilled tuition in a homely atmosphere for acceptable young
gentlemen academically stranded by their failure to matriculate while
still at school? The success of reading parties had depended on accommodation at some agreeable inn. The lads he had in mind would require
closer supervision and a less distracting environment. What better than
to board these slow but well-born starters with this gifted young tutor
and his mettlesome wife for as long as was necessary to enable them,
with care and coaching, to gain entry to his college? The Smiths, glad
enough to supplement their modest income, at first demurred only
because they were planning a holiday abroad and were expecting their
first child to join them in the course of it. The bachelor Master saw no
obstacle in this, and had a young peer in mind ready for immediate
experiment. In due course the Smiths' child was delivered in Baden-
Baden, and their pupil to his examiners, to everyone's satisfaction.
Thereafter the Smiths' home, in addition to the regular arrival of further
babies, was rarely without a lodger or two, most of whom came to
look back upon their eccentric hosts with gratitude and affection.

The reader might reasonably assume that this scene has been set for
a romantic *dénouement* in which the Baird girls in turn marry handsome
if not brilliant lordlings and, by quartering their boars' heads and
bugles with nobler arms, rescue the Bairds of Bowmont River from
heraldic oblivion. Although as constant visitors to Crick Road and to
the seaside lodgings of vacational reading parties the doors of the House
of Lords seemed wide open to them (for they were lively and good-
looking girls), in the event it was scholarship rather than escutcheons
which won their hearts.

This period at Oxford was celebrated by a jingle long remembered
at the Union which included the lines

'...in the palmy days of Milner,
Curzon, Cook and Wise.'

Each of these young men had in turn been President of the Union and had presided over debates unmatched until Hilaire Belloc and John Simon faced each other across the despatch box in the nineties. Milner in 1875, Cook in 1879, Curzon in 1882 and Wise in 1884 exercised gifts of oratory rarely found in undergraduates. All were equally accomplished speakers; they differed only in style—Milner dry, witty and precise; Cook graceful, humorous and merciless in logic; Curzon studied and ornate. Wise appealed to his hearers with his boyish eloquence; he was less serious of mind than the others, cutting something of a dash with resources denied to his friends and gaining an athletic blue, distinctions that led them to nickname him affectionately the Bloody One. All except Curzon have their place in this story, for each wooed or won one of Mary's sisters. Milner was much attracted to Emmie, though they were never engaged. Bernard Wise married Lilian and carried her off to Australia, where he became Attorney General for New South Wales. Evie, while on a visit to the Wises, met and married a promising young scientist, Richard Threlfall and so placated the shade of John Forster Baird by giving him at least one Cantabrian son-in-law. Cook, after a youthful engagement which came to nothing, fell deeply in love with Emmie and she with him. Of them all, we are concerned most with Edward Tyas Cook, for it was upon him that Dolly Baird would depend for the wise and affectionate guidance that she might have expected from her father.

III

J OHN FORSTER BAIRD'S choice of a home for the family he left
disconsolate behind him could not have been more conveniently
placed for the education of his sixth daughter, Dorothea. A short
walk from the house in Fitzjohn's Avenue over the hill to Maresfield
Gardens brought first her prospecting mother and, in due course, the
eager child to the South Hampstead High School for Girls. There
Dolly began her school life in the summer of 1886. She was the first
of the Baird girls to attend school regularly; if she seemed to her
mother less gifted than her elder sisters, who had managed very well
without such advantages, the keen appetite she showed for communal
life would justify the experiment. Dolly was eleven years old when
she began those daily journeys in term-time, outward bound brisk
with the day's prospects, homeward more leisurely with time for
welcome distraction and to contemplate the homework in her
satchel.

She was tall for her age and inclined to be plump, but her large
hands indicated that she would fine down as she grew taller. Her brown
hair fell loosely over her shoulders; beneath a full fringe veiling her
high forehead the steady gaze of her grey wide-apart eyes was at once
direct and scrutinising, yet with a hint already of an innocent pathos
that later would move her audiences to tears. Beneath a strong, finely
moulded nose her generous mouth, animated with humour, belied her
wistful glance and, in smiling, accentuated the chubbiness of her cheeks.
The observant would have discerned a strong chin as yet modified by
her childish fullness of face, indicating that she would not be deflected
easily from actions prompted by pity or conviction. There was something about her of Slavonic gravity and strength of feature. In her
smocked summer frocks, full-sleeved and sash-waisted, and in her
heavier winter dresses, severely cut, with dark velvet bands at neck and
wrists, she would not have been out of place in an album of Turgenev's
pensive and reticent young ladies. Yet she was essentially extrovert and
naturally gregarious—the answer to the prayer of Mrs Grey and her

fellow-founders of the Girls' Public Day School Trust for the ideal schoolgirl. In fact, she was a pliant twig ready to be bent by a curriculum designed, as Miss Buss professed, to 'inspire its pupils with a feeling of membership of a great body helping to cultivate that collective as opposed to individual feeling which has various forms—domestic, affection, charity, public spirit—but in the fulfilment of which consists the highest happiness'.

All these things would, in due time, colour Dolly's natural predisposition to happiness. Yet she may already have been conscious of an artistic urge that was not in Miss Buss's catalogue, and one that her friend, Miss Beale, would have suppressed firmly had she diagnosed it in any of her Cheltenham girls. For four years she was in all respects a model high-school girl; at the end of them she earned modest distinction by winning prizes for scripture and swimming. The practice of reading out every week the names of the three top girls in each form was an incentive to hard work. There was little religious instruction but, in Dolly's case, this shortcoming was amply remedied at home. In 1889, for her a bumper school year full of honours in a wide range of subjects humane and scientific, she recited on Speech Day, with two other girls, a scene from *Henry VIII*. The trustees of the South Hampstead High School, though less suspicious of the drama than Miss Beale (whose only concession was to invite the Benson company to give her pupils a performance of *The Merchant of Venice* in evening dress and with the unedifying part of Jessica omitted), did not in those early days encourage play-acting. They were, perhaps, aware of the heady effects that the recent elevation of the stage and the recognition of acting as a genteel profession would have upon impressionable girls in their adolescence. If this Speech Day recital first whetted Dolly Baird's theatrical ambition, the means of furthering it were not to be found in Maresfield Gardens. Yet they were not far to seek. Hampstead had already become a mecca for immigrants from Europe. Foreigners were arriving and settling there in force, and many of them were anxious to modify their accents. Consequently, a teacher of elocution, Mr Child, with a small native clientèle in the neighbourhood, began to find himself in unexpected demand. The High School, stoutly opposed to religious, social or racial discrimination, had its quota of immigrant children and through them, no doubt, Dolly discovered that Mr Child could teach her the rudiments of acting.

It would not have occurred to her that she was to be the thin end of a theatrical wedge driven into new and promising material. She was neither Bohemian nor rebellious. She had, if anything, too great a respect for authority and herself a tendency to bossiness. When she complained to her devoted nurse that some girls had remarked on this, Duck had replied: 'Well, Miss Dolly, it may not have been polite but it is neither more nor less than the truth!' Her teachers were evidently aware of this:

> *We've had such a row at our school lately* [she wrote to her mother]. *One of the Girls in the L.V. called Annie Voght said that at the monthly exam. of Arith. one of the girls called Ethel Wolfe copied the sums off the board, but it wasn't true, and Annie Voght got no end of rowing and Miss Tammage called Annie Voght no end of names.*
>
> *Miss Firth also is extremely horrid for one day before she came in to give us 4th lesson I stood up and said 'Hush'. Some girls laughed. Miss Firth came in, she saw me standing up saying hush and sent me out of the room; wasn't she a horrid old thing? and I had to take nought for conduct (I didn't do anything).*

If Miss Firth and Miss Tammage now and again tried her patience, her devotion to her tweedy and whale-boned headmistress, Miss Benton, was whole-hearted and lifelong. Miss Benton, weighing up the value to her school of such an exemplary pupil against the risk of other less stable girls becoming stage-struck, may have encouraged a talent that could be useful on Speech Days. Later, during her long reign, the school won quite a reputation for turning out actresses. Successively, Lilian Braithwaite, Gwen Frangcon-Davies and Glynis Johns followed the trail that Dolly Baird blazed through the virgin groves of that academy, and found theatrical fame at the end of it.

In contrast to the intensity of her school-days, Dolly's home life was uneventful, quiet and, at times, dull. Her enthusiams were shared by Margaret. Much of her time was spent helping her sister to enjoy as full a life as her disabilities allowed her. Margaret, by now nicknamed Daisy by her family, had an unquenchable sense of fun, and such pertinacious courage that she was learning even to play the piano with her stricken and almost inert hands. She was a bright child and an avid reader, and with the help of a governess was keeping pace with Dolly in her education. These sisters were, then, perfect companions as far as their physical disparity would allow.

But my grandmother seemed no longer to have the heart to make new friends or to encourage visits by other children of her daughters' age. She had an abiding sense of bereavement and Daisy's condition was to her an unending sorrow. She had ceased to attend the painful ritual as daily the invalid was lifted and harnessed into a sitting posture. 'I can't go...I've now *forgotten* the sad sight and see dear M. as she was...it just kills me to look at her and I do *no* good at all. I'm nervous having "suffered many things".'

Happily Dolly could count on an affectionate welcome to an altogether happier and more normal environment—one as entertaining, amusing and stimulating as any girl could wish for.

E. T. Cook and Emily Baird were engaged some time before Dolly went to school. Teddie, as he was known in the family, came down from Oxford in the winter of 1881. He had won a not unexpected first in Greats but had been a little chastened by failing in 'Divvers',[1] and for this lapse being fined £10 he could ill afford by inquisitorial dons culpably ignorant of his character and capacity. Whether or not his subsequent failure to get a Fellowship at New College was due to the lingering prejudices of his examiners, the suspicion of it put an edge on his financial anxiety. Like his brother-in-law, Arthur Smith, he ate his dinners at the Inner Temple dutifully but without relish; he found he had no appetite for the Law and was not called to the Bar. He took the Civil Service examination, and passed high on the list, but when a Treasury post was not forthcoming he turned his back on Whitehall. Discouraging as these setbacks were, he may have decided already that Fleet Street was his ultimate destination.

At that time John Morley was editor of the *Pall Mall Gazette*, an evening paper of twenty years' standing and now a witness to the Liberal convictions shared by the editor and the proprietor, Henry Yates Thompson. Before he left Oxford Cook had an interview with Morley, whose style and utterances appealed to him. At the editor's invitation he had, since then, contributed articles to the paper fairly regularly. Morley had further endeared himself to the spurned graduate when later he asked him if he was a Fellow of a College, adding: 'No?...then there is some hope for you.' Even then Cook's situation as a free-lance journalist would have been precarious had he not been able to rely for his bread and butter on his secretaryship to the London University Extension Lectures. His duties took him all over London, brought him into the orbit of Arnold Toynbee, and gave him an

---

[1] The Divinity part of Moderations.

insight into the growing demand for adult education, but left him time
to practise his chosen craft.

Morley's editorial staff included two men of radically opposed
temperaments. His assistant editor was William Thomas Stead, an
evangelical liberal, an uninhibited publicist, a turbulent crusader
wearing a sense of outrage as a hair shirt, and ready to accept martyrdom with voluble resignation when, inevitably, he had to endure it.
It was to Morley's credit that, though he detested the kind of sensa-
tionalism his assistant gloried in, he realised that Stead's genius for
journalism could enliven a paper concerned more for its conscience
than for its circulation. As a stable companion Stead could hardly have
had a darker horse or one less of his own mettle than Alfred Milner.
The pattern of Milner's career at Oxford had been similar to Cook's.
He, too, on coming down with equal honours had no very clear idea
of the course he should pursue, and had welcomed Morley's suggestion
that he should try his hand at journalism. As an undergraduate he had
been cool, aloof and old beyond his years; in his precocious gravity he
may have taken after his German mother. He was not the only eminent
Victorian who, by omitting youth, had reduced the stages of life to six.
Though he had left New College before Cook entered it the two young
men had met several times, and, as a result, Milner had kept an eye on
the brilliant undergraduate whose performance as President of the
Union was an echo of his own. Having through his friendship with
Toynbee been concerned in the University Extension scheme, he may
have drawn attention to Cook as its possible secretary. Certainly it
was he who in 1883 wrote from the office of the *Pall Mall* to
Cook:

> *Should you be prepared to consider the idea of coming on here at a
> salary? It is quite in the air as yet and I am not empowered to make
> you any proposals, though Stead knows that I am mentioning the
> subject to you. The sort of notion is that you should come here every
> morning with notes, if notes were wanted—if not, be prepared to do
> any other work, middle articles on general subjects or descriptive
> articles on anything that was going on. It would not take your whole
> time or anything like it, but would be a sort of first charge on it. Waste
> of time, like that involved in your writing good articles which don't
> happen to be wanted, would be avoided. Arrangements might be made
> to prevent its conflicting with University Extension.*

The offer of the appointment was confirmed and Cook gladly accepted it. He had scarcely set to work when Morley, now a Member of Parliament, resigned his editorship. Stead naturally succeeded to the Chair. Beneath Cook's calm and correct bearing there lurked a prankish humour and an inner gusto that may have led him to welcome an editor likely, in his own words, 'to make things hum'. And hum they did during the years when Dolly was at school and her brother-in-law, first as Stead's assistant and later as editor, made the *Pall Mall* a political organ to be reckoned with.

His position, professionally and financially, was now secure enough for him to marry Emily Baird. Though in later years he remarked that Milner's 'bitterness was his weakest point', his colleague seems to have borne him no ill-will for winning the girl he himself had wooed unsuccessfully. As, in the event, Milner did not marry until late in life, his ardour may have been tempered by a cautious instinct not to encumber himself with responsibilities that might confound his ambition. Cook's salary from the *Pall Mall* enabled him to resign as secretary of University Extension Lectures, and to devote such spare time as he had to the study he had already begun at Winchester of Ruskin's vast heterogeneous and uncoordinated works—the prelude to his lifelong service to the master. About this time Stead, following the publication in his paper of his assistant's summaries of Ruskin's Oxford Lectures, received a letter from the lecturer calling his attention 'to a man on your staff who knows more about my works than I do'. Later Cook called on the now frail old man at his London hotel, where he was staying prior to having a minor operation. Though Ruskin by now bore the scars of his mental affliction, though the signs of his physical decay and spiritual dejection were apparent, and though he rebuked the representative of the *Pall Mall* for the vulgarity of its illustrations, the admiration of his devotee was unimpaired. A full account of this meeting was the first entry in a diary begun by Cook in 1887 and kept conscientiously until his death.

The Cooks returned from their honeymoon to a house on the east side of Russell Square. The rent was low, as the block was already doomed to be demolished to make room for the new Imperial Hotel. When the short lease came to an end they moved to No. 6, Tavistock Square. They had been attracted to the house by finding in its small garden an outbuilding that would serve their hobby of photography as studio and dark-room. It soon, however, became apparent that they were not the only tenants of the property. Now and again when they developed plates of portraits they had taken in the studio vague ectoplasmic shadows were seen to be lurking behind the sitters. The place, undoubtedly, was haunted, and they were driven to find less ghostly backgrounds in the garden. Later they discovered that one of the previous occupants of the house had been a surgeon and that it was to the garden-room that body-snatchers had brought illicit cadavers for him to dissect.

Emmie was less disturbed by these manifestations than by seeing one day her old bedroom in Russell Square exposed to public view as the housebreakers picked their first home to pieces. Their increasing resources, and the prospect of living there for some time to come, enabled them to furnish the new house modestly but well in a style reflecting their shared taste for the products of William Morris and de Morgan—one complementary to the glazed book-cases and heavy mahogany writing-desk to which all his life Teddie would be securely moored. Any money they could spare was set aside for summer holidays abroad following Ruskin's tracks and through his eyes re-assessing the treasures of European art.

Emmie was much concerned for her younger sisters. She was naturally at ease with young people and quickly gained their confidence. As time went on she would sublimate her grief at having no children of her own, in winning the affection of nephews and nieces susceptible to her rare gift for entering into their own fantasies. Dolly found in her a receptive and appreciative audience, an amused critic and a mentor more in touch with the outlook and problems of her generation than her mother was ever likely to be. Thus, during those early years, 6, Tavistock Square was a warm refuge from the tensions of Fitzjohn's Avenue.

A letter from Dolly brought Emmie the first whiff of an education so bewilderingly different from her own:

> *I have begun at the High School this Christmas. I like it very much.*
> *Mother can't teach me any more. She used to help me with French*
> *but French isn't what it was. The teaching in the shool is quite equal*
> *to harrow winchester and eton.*
> > *I am your loving sister,*
> > *Dorothea.*

Similar reports were sent from the fleshpots of Tavistock Square:

> *My dear Mother,*
> *   ...We had Alec and Mr Vincent and Alfred and Mrs Cook to*

tea yesterday…[1] *I've got 2 new pieces, all chords. I sang 'Jenny' and all of us sang 'Ring the bell watchman'. Ted Vincent said I mustn't say I made eyes at him. They went away at half past 10 and I went to bed. We had for Menu*

I. Fish Cakes
II. Mutton Cutlets
III. Peas New Potatoes
IV. Roast Beef
V. Red currant tart; cream
VI. Pineapple cream bread Jam
VII. Cut egg and bread
VIII. Cheese
VIIII. Dates oranges.

It's been showery all the morning. We went St Pangrass [sic]. We went out before the sermon. Teddie says I ought to put my Things like this

1 Duty
2 Other people's pleasure
  My own.
He wrote that after Dinner.

                    I remain
                    Yr Affectate
                    Dorothea Francis Forster Baird.

Teddie's postprandial precepts did not fall on deaf ears, though the conscientious practice of them was deferred until the exuberance of adolescence had subsided.

During the summer holidays, when the rooms in Tavistock Square were shrouded in dust sheets while Teddie and Emmie were abroad, Dolly visited her sister Mary at Oxford or the Crossleys at Somerleyton. On the whole she preferred the bustle of Crick Road—helping Mary with her punctual babies, learning to cut out and stitch Ralph Caldecott sun-bonnets and to smock the children's summer dresses—to the decorum that her Aunt Martha (or Aunt Frank, as they called her) insisted upon. This separation from Emmie promoted a lively correspondence. In the summer of 1885 Teddie had gone on holiday shortly after Stead had published his challenging article 'The Maiden

[1] Alec, Teddie's sister, had married Edward Vincent, then upon the editorial staff of *The Times*; Alfred, Teddie's brother, was a master at Winchester.

Tribute of Modern Babylon' in support of a Bill drafted to protect young girls from the dangers of juvenile prostitution, to raise the age of consent, and to permit the victims of this prevalent traffic to give evidence against their seducers. To force the issue Stead had, with the knowledge and approval of several promoters of the Bill, including the Bishop of London, purchased a child from her mother for £2. The child was immediately placed with reliable foster-parents. The opponents of the Bill, however, forced the Attorney General to prosecute Stead for committing a technical offence. It was while the proceedings were pending that Teddie, with cool detachment (for the case was bound to have distasteful repercussions in the event of his Editor's conviction), set off with Emmie for the Tyrol to rediscover scenes familiar in her childhood, her nostalgia sharpened by references to Bradshaw's first Guide to the neighbourhood written by her father and illustrated with his sketches.

A letter from Cortina conveys the affinity between the sisters, bridging their disparity in years.

Sweetest of Children (Don't be offended at my calling you a child will you?), We were so delighted with both your letters, especially the last ones and we felt very ungrateful not to have answered them before—but one never seems to get time when one is travelling about.

I'm always wishing that you were here to see all these lovely places, and we often wanted you, in Venice, particularly when there was a grand fête on the water one night and a splendid show of fireworks, some of which fell into our boat and nearly burned a hole in my frock! —at which I shrieked and held up an umbrella!

I am quite sad to hear that you have already gone to Somerleyton and we shan't see you when you get back...I hope Aunt F. will withdraw the prohibition about the garden now that you are provided with six brown holland pinafores.

The day before yesterday coming in the train from Venice, an Italian lady got in with four nurses, 2 mangy-looking infants and endless bags and boxes. The babies, aged about 2 and 6 months were spotty and sad looking and no wonder; for they were only in the train ½ hour and cried all the time, notwithstanding the 4 nurses; their fond parents supplying them in succession with sips of beer, raw apples, chalk pencils to suck, leather shoes, bottles and penny whistles. The penny whistles were the last straw, so you can imagine what relief it was when they got out. The nurses were terribly grand and well dressed but didn't appear to be of much use. The mother gave the baby the apple when she found it was too raw to eat herself.

We went up a lovely hill this afternoon leading to a pine wood and Teddie found some Alpine roses and wild strawberries…There are lots of peaches, melons and grapes eaten up here, as well as at Venice; and oh! it was so hot there, though it was delightful too for it didn't matter being hot as long as one could be lazy too and just loll about in a cushioned gondola. I wore as few clothes as I possibly could, fewer than ever in my life, and Teddie sat and wrote letters in his shirt-sleeves…he is just as silly about stamps as ever! His hair is nice and long now, and he wanted to go and get it cut every day in Venice but I wouldn't let him.

As Teddie let his hair grow he shed all cares and responsibilities but those avuncular rather than fraternal obligations he had now assumed.

My dear Dorothea,

It was a great pleasure to your kind brother-in-law to receive such a nicely written letter from his little sister-in-law and to hear a good report of her school-work. Now is the time for self improvement; hours mis-spent (and words mis-spelt: 'grammer') can never be recalled and little Dorothea will never regret any trouble she takes to be a good girl and learn her lessons. Little Agatha will agree with this, I am sure, and will not say anything about 'prim and priggish'… This afternoon Emmie insisted on my paddling in one of the brooks and said she would do so too so I took off my shoes and stockings, tucked up my trousers and paddled. But Emmie basely left me in the lurch, and there I was solemnly paddling about with her looking on and the villagers laughing.

He returned refreshed to the *Pall Mall* offices in Northumberland Avenue, and in the robust frame of health and mind needed to face the heroic music that Stead was conducting and was now reaching its clamorous coda. As Teddie had shrewdly foreseen Stead, on a point of law, was committed at the Old Bailey to three months' imprisonment in Holloway Gaol, where, from his cell, he continued to conduct his campaign with pardonable self-righteousness, and to edit his paper without much consideration for his staff. Milner had left the *Pall Mall* discreetly on the eve of the prosecution. Cook took his place as assistant editor. But Stead's behaviour after he had served his sentence strained the loyalty of his colleagues and exasperated Yates Thompson.

At a stormy interview with his proprietor Stead resigned, exulting in dreams of higher endeavour, which materialised in his becoming founder-editor of *The Review of Reviews*. On New Year's Day 1890 Cook was appointed to the chair with Stead at his elbow as political editor. This impractical and uncomfortable arrangement happily was short-lived, for after a week or two Stead did not return to the office.

In the autumn Dolly spent her mid-term holiday with the Cooks, and with them went to see Henry Irving and Ellen Terry in *Macbeth* at the Lyceum Theatre. She must have been lost in wonder at the sumptuous production, at the wide gloomy Scottish landscapes, at the tenebrous interiors of Dunsinane and at the eerie supernatural effects. In her critical innocence she was blissfully unaware that she was seeing these two great players for the first time in parts that suited neither of them. If she surrendered to Irving's magnetism and to Ellen Terry's inappropriate charm as Lady Macbeth, she was the more puzzled to hear Emmie and Teddie discussing the play when they got home. They agreed that Ellen Terry was better than they expected but that Irving's conception of an 'aesthetic drawing-room Macbeth' was absurd and that his diction compared unfavourably with his partner's; in ironical and semi-humorous passages he had been very good, but for tragedy they found him lacking in reserve and his 'clipped words horrible'. But whatever second thoughts their criticisms gave rise to, this first experience of the enchantment of the theatre awoke in Dolly the stirrings of a new and irresistible allurement.

During those Christmas holidays she visited her Uncle John at Moor Hall, Stourport, where the Brintons had established themselves on an estate conveniently close to the carpet mills of Kidderminster, but as well out of sight of them as Somerleyton was from those of Halifax. There John Brinton presided over her mother's clan—a handsome and genial patriarch as elegant in manners as in appearance, his disposition as inflexible as his waxed moustaches, and his figure so shapely for his age as to lead his irreverent grandchildren to suspect him of wearing corsets. He was, however, by no means strait-laced, and encouraged his children and his guests to celebrate Christmastide with Dickensian exuberance. Dolly found all this a pleasant change from the rather self-conscious rectitude of Somerleyton, where even the sportive Savile had begun to show signs of being weighed down with hereditary dignities and responsibilities. She was soon caught up in a whirl of festivities, including house-party theatricals, a visit to the pantomime in Birmingham, and a full programme of dances in the neighbourhood;

the best of them given every year by the Broomes, who, by providing
the yarn for the Brintons to spin into carpets, were sharing and
thoroughly enjoying a prosperity that nothing but linoleum could
threaten. Dolly blossomed in this frivolous environment, and made
the most of the unaccustomed attention of a lady's maid devoted to
her appearance.

I got here very well [she wrote to her mother] *after a very nice and
warm journey. It is very jolly here, we skated this morning on a 2 ft
pond, a hard frost but the ice waved like billows on the briny ocean.
Ask Daisy if she remembers Emma. She is very nice and does my
hair and sees after me in a magnificent way.*

*I am sorry I have not written before but we have been so busy and
everybody has been ill. Reg. has congestion of the lungs so Bob had
to take his part. Kitty has bonafide Russian Influenza and everybody
takes a turn at being in bed.*

*Thanks very much—the gloves fitted beautifully. On Wednesday
The Tomkynsons gave a mixed grown and children's dance. There is
a Cinderella ball at the Jones tonight. Jack asked Uncle John if I
might go. He said I might. I think I shall want another pair of white
satin shoes for the Hayman's dance.*

She and her cousin Jack, now an ensign in the 2nd Life Guards,
evidently were inoculated by gaiety against any morbid infections.
She found her cousin, Cis, 'a darling' and Patty too, though on closer
acquaintance the latter proved to be 'a regular little demon of the 1st
order...always either rowdy or unhappy. I am very sorry for her because
she gets snubbed so but she really requires snubbing.'

We had skating for three days [she wrote later], *and then the frost
gave which was a good thing in its way as we have so much to do
rehearsing. I am to be the good Fairy Pantarista, a very nice part,
with plenty to say! By the way I never told you what the play is going
to be—The Sleeping Beauty. Patty is going to be it (Sleeping Beauty)
and she has only two lines to say. Sibyl is going to be a Duchess, Bob
the Queen Wasabella, Roger King Whatwazee, Mr Clarke Pactotum.
Mr Clarke is a friend of Jack's, he is very nice and most funny.*

*The Broome's party was very nice. We went a party of ten, three
carriagefuls. Kitty frizzed my hair and consequently the whole family
(Uncle John included) begged me always to wear it so. I can waltz
quite well. I danced 2 dances with Reg, 2 with Mr Clarke, 6 with Bob*

and 1 with Walter, Patty and Sybil. The reason I danced such a lot
with Bob is (1) because he suits my style and (2) because our vacancies
fitted. Everyone admires my fan and I never enjoyed anything so much
as staying here. I have made my dress (for the fairy Pantarista), at
least not the seams and the cutting out all the sleeves. It is extremely
pretty, the skirt is a white muslin petticoat trimmed round the edge
with gold fringe and Brussels net skirt draped over it covered with
gold stars and a white muslin body trimmed with gold fringe...

Yet in the midst of all this unprecedented fun, she found herself looking
forward to the end of the holidays and to the delightful and thrilling
duties that awaited her at Maresfield Gardens. An invitation from
Mary to Oxford was refused '...as I'd rather not miss the first days at
school'. When the house-party dispersed Uncle John escorted his
niece to London, marvelling that beneath those frizzed curls there
lurked so serious a mind, and that this pretty and talented young
woman who had entered into the junketings at Moor Hall with such
gusto could be transformed, as by the Fairy Pantarista's wand, into
the earnest schoolgirl he parted from at Euston Station.

No wonder that Dolly was eager to be back at school. The two last
terms ahead of her were full of promise. She was now head girl,
enjoying the trust of the staff, the love of her friends and the adulation
of her juniors. With any luck she would win prizes for Geography,
Scripture and Maths; she would lead the school teams in games sym-
bolic of the modern girl's emancipation. When the time came for the
last emotional farewells, all these things had been fulfilled. She had
rewarded her adored Miss Benton by gaining the Board's Certificate.
On her last Speech Day she had recited a passage from *Coriolanus* and
had measured the validity of her still secret ambition by the applause
of her audience. That she would be long remembered by her schoolmates for her zest, her beauty and her good nature never entered her
head.

IV

A T THE END OF THE SUMMER TERM Teddie and Emmie decided that the time had come to take Dolly abroad with them. This was a holiday they had all looked forward to; for none of them did it turn out at all as they had imagined. Emmie confessed to herself that the idea of taking Dolly with them was a partly selfish one prompted by a curiosity to see the effect of travel on 'a young mind fresh from the stimulating power of a High School education'. When they all met at Charing Cross Station Dolly was still trailing the clouds of her end-of-term glory, and evidently only partially aware of the magical significance of the train that would take them to Dover. Emmie noted with pleasure how many people looked at her sister admiringly. Dolly's striking beauty and youthful grace, without a trace of gawkiness, was set off by a simple travelling dress of blue serge picked out in red. She enjoyed the breezy crossing, and did full justice to a delicious lunch at the Calais Gare Maritime. But once in the train on the journey to Basle she saw through the window, not the wide sweeping landscapes of France, but a mirage shimmering with nostalgic visions of the South Hampstead High School. She had brought with her two school books—one on history, the other on experimental chemistry—and for Emmie's benefit she made a show of studying them. Her sister was unimpressed, though fascinated and a little disconcerted by these first reactions to her experiment. Laying the books aside, Dolly gazed once more out of the window.

'Dear me,' she said. 'How like abroad is to England!' And as they neared Basle and dusk began to fall, she murmured wistfully: 'This time last week the Upper Sixth would have been going down to prep.' The night journey interested her, until, while Emmie sat through the night racked with headache and pondering on the mysteries of higher education (how could one practise chemistry on a train?), she fell into a deep sleep and was only roused with difficulty in the early hours of the morning—no less radiant and rosy than the dawn.

Yet the letter she wrote to her mother from Locarno would have reassured Emmie that her experiment was already a qualified success.

Friday August 29th/90
Hotel Locarno
Suisse
Lago Maggiore

My dearest Mother,
    We are now immersed in mountains and most unfortunately also rain, thunder, mist and lightning. We got to this beautiful place at 4 p.m. yesterday, have been exactly 30 hrs. on our journey.
    It was very exciting (the journey I mean). The crossing was not rough, only a ground swell. It rained hard all the time so we were obliged to retire to the covered deck. Those French people are horrid; directly we got on board and even before the Calais-Douvre had begun to paddle, they called for basins and remained in that condition for 1¼ hrs. after which they managed to eat more than us at the Calais dinner.
    We got to Calais about half past one and started for Basel at two p.m. The scenery of this part being nothing particular I composed myself to try to sleep and Em and Teddie read.
    Teddie bought us each a delicious French roll and butter at Amiens, and we managed to keep ourselves together until Table d'hôte at Tergnier 7 p.m. (25 minutes allowed for everything). How we gobbled! 5 courses—soup, meat, chicken etc. etc.
    At Laon we each got a dear little white pillow, with a small engine worked in red cotton. We composed ourselves to sleep, for my part rather to rest as to sleep is rather a difficult occupation in the train. The hrs. dragged on, and after we had passed Chalons (2 a.m.) I fell asleep. Roused by Em at 3 a.m. 'Come wake up'. Hot coffee and rolls.
    I stumbled up and reeled on the platform. It was a queer sight, about 50 dishevelled looking people clustered round a long table in the centre of the platform. Quite dark except for one little light (it was the hour before dawn). We began our hot coffee (and before 2 hrs. how we wished we had not).
    The guard of the train is like Arthur when he times us in the Geography Game. 'Cinq minutes, quatre...trois...partenza...Deux...partenza...un minute PARTENZA...'
    Soon after 3 Teddie and I were attacked with spasms and for about 3 hrs. great were our sufferings.

Watching the dawn breaking was very pretty.

9.13. Arrived at Lucerne. The chalets of Switzerland are very pretty indeed. We changed at Bâle, I forgot to say, and went first class, the carriages are very good indeed only five seats in one compartment (sometimes you have green velvet armchairs).

The St Gothard was most exciting. You can see the line you go on ever so high above you...you wonder how you get there.

Em has been awfully sick and there was a lavatory in our carriage and she went there three times and was sick—very.

We were exactly 18½ minutes in the St Gothard tunnel 9 miles long.

This is a huge hotel with 200 bedrooms and last night there were 12 people at table d'hôte only. However Em has just told me to come to the window to look at the 'arrivés' from the station.

Please don't forget to bring that pink frock home and send it to school.

Menu last night:
Soup.
Fish.
Beef Roast with tomatoes and new potatoes.
Aspic Jelly with pate de foie gras.
Chicken and salad—Celery and sauces.
Ice pudding and cake.
Dessert. Wine.
Before we went into the tunnel we had a quarter of an hour's Luncheon at Goschenen at the very top of the mountain.
Menu:
Soup—
Salmon—
Roast beef—
Chicken—
Pudding—
Dessert—

Your very loving
D. F. B.

My grandmother, noting that the last sheet was almost unused, wrote fretfully on it 'Then why all this left blank—perhaps to leave room for the next menu!' If the modern schoolgirl seemed unduly preoccupied with food, she was, after all, but a pioneer of the vast army of British travellers who in years to come would boast of their gastronomic discoveries, and at long last would awaken the nation's conscience to the shortcomings of its own cooking.

On the climb towards the mountains Dolly chattered away about her geometry mistress and school friends. When Emmie called her attention to the first view of the Alps, she broke off to remark: 'They don't look very high.' They settled for a day or two near Monte Rosa. Emmie and Teddie were keen walkers. Dolly, after a tentative sortie, declared that walking knocked her up.

'Nobody goes in for walking now. We play fives and cricket!'

On the last stage of their journey to Venice Emmie made a final attempt to improve her sister's wayward mind.

'There,' she cried, as they came upon the promontory of Sirmione and the blue Garda glittering in the sun, 'is Catullus's villa!'

'Do you know him?' asked Dolly, with a flicker of interest.

When Dolly yawned at the first glimpse of the Lagoon, Emmie, remembering vividly her own wonder when she first saw the golden prospect, knew that her hand-to-mouth education had had its advantages. In Venice Dolly found much to excite her interest—though little that needed interpretation by Ruskin. 'What a heavenly place!' she exclaimed as she led Emmie from one sham jeweller's shop to another. San Marco did not distract her from window-shopping. Looking at churches made her so giddy that often she had to be helped back to their gondola. The Palace of the Doges seemed to impress her.

'How many Doges were there?' she asked.

'Only one,' answered Emmie. 'They reigned in order like kings.'

'What a very big house for one Doge,' was the comment of the Shakespeare reciter.

Dolly found Venice too enervating for letter writing.

> *Fondamenta Bragadine*
> *San Vio—609*
> *Sept. 15. 1890.*

My dearest Mother,

> *We are all very well and hope you are well too, except I feel very dobsy. I am going to bathe. I don't feel like letter writing at all. I like this place very much indeed and I'm going out now.*
>> *With much love,*
>>> *Yr. ever loving*
>>>> *Dorothea Baird.*

On this my grandmother commented: 'This letter is a disgrace to the High School. It ought to be shown to Miss Benton.'

Dolly was critical of Venetian family life. Of the lightly-clad but robust-looking children she remarked cheerfully: 'They'll die!', in the firm belief that life without Jaeger was a chancy affair. The sight of them eating *gelati* in the *trattoria* far into the night while their parents gossiped and sipped *grappa* appalled her. Emmie's tolerant dissent did not alter her conviction that in hygiene and higher mathematics lay the hope of the new world the Girls' Public Day School Trust had inspired her to serve. On the way home the cooler winds of Bergamo dispelled her dobsiness and roused her to write a letter that would have gratified Miss Benton.

> *Bergamo.*
> *Monday, September 22nd.*
>
> *My dearest Mother,*
>
> *I know it is somewhat in the past since I wrote last also we have had no letters from you so I cry quits...we had nice lodgings at Venice, kept by two poverty-stricken old maids, one of which went by the name of Luiga Dante. They had a fresco of Dante in the hall so must have been some relation to him.*
>
> *Our gondolier Antonio was quite a charming person, and dark but not sulky. It was very curious having all one's meals at a Restaurant. You will feel for me I am sure when you learn that I didn't have any fruit for six days, I felt like Tantalus surrounded by water and never drinking. Grapes 1d and 2d a huge bunch, large figs 8 a 1d, peaches equally cheap.*
>
> *We left Venice at 4 p.m. Saturday and got to Verona at 7 p.m. It is a lovely place and we went to a very swell expensive hotel. We encountered a very Suffolky county family. You know the sort of manners and customs of the B—s and D—s, a very loud voice and striding manner—horrid people. The cooking and everything there was excellent and therefore our feelings were slightly outraged by our arrival at this inn (very Italian it said in the Guide Book, very unclean in reality). However we are going on to Como tomorrow and the people are obliging.*
>
> *The weather in Venice was quite cloudless and therefore we are surprised in finding that it has rained more or less elsewhere in the hills...Em and Teddie bathed five times at the Lido and I did twice for I was not up to it the other times. Our packages have now*

*increased wonderfully. What they will ascend to at Paris I really
don't know, however I have not spent all my money yet though Venice
shops were very tempting…I am quite 'up' in school news having had
a letter from Nellie Taylor.*

With heaps of love to yourself and everyone.

Yours ever lovingly,
Dolly.

Emmie and Teddie were not disheartened by the unexpected reaction
to their experiment. The following summer they took Dolly to
Germany with much the same result.

*Emmie and I have been buying Xmas presents. The German shops
have such jolly toys. I am knitting a pair of 'Pulzwarmen' you will
be glad to hear (or rather sorry I suppose). One I will send to Mary
as a sample.*

Yet, long after this innocent abroad had forgotten these perverse
attractions, an incident of not much significance at the time became
the most vivid recollection of those memorable holidays. Somewhere
near the slighted Monte Rosa the party came upon an elderly English
gentleman resting near a wayside *ex voto*. He had a bristling grey beard
and moustache clipped back from his full sensitive lips; under heavy
black brows his tired whimsical eyes appraised them; a sparse wiry
forelock strayed across his damp forehead. He greeted Teddie as a
friend. What passed between them had been over Dolly's head. Yet
her impression of this encounter was lasting. The old man was Samuel
Butler. Perhaps he managed to convey with a twinkle his sly sympathy
for this tall, self-assured girl who was not taking anything on trust.

The early nineties were years of upheaval and readjustment for the
Cooks and the Bairds. In the summer of 1892 the Liberal party was
preparing for a General Election with high hopes of defeating the
Unionists, in spite of the hurt it had suffered through Parnell's betrayal
of Gladstone. Cook had a flair for political diagnosis; he had earned
Gladstone's gratitude for the way he had handled that affair, and had
done what he could to put heart into the Liberal candidates, but he
was not very sanguine of the party's chances. In the event the Unionists
resumed their long tenure of office; the Liberal leaders despondently
licked their wounds. Teddie and Emmie set off by themselves for
their holiday—well earned not only by the editorial stresses of the

past months but by having for the last two years shared their treasured weeks of escape with their beloved ingénue.

Their holiday was more than half spent when, on a sparkling September morning as they were starting on a drive from Biella to Varallo, the landlord of the inn where they were staying ran after them with a telegram. It was from one of Teddie's staff. Ominously it warned him to await the arrival of a letter that had been posted to Biella. Even if he had an inkling of what was afoot he was quite unprepared for the shock of the news the letter brought. The *Pall Mall Gazette* had been sold over his head. He hastened home. If the new proprietor proved to be of a Liberal turn of mind it might be possible to ride the storm of change, and to adjust everything but his conscience to the new conditions. But he found that the negotiations had been devious— as distasteful to him as they were bizarre.

The manufacturer of a non-alcoholic beverage, Kops's Ale, by name Lowenfeld, had made an offer for the paper to Yates Thompson, ostensibly on behalf of a Mr Dove Keighley of the National Liberal Club. So far so good, though it was hard to understand why Yates Thompson, after meeting the paper's losses for so many years, was prepared to sell it as soon as it was making a profit. But the dove was no more than a stool pigeon. The true and ultimately successful bidder was an American, Mr William Waldorf Astor, until recently United States Ambassador at the Court of King Humbert I in Rome and now permanently settled in England. Cook must have been puzzled to know why this retiring and scholarly American should wish to burden himself with the conduct of a London evening paper. His friend Milner could have enlightened him. Many years later Milner's widow described how Astor, who had suffered a good deal of criticism and unwelcome publicity in the New York Press, had, when he decided to make his home in England, asked Milner how he could avoid being similarly vexed in London. Milner replied that he could ensure against this by purchasing a newspaper, for by tradition the dogs of Fleet Street did not bite their own species. He may not have foreseen that Astor, in buying the only London newspaper on the market, would put his old friends and colleagues in jeopardy, or that a paper written 'by gentlemen for gentlemen' (and under Yates Thompson and Morley more precisely for Liberal gentlemen) would under its new proprietor strike its flag for one of Tory blue. Though later Astor stipulated to his new editor, Harry Cust, that he should control the policy of the paper, the only reason he can have had for favouring one party rather than another in the country of his adoption was a rich man's disapproval of the Liberal advocation of death and estate duties and graduated taxation. Such speculations, and the rumour that Astor had suppressed literary ambitions now assured of fulfilment in a paper of his own, can have been little comfort to Cook in the immediate crisis. Yet within a few weeks he and the shipwrecked staff of the *Pall Mall* were to find refuge in a green sanctuary.

Scarcely had Cook digested the commiserations of Gladstone and the leaders of the Liberal Party when Mr George Newnes, the publisher, encouraged by Lord Rosebery and Mr Bryce, proposed to Cook that with their backing he should start another evening paper of the same quality, and adhering to the same political creed, as the now violated *Pall Mall* had professed. Cook more or less dictated the terms, moral rather than financial, on which he could accept this proposal. Newnes readily agreed to them. On January 31st, 1893, the new pale viridian evening paper made its first afternoon appearance on the London streets. For three years Cook made the *Westminster Gazette* the expression of his personality, principles and convictions, and the most respected and readable evening paper London has ever had.

Meanwhile, in 1893, Mrs Baird had decided to move her fledgling family to Oxford. Now that Dolly had left school Hampstead had little attraction for them. They had made only a few friends, though among them was an interesting young couple living in the Vale of Health. Dolly had taken to them as she had to the child of the wholesale hatter. For Mr and Mrs Harmsworth made no bones about canvassing sales of Alfred's publications in the neighbourhood and pushing sample copies of his latest venture, *Answers*, into local letter-boxes.

In Oxford they would be near Mary and her seven children, and through them Dolly and Daisy would be more likely to meet friends of their own age. Oxford had begun to spread its tentacles along the Banbury and Woodstock Roads, and on the land between them comfortable houses with large gardens were being built along the side roads. One of them, in Rawlinson Road, was suited perfectly for the conditions that Daisy's needs imposed upon them. A wide gate opened on to a drive leading to a porch giving straight into a hall with no intervening steps. The ground-floor rooms were ample and well proportioned, a large drawing-room having direct access to the garden through a conservatory later to become an evergreen cork grotto. A broad staircase gently ascending from the hall reached a generous landing with a bedroom leading from it large enough to accommodate Daisy and Duck and all the orthopaedic gear that was now part of their life. About this time the Smiths had re-established the family links with Bamburgh. Mary, not without anxiety, for Arthur responded best to a warm holiday climate, had taken a cottage there for the summer. This had proved such a success that when her aunt, Martha Crossley, left her a legacy she bought a rather bleak but serviceable house standing below the castle on the other side of the road from Alnwick. This house the Smiths had named St Aidan's, so it seemed natural to my grandmother to dedicate the house in Rawlinson Road to the same saint, so closely identified with the village where, on the whole, she had been happier than in any other of the bivouacs she had made with her errant but beloved husband. In the hall she raised a shrine to his memory in the form of a trophy displaying the arms and accoutrements of an officer in the militia—a grey spiked helmet supported by a breech-loading rifle and a tasselled sword amid an array of belts, pouches and equipment. To a small boy such a display was irresistible, and in due course it taught me dramatically and effectively not to indulge in mischievous curiosity. Happier lessons were learned from my grandfather's sketches, now reverently framed and hung about the house. And in the drawing-room the sweet resonant chimes of a large ormolu clock reminded Emily Baird of the hours she and my grandfather had shared in the past, and of the passing of each one that brought nearer their reunion. Chimes and the bells of schools and churches are, perhaps, the most evocative sound recorded on the tape of memory. In contrast to the nagging peal of school bells and the ominous tocsin of Big Ben I still hear the mellifluous striking of my Aunt Daisy's clock against a background of music, laughter and peace.

V

IN THE SPRING OF 1893 the University ladies of Oxford were startled to see a goddess on her machine whizzing down the Banbury Road, flashing through the broad reach of St Giles, and dismounting and remounting with accomplished grace as she flitted from shop to shop along the High. It was not so much the sight of a young woman on a bicycle that shocked them (though, in fact, she was the first they had seen) as her unconventional attire. For her skirts, already immodestly abbreviated, as they streamed in the breeze of her passage were quite inadequate for their intended purpose. It was more distressing to know that this girl was the sister of Mrs A. L. Smith of Balliol, sharing, if nothing else, the latter's striking good looks. Happily the Master was unlikely to hear that such a breach of decorum was associated with his college, for it was generally understood that his life was now drawing peacefully to its close. The girl's name was Dolly Baird. She lived with her sister (a sweet afflicted child, said they who met her being wheeled into the town to do her shopping) in one of those new houses in North Oxford, and confirmed the doubts of many of the older residents about the sort of people this suburban development might attract.

Dolly was well aware that she was the subject of adverse comment. She soon became inured to 'unpleasant remarks and querulous policemen'. For she had taken up cycling with missionary zeal and was not impressed or discouraged by such idiotic criticism. Had she not, on discovering that ladies' models were designed for less Junoesque riders than herself, set Messrs Singer to work dismantling a man's machine, reassembling it to her specification, and fitting it with special pedals to suit her feet? In any case, it was the most convenient and up-to-date way of getting to her place of work, where happily her enterprise was much admired and made her something of a heroine. For every morning she could be seen swerving into Banbury Road, speeding down hill until she swung left into Norham Road, then, banking gracefully, taking a right and left turn which brought her into Crick

Dorothea Baird, aged 18.

Emily and Margaret Baird, *circa* 1890.

Dorothea Baird as Galatea in *Pygmalion*.

As Viola in an open-air production of *Twelfth Night* at Oxford.

Road, past Mary's house to the gate of the Oxford Preparatory School for Boys.

Soon after they had settled down in St Aidan's she had been offered by the headmaster, Mr C. C. Lynam, a post as under-matron and arithmetic mistress. No doubt her sister Mary had a hand in this, for she was friendly with her neighbour Lynam and had sent her first-born, Lionel, as a day boy to the school. Dolly accepted the offer enthusiastically, not for any prospect it offered of an academic career but because it would bring her into touch with the less moribund circles of Oxford society. Moreover, Mr Lynam's ideas of running a prep. school were novel, to say the least. Did he not take favoured boys, parents but not weather permitting, to cruise with him in his small sailing yacht during the summer holidays—as far afield as Scotland and France—thereby earning the enduring nickname, 'Skipper'? Did he not, in the faith that whatever boys did at work or play they must do well, attach as much importance to the production of the annual school play as he did to preparing the most promising of them for scholarships? A year or so previously Dolly, while staying with the Smiths, had been taken to see one of these zealous performances. Now she looked forward eagerly to taking a back-stage part, as all the staff were expected to do, in the next. So the daily rides to Crick Road became her routine, and gradually the novelty and shock of her equipage wore off until only the rapt gaze of impressionable undergraduates lingered on the comely cyclist as she pedalled by.

In March, before she took up her duties at the school, Dolly had gone with Emmie on a visit to Eastbourne. Teddie had his hands full in London, striving to justify Newnes's confidence and investment in him and his *Westminster Gazette*. Emmie was evidently in need of a change.

We got here all right [Dolly reported to her brother-in-law], *but it was very cold and snowing frightful pills. We found lodgings quite easily, this being the first house we stopped at. Emmie wanted to go out in the snow right away but I would not let her so I went out with Beauty. It was not snowing when I started but before we (the dog and I) reached the post office it came down a Blizzard and I could not see in front of me.*

I am quite a mature house-keeper and bought oranges, cake, cheese, biscuits etc., but I forgot the dog's biscuits and I could not imagine why it pulled and tugged before going out of every shop and looked at me with pitiful imploring gestures. I understand it all now.

We have awfully swell lodgings and are cosy despite the weather. We even have a piano. I'm going to write to mother for the music. Mind you come on Saturday. We have a fire in our room. Beauty was such a bother at the station, it is against the law to have a dog in the carriage, so we had to hide him, and when an official came in I covered him up with rugs and held him fast, but to my horror I had only got his two back legs and his nose was half a mile away, peering into the ticket man's face.

Emmie found the sea air and her sister's brisk management equally bracing.

Thank you very much for your letter [Dolly wrote again to Teddie]. *Emmie was rather in a wax this morning because you'd not written and said she would go back home...She has only mentioned nerves twice today.*

We were photographed today. Beauty has too much to eat, it has found out a sure method of being fed. It grunts and groans all the while we dine, breakfast, tea and supper, and pretends to be starving. While the chickenhearted Emmie, unmindful of the big plate of a former meal, gives it ever such a lot to eat. It sleeps at the foot of our bed and snores.

Emmie is much better except that she woke me in the middle of the night and told me she was in a consumption. She looks well today in spite of that woeful intelligence.

Mind you come on Saturday. It will be awfully mean if you don't.

Emmie makes quite a pig of Beauty, but I nearly fainted on the rocks because she would not give me some gingerbread cake and she has told mother I do nothing but eat. Anyrate she has eaten ever so many peardrops more than me.

Noble Tyas,
Good night and good repose (Shakespeare)
                                        Yours,
                                        Dorothea Frances Forster Baird.

But St Aidan's was never for long out of Dolly's mind. A letter to her mother disclosed a subtle change in their relationship. My grandmother may well have taken alarm at its ominously authoritarian tone.

We are all quite well and so is the weather...I am sure Daisy did

*not say that about going to plays in Lent. I think it's a great pity.
I wish you would get a new dress, if that old rag-picker's costume is
not gone by the time I come back—I'll contrive to throw it in the rag
bag. Please don't go to the post in your Shetland spencer or talk to
the Hamiltons through the W.C. window. Please send Bright's
'History of England' at once, also tell me the next sketching class
subject.*

*It's lovely here and would do you much good to get away from
the region of perpetual church-going, you always do get knocked up
in Lent. You must eat butter—mind. It poured yesterday hard. We
ventured forth in the afternoon but we were nearly blown off the piers.*

At this time Oxford was a hive of amateur dramatic activity. It was
twelve years since Jowett had made Oxford theatrical history by
allowing Frank Benson and his friends to perform the *Agamemnon*
of Aeschylus in Balliol Hall, with the safeguard that it should be
played in the original Greek. Four years later the Undergraduates'
Dramatic Club, under the Presidency of Arthur Bourchier, had given
its first performance in the New Theatre—itself the fulfilment of another
of the Master's liberal dreams. Since then the Oxford University
Dramatic Society, as it came to be called, had presented classical plays
annually, and had recruited as members more and more of the most
lively and intelligent undergraduates. During the past four years
Alan Mackinnon, as President, had improved the quality of the productions and had attracted a wider public for them with the help of
his friends E. Holman Clark, W. H. Goschen, W. J. Morris and
H. B. Irving, the latter enlisting his eminent father's help in putting
at their disposal the armoury and wardrobe of the Lyceum Theatre.
Julius Caesar, Strafford and *King John* had vastly entertained partisan
audiences, and earned a good deal of indulgent comment in the
national press. As a result there was such a surge of interest in the
drama (now that it could be discussed freely between the sexes and no
longer in the original Greek) and such a burgeoning of amateur talent
for the stage that the young people of Oxford were forming themselves into clubs and societies for play-readings, for the earnest
exchange of theatrical gossip, for unchaperoned rehearsals and for
the actual production of plays, not only in private houses and public
halls but in the pastoral setting of spacious country estates. And amid
the simmering of kettles and the clatter of teacups the newcomers to
North Oxford were busily exploiting this breach in the defences of

the University enclave. Little was heard of not so ancient prejudices; many of the dons were delighted to dither on the fringes of this fashionable frenzy, and even to extol a pupil's success in the O.U.D.S., though it might lessen his chances of distinction in the Schools. The memorial addressed by undergraduates to Henry Irving after the lecture he had recently given at Dr Jowett's invitation had ended with the words: '...to your influence we owe a deeper knowledge and more reverent study of the master mind of Shakespeare.' Be that as it may, they certainly owed him a tremendous amount of fun in a new and less monastic environment than Oxford had hitherto afforded.

For Dolly Baird this change in the social climate of Oxford was timely. Soon she had many friends in circles once segregated from one another but now meeting on the common ground of their amateur theatricality. In the autumn she found herself committed to two very different enterprises of this kind. At Lynam's much of the winter term was spent by the boys and by the staff in rehearsals for *The Tempest*. Her duties were to be those of dresser and wardrobe mistress. At the same time she was much preoccupied with her membership of the Christmas Dramatic Wanderers who planned, under the direction of Mrs H. M. Dowson, to give a performance during the holidays of *The Taming of the Shrew* in the Holywell Music Rooms. Dolly had been cast for Petruchio or had, perhaps, in her own forceful way appropriated this leading part.

Mrs Dowson's maiden name was Rosina Filippi. Her father, Filippo Filippi, was an Italian music critic. Shortly after Rosina's birth her family left Venice and made their home in England. She was a born actress. Her warm extrovert nature and her intuitive sense of artistic fitness were matched by a natural talent for mime and elocution; and her plump comely face was a malleable mask of comedy. At seventeen she was studying acting with the veteran tragedian, Herman Vezin, and later served her apprenticeship in the provinces. She had just begun to make her reputation on the London stage as a competent and versatile player when she married H. M. Dowson, a brewer, and retired to Oxford. Dowson was one of three brothers and Rosina was happy in her choice of him for a husband; for the other two, one of them the poet Ernest, were too wayward to be the foil of her exuberant maternity. When Dolly met her she was bearing her children and endowing them with a share of her own gifts and of her good-humoured common sense.

The school play at Lynam's went off with well-ordered gusto, the boys proving anew that Shakespeare is safe in the hands of innocents or of accomplished professionals but hazardous for lesser talents between these extremes. Dolly's particular charges were the shepherds and reapers—the 'sunburnt sicklemen'—whom Iris, conjured up by Prospero to amuse Ferdinand and Miranda, summons to attend on Juno and Ceres. At least one reaper never forgot how grateful he had been to her for getting him on the stage properly tanned and, as the poet directed, 'suitably clad'.

On the other hand all trace of the productions by the Christmas Dramatic Wanderers might have vanished with the winter's snow but for the presence of an elderly graduate, as assiduous a playgoer as he was a collector of protégées, one of whom, Edith Lucy, was playing Bianca. Their friendship had begun, as was usual with him, when she was a child; less usually it had survived her transition to adolescence. She was now the same age as Dolly Baird; her friend was the Reverend C. L. Dodgson.

> *Jan. 12th 1894. Fetch my pet Enid* [wrote the creator of Alice in Wonderland in his diary] *to dine with me and go to The Taming of the Shrew at the Holywell Music Room by the Christmas Dramatic Wanderers. Edith Lucy was Bianca but nearly all she said was lost owing to bad enunciation and extreme rapidity of speaking. Most of the performers had the same fault: so that they were very poor as a whole. Miss Dolly Baird was a spirited Petruchio and Miss Nellie Macdonald a droll Grumio...Miss de Brisay might have been a good Kate if she had not looked so woebegone all through: she would do Jane Shore fairly well.*

Though Edith Lucy had herself no ambition for the stage, her mentor, in all things a perfectionist, the next day wrote to her a long criticism of her performance. She had made Bianca something of a shrew herself, but he would not accept her excuse that she had done so to please Mrs Dowson. 'Petruchio' he added 'was played with real spirit. Miss Dolly Baird is *good* in action and in stage business and, if she learns to speak about half that rate and to recognise that she has a decided lisp, so as to give extra force to the S, she would do well.' Two months later he recorded that Edith Lucy came to tea 'bringing a new friend for me, Miss Dolly Baird. She is very pleasant: she wishes to try the stage.'

Perhaps it was to Edith Lucy that Dolly first confided her intention of going on the stage. She would have to earn her own living and this seemed the most attractive way of doing so. Her mother, faced with the problem and expense of Daisy's growing needs, could only afford to give Dolly an allowance of £2 a month, some of which went towards her keep when she stayed with Emmie. Her work at Lynam's was, she realised, only a stopgap; what she had seen of the academic world did not particularly attract her. She was modestly unaware that her looks and radiant charm were more than likely before long to resolve her doubts. And all that had happened since that evening at the Holywell Music Rooms encouraged her to believe that her decision was a sensible one.

This critical year of her life, her nineteenth, was ushered in by an invitation from the O.U.D.S. to play Iris in their producion of *The Tempest* at the end of January. Thus, unexpectedly, she summoned rather than despatched the shepherds and reapers and found herself among Oxford's theatrical élite. She brought several of her new friends to St Aidan's so that Daisy, already vicariously stage-struck, could enter into her enthusiasms, and that her mother might be conditioned gradually to accept her choice of a profession. But it was Edith Lucy who suggested the first practical step she should take in that direction.

Edith's elderly friend, the Rev. C. L. Dodgson, had long been famous as Lewis Carroll, but, being shy and hypersensitive, though well known in Oxford as a preacher and as a mathematician, he was known intimately only to a small, predominantly feminine, coterie of his own meticulous choosing. But outside Oxford he kept his many and diverse friendships in good repair, particularly those he had made among theatrical folk. To them he was drawn by a genuine fascination for their work and way of life, and to some extent by the missionary field they offered for the propagation of his Ruskinian faith in the mutualism of morality and art. It was nearly fifty years since he had first seen Ellen Terry as a child playing Puck to her sister Kate's Titania at the Princess Theatre with Mr and Mrs Charles Kean. Through Kate he soon came to know that united family, and had no difficulty in enlisting them as willing and co-operative models for his early experiments in photography. Since then the managers of most of the London theatres had become well acquainted with the clerical gentleman who booked his seats through his publishers, Messrs Macmillan, and was evidently *persona grata* at the stage door. His taste in plays was catholic; yet if anything he saw or heard offended his sense of moral or Christian propriety he was uncompromisingly protestant. After seeing E. A. Sothern in a double bill, he wrote: 'The other piece is very poor: wit low and vulgar. I shall *not* take any children to a London theatre without first ascertaining that the pieces acted are unobjectionable.' He had protested recently to Ellen Terry that her Portia was too 'forward' with Bassanio, and after seeing her as Margaret in *Faust* begin most discreetly to undress on the stage had sternly asked her: 'Where is it going to stop?' He had even suggested that she might persuade Irving to play the love scene between Benedick and Beatrice *outside* the church. At this very time he was taking to task Mrs Ben Greet, the wife of the highly respectable actor-manager, for certain 'comic allusions to serious things, i.e. baptism and the soul' in a play called *The Little Squire*. She replied spiritedly to what she protested, and he in turn denied, was 'a Christian rebuke'. But he had the last word. If his closest friends on the stage were party to such improprieties, he considered it his duty to wrestle with them, and, on the whole, their respect and affection for their gentle censor suffered not at all. Often his concern for the well-being of the theatre took a practical form. Five years earlier he had, in a letter to the *Sunday Times,* proposed a charter for the employment of children on the stage. He approved of this in principle, subject to conditions ensuring that they had proper care and education—conditions that many years later became statutory. So, as Edith Lucy explained to Dolly, one way and another nobody in Oxford had so many friends at the theatrical court, and already he had helped several girls she knew to start their careers as actresses. If Dolly was determined to go on the stage, he was the man to be consulted.

Dolly's impressions of her host at that tea-party may have been mixed. Others at that time visiting the ageing master of fantastic and precise arts found his ever-green fancifulness a little disconcerting. Often he would entertain the now middle-aged women who, as children, had been of his privileged kindergarten and had first heard the adventures of Alice at his knee; if an outsider happened to be present he found their affectation of whimsies long past and now, to flatter their author, kept up with desperate *naïveté*, embarrassing, if not a bit macabre. But she and Edith were his only guests on that occasion. She found him kind, and so far the only grown-up person she felt she could talk to frankly who would consider her problems with sympathy and understanding. She had little difficulty in persuading him to come to St Aidan's and, with his odd credentials as a man of God and a friend of the players, to help her mother to see reason when the issue had to be faced.

The outcome of that meeting was remarkable, less for any practical help it was to Dolly than for the clear light it threw on Dodgson's perplexing character. The next day he wrote to my grand-mother:

> *Christ Church*
> *Oxford*
> *April 12th 1894*
>
> Dear Mrs Baird,
>
> *There are two questions that I want to put before you for considera-tion.*
>
> *The first is as to that friend of mine to whom Dolly wishes to be introduced. I have now introduced to her four of the daughters of my friends of ages between 18 and 25; but in every case, before doing so, I told the mother the history of my friend and asked her whether, now she knew all the circumstances, she still wished her daughter to be introduced. In each case the answer was 'Yes'—So now, before giving any more promises to introduce Dolly, I would like to know what you think about it.*
>
> *If you already know what is popularly said against my friend (which is usually a good deal more than the truth) and if, knowing it, you still wish Dolly to be introduced, I am quite satisfied and no more need be said.*
>
> *If you do not know of any such tales, current in society, then I think I had better come and tell you the true history (you yourself, I mean; I had rather not talk about the matter to your daughters) and then you can settle what you wish to be done.*
>
> *The other question is, may Dolly come and dine with me? I ask this, not knowing your views as to 'Mrs Grundy'. And you may be sure I shall not feel in the least hurt if you think it best to say 'No'. It is only in these last two or three years that I have ventured on such unique and unconventional parties—Winifred Stevens was my first guest.*
>
> *If you say 'Yes' and will name a day (I've no engagements) I would come for her about 5½ and would escort her back at any hour you named (but I hope you would fix it as late as you can).*
>
> *Believe me sincerely yours,*
>
> C. L. Dodgson.

The friend was Ellen Terry. Lest Mrs Baird should be in any doubt about this 'true history', he decided, instead of imparting it in conversation with this rather distrait lady, to enclose with his letter this extenuating record of his friend's fluctuating marital fortunes.

When she was scarcely more than a child (17, I think), a man nearly three times her age professed to be in love with her. The match was pushed on by well meaning friends who thought it a grand thing for her. From the first, I don't think she had a fair chance of learning her new duties. Instead of giving her a home of her own he went on living as a guest with an elderly couple and the old lady was constantly exasperating the poor child by treating her as if she were still in the schoolroom and she, just like a child, used to go into fits of furious passion.

Quarrels began at once and very soon a separation was agreed on. He cynically told his friends that he found he had never loved her; it had only been a passing fancy. He agreed to make her an annual allowance so long as she lived respectably.

This she did for a while, then she rebelled and accepted the offered love (of course without ceremonial of marriage) of another man.

I honestly believe her position was, from her point of view, this:

'I am tied by human *law to a man who disowns his share of what ought to be a* mutual *contract. He never loved me and I do not believe, in God's sight, we are man and wife. Society expects me to live, till this man's death, as if I were single and to give up all hope of that form of love for which I pine and shall never get from* him. *This other man loves me as truly and faithfully as any lawful husband. If the marriage ceremony were* possible *I would insist on it before living with him. It is* not *possible and I will do without it.'*

I allow freely that she was headstrong and wild in doing so; and her real duty *was to accept the wreck of her happiness and live (or if necessary die)* without *the love of a man. But I do not allow that her case resembled* at all *that of those poor women who, without any pretence of* love, *sell themselves to the first comer. It much more resembles the case of those many women who are living as faithfully and devotedly as lawful wives without having gone through any ceremony and who* are, *I believe, married in* God's *sight though not in Man's.*

A lady (wife of a clergyman) to whom (before I would introduce her daughter to my friend) I told this story said 'She has broken the law of man; she has not *broken the law of God.'*

She lived with this man for some years and he is the father of her

*son and daughter. Then came the result she must have known was
possible if not probable and which perhaps her mad conduct deserved;
the man deserted her and went abroad.*

*When her lawful husband found out what she had done, of course
he sued for and got a divorce. Then of course she was, in the eye of the
law, free to be legally married and if only the other man had been as
true as she, I have no doubt, meant to be to him, they would have
married and it would have gradually been forgotten that the children
were born before the ceremony.*

*All this time I held no communication with her. I felt that she had
entirely sacrificed her social position that I had no desire but to
drop the acquaintance. Then an actor offered her marriage and they
were married. It was a most generous act, I think, to marry a woman
with such a history and a great addition to this generosity was his
allowing the children to assume his surname.*

*The actor's father, a clergyman, so entirely approved his son's
conduct that he came from the North of England to perform the
ceremony. This second marriage put her, in the eyes of Society,
once more in the position of a respectable woman. And then I asked her
mother to ask her if she would like our friendship to begin again and
she said 'yes'. And I went and called on her and her husband.*

*It really looked as if the misery of her life was over. But another
misery came on of quite another kind. The man drank. She knew he
was addicted to it before she married him but she fancied (very
foolishly, I fear) she could cure him. This got worse and worse till
they had to live apart and I believe he drank himself to death.*

So she is now a widow.

It's hard to guess whether Ellen Terry, had she known that all the
mothers of the girls that Dodgson had introduced to her had been
served with such a dossier, would have been hurt or amused. The
facts were more or less accurate and his comments, according to his
own curious conscience, were fair. Probably, since he was friendly with
the Camerons and the Prinseps, his report of G. F. Watt's feeble
disavowal was correct. His own pity, too, was genuine enough,
thought it lacked the saving grace of compassion. Ellen Terry had, it
seemed, generously forgiven him the withdrawal of his friendship for
those twelve unhappy years when she was most in need of it; the fact
that he was constantly in the company of Kate and her other sisters can
only have sharpened the edge of her resentment. Mrs Baird may have

missed the significance of his reference to 'tales, current in Society'. These, of course, were conjectures as to her relationship with Henry Irving. He had never sought Irving's acquaintance. He admired him as an actor and as a champion of his profession; but his entrée to the Lyceum was through the favour of its leading lady. Who was he, when so many of his distinguished contemporaries of unquestioned rectitude ignored such gossip and accepted socially these two great players, to add fuel to any smouldering fire that might conceivably be generating uncharitable smoke? Certainly no whiff of it would have reached the Bairds of Rawlinson Road. Thus, like so many of his Victorian kind, he helped unwittingly to confuse those searching, in time to come, for the answer to this romantic riddle.

The invitation to dinner was not accepted. Either Dolly demurred or her mother was persuaded that, although Winifred Stevens, a fellow Dramatic Wanderer, had come to no harm, it would be unwise for her to go. At that time there was a faction among the University ladies that saw this deacon, if not as a wolf, as a greying satyr in sheep's clothing given to entertaining little girls in his bachelor rooms, and even photographing some of them in the nude. A year or two previously the wife of a fellow don of Christ Church had paraded her outraged sense of propriety when her daughter, in appearance deceptively childish for her seventeen years, had confessed that she had exchanged a kiss on parting from her eccentric host. Dodgson, patently innocent of intent to harm anybody, was painfully aware of this gossip and did his best to ignore it; but thereafter he abandoned photography lest it might lead to consequences that both he and his detractors might regret. It was more than likely that Mary Smith, with her addiction to moral prejudication, had warned her mother that Dodgson's concern for Dolly's future might not be altogether wholesome. It was agreed, however, that as soon as possible he should take her up to London to seek an interview with Ellen Terry.

On May 26th Dodgson set out for London with Dolly properly chaperoned by the mother of another of his young friends, and with tickets for them all for the matinée of *Faust* at the Lyceum. The morning was spent at the Royal Academy, where they fell in with Norah Quin, who, thanks to his earlier importuning of Ellen Terry, was now a 'supernumerary' in Irving's company. *Faust* was altogether simpler fare than the much criticised *Macbeth* Dolly had seen five years ago, since when she herself had become a more sophisticated playgoer —better able to appreciate the subtleties of Irving's Mephistopheles, with his mocking eyes and the flash of his cruel teeth, to assess his mastery of theatrical contrivance, and to marvel at the realism of the scenes in Nuremburg. If the antics of its wine-swilling citizens were a bit forced, she remembered the boisterous but unconvincing performances by members of the O.U.D.S. of Trinculo and Stephano. She found it hard to believe, as she watched the fated Margaret trapped by Faust and his accomplice Fiend, that this raptured and enchanting actress could, in a few minutes, condescend to an interest in her own humble theatrical ambitions.

After the second act her host took her round to the stage door. Apparently he had not made an appointment with Miss Terry. In the passage they met a friend of his, Nellie de Silva, whose husband, Martin Harvey, though still young enough to play boys' parts, was one of Irving's veteran troupers, and now, in *Faust*, had been promoted from a speechless and anonymous soldier to the reveller, Fosch, with a few incoherent lines to say. Miss de Silva did not feel that she herself could take them to Miss Terry, but suggested that they ask the manager, Mr Stoker, to arrange it. This they did, and later received a message from him that they would be taken round after the next act. When the curtain fell on the shamed Margaret lying senseless on the steps of the church, they were escorted to the pass door, on to the stage and through the ordered chaos of the scene change. Dodging the lumbering trucks loaded with swaying scenery, ducking their heads as assistant stage managers warned them of ascending or descending cloths and battens, they reached an oasis of calm and safety—stage centre immediately behind the drop curtain. There stood Margaret, already wide awake from her trance of her performance. Ellen Terry greeted her old, if intermittent friend, and immediately enveloped Dolly in the warmth of her personality. They chatted away while Nuremburg was dismantled and Telbin's masterpiece, the Brocken scene, was swiftly assembled in its place. A few infant players of imps and monkeys scampered around their feet. Dolly managed to blurt out her misgiving that she was too tall to be an actress. Ellen gaily suggested that they stood back to back while Dodgson measured them. They were exactly the same height.

Dolly was dazed by new and confused impressions—the radiance of the great actress's personality, the music of her perfectly articulated questions, the gay sincerity of the consideration she gave to distracted replies, and through all this the muted playing beyond the act drop of the entr'acte against the ground-bass of conversation in the stalls. Stage hands were shouting out directions to their invisible mates in the flies as cut cloths and borders were lowered to their deadlines. Toppling wings and ground rows were skilfully manoeuvred and braced into position. As soon as the scene was set, property men brought in their bits and pieces and dumped them on their allotted marks. Hissing limelights focused on their particular areas to the snap and crackle of the changing of their mediums. 'Clear please!' The stage managers clapped their hands. The busy stage was hushed as the players began to take their places for the opening tableau. An escort appeared at Dodgson's elbow and ushered the little group towards the wings. Irving had not appeared, so the spell of his acting would not be broken. As they left the stage they were met by a surge of supernumerary witches and demons—among them Norah Quin. Ellen Terry bade them a fervent farewell and disappeared towards her dressing-room. The pass door closed behind them to the last chords of the entr'acte; the chatter of the audience diminished to an expectant susurration. As they reached their seats the auditorium lights were dimmed until only the footlights flared along the fringe of the heavy curtain. 'Scurry music' heightened the suspense of an audience already half enthralled. When the curtain rose on the Brocken the illusion was perfect—the vast distances, the craggy heights poised over precipitous depths, and the deadly chill of wreathing mountain mists that made Dolly shiver delightedly in her seat.

Instantly she recognised the source of Irving's inspiration, derived as it was from the illustrations by Doré in those great volumes her father had left for herself and Daisy to pore over with awe and wonder. When the curtain fell on Margaret ascending magically with an escort of angels to a limitless heaven, and on the evaporation of the cheated Mephistopheles, she applauded ecstatically as the tall crimson figure led Ellen Terry forward to take her calls; and when the curtain fell with seeming finality to sustained clapping, it parted in the middle to allow the actor-manager and his fascinating leading lady to take their last bow on the narrow strip of stage between the footlights and the green wall behind them.

Dolly returned to Oxford firm in her resolve to become a professional actress, and as firmly convinced that Norah Quin's way of approach to the stage was not for her. It was hard to see how by 'walking on' at the Lyceum time could be found for learning the rudiments of acting, or, in so large a company, opportunity to catch the eye of the dispenser of small parts. Undoubtedly Ellen Terry was captivating, but Dolly had seen and heard enough to guess that the price of her patronage could be an enervating adulation, robbing the spell-bound of initiative or ambition. Though she was grateful to Mr Dodgson for the trouble he had taken, and for the salutary glimpse he had given her of the back stairs to Olympus, she knew now that she must fend for herself, and somehow or other find a humbler workshop where she could serve a more realistic apprenticeship.

Meanwhile she had little time to worry about the ways of starting her career, when the means were abundant and ready to hand. For within a few weeks of her appearance in *The Tempest,* she found herself much in demand for leading parts in the spring spate of amateur productions. Philip Carr, of Brasenose, had invited her to be his leading lady in Gilbert's *Pygmalion and Galatea,* which he planned to present at the New Theatre in early June.

Philip Carr was the son of Joe Comyns Carr, a witty and popular dilettante, the begetter of the New Gallery, which was now challenging the supremacy of the Grosvenor Gallery as a shop window for the best of contemporary art; as a dramatist and as dramatic critic of the *Pall Mall Gazette* he had both interests and influence in the theatre, to say nothing of the immediate prestige of a commission from Henry Irving to write a verse play on the Arthurian legend. Philip Carr's home, during his childhood, had been thronged with literary, theatrical and graphic artists. His mother was the gifted Alice Strettel, with a flair for costume design and with the rarer talent of being able to win the regard and affection of her husband's brilliant friends, providing in her drawing-room in Blandford Square a congenial rendezvous for an eclectic circle to which the password was wit and the subscription laughter. So her son, a freshman and too junior a member of the O.U.D.S. to have had a speaking part in *The Tempest,* was determined to show his theatrical mettle by producing on his own account a play that the Vice-Chancellor of the University would certainly have vetoed for its Dramatic Society. It was a play that, a few years later, exasperated Max Beerbohm into taking the button off his well-tempered foil and doing his best to wound the author, probably in gallant defence of the leading lady, Gilbert inexplicably but characteristically having written 'a rather mean letter about her to the Press'. But for ten years the American actress, Mary Anderson, had given it pride of place in her repertory, and had played it with success during her recent season at the Lyceum. All this was of very little account to Dolly; it sufficed to give her the chance to play the lead in a commercial theatrical venture. One of the company, Nigel Playfair of University College, remarked that, though she was passing through a plump stage and had not then quite developed her bewitching beauty, she showed more promise of good acting than perhaps she ever achieved. Her performance was briefly reported in *The Era*. If she was becoming increasingly aware of her shortcomings as an actress, she was discovering that she had an unusual capacity for learning lines. For since her début at the Holywell Music Rooms she had been studying with Rosina Filippi the interpretation of shakespeare's heroines, and in several of those parts was already word perfect.

It so happened that for the week following the run of *Pygmalion and Galatea* the bills of the New Theatre announced the appearance of the Ben Greet Shakespeare and Old English Comedy Company in Sardou's *Diplomacy* and in *A Midsummer Night's Dream;* it would also give a performance of *Twelfth Night* in the gardens of Worcester College. Greet had arrived in Oxford in time to see Philip Carr's production. He was sufficiently impressed by Dolly Baird's acting to call upon her afterwards and to offer her an engagement for seven months at a salary of ten shillings a week on the understanding that she provided her own wardrobe, as had been the custom of players in the old stock companies. She was sensible enough to realise that such a nominal salary could be looked upon as a remission of fees for learning, at the hands of an experienced teacher and in a workmanlike school, the technique of acting and at the same time gaining the experience necessary to any future engagement. It was no longer possible to find employment in provincial stock companies—the schools in which the great players from Garrick to Irving had learned their business; all of them had wilted and wasted away in the changing theatrical climate, and with them the training grounds that had served the profession for centuries. It was with the idea of providing something of the kind that Frank Benson and Ben Greet had formed their touring companies. Already the English stage had cause to be grateful for their enterprise. Dolly knew that this chance that Greet offered was not to be missed. If she needed further inducement to accept his offer, the performance of his company in *Diplomacy* may have been the spur. For, as Beauclerc, Mr Henry Irving junior returned to Oxford for the first time since his triumphs in the O.U.D.S., as a professional actor. Though the part was a small one, his playing of it confirmed all she had heard of the grace and distinction of his bearing from his many friends in Oxford, now curious to see how his promising talent had developed. In any case she had to make up her mind quickly, for Greet wished her to join him at the end of the month at the Metropole Theatre, Camberwell, where she would be expected to be ready to play Emilia in *The Winter's Tale*. She accepted his offer there and then.

During the next few days there was much to be done. The news of her decision had to be broken to the family. Her mother accepted the inevitable with bewildered calm. From Somerleyton came protests and urgent pleas that she should think again before compromising her relatives by adopting such a questionable profession. The reaction from Moor Hall was more favourable. The Brintons could hardly be surprised if cousin Dolly's success as the good Fairy Pantarista had put such ideas into her pretty head. Reg, moreover, now at New College, was basking in the reflected glow of her popularity, while Jack could foresee delightful possibilities in having a cousin on the stage. Dolly left her mother to deal with these conflicting repercussions. She was concerned only that Teddie and Emmie should approve and support her decision. This they did.

The collection of a wardrobe took longer than the memorising of Emilia's lines. From Tavistock Square she and Emmie made several sorties to cheap sales and to the haunts of secondhand clothes dealers in narrow by-ways off the Strand. There, so Dolly had been told, was to be found a female pawnbroker well known to the profession for specializing in buying cast-off dresses from ladies of the aristocracy or, more probably, from their maids. And, sure enough, she found at the head of a dark staircase in a dingy and dilapidated house a friendly woman in a room lined with closely fitted chests, eager to sell at a knock-down price creations scarcely worn and elaborately embroidered, that could be easily adapted to dress any part in a tragic or comic repertory. One of them was a silken evening gown stiff with panelling and foaming with fichus and flounces of gossamer lace; it was sadly creased and crumpled after scintillating, like a butterfly, through its brief life at a single ducal reception. As Dolly stepped into it, the snapper-up of out-moded and discarded finery remarked that she exactly matched the build of the Countess it had been made for. One of the chests was full of her dresses; her fancy for trimmings was not to everyone's taste, but it would be easy enough to alter them. By the time Dolly's purchases had been packed up and paid for the pawnbroker had a shrewd idea of her purpose. She asked if she had been in the profession long. No? She guessed as much. She herself had a son on the stage—comic songs and dances, the variety line. If they happened to meet they'd get along famously together. Emmie was impressed by the unaffected cameraderie of the make-believe world Dolly would soon be entering. Would those crushed creations from the Rue de la Paix as quickly accept their transmutation and come to enjoy a new and almost everlasting life at the lime-lit court of a player king?

Emmie soon learned, too, that sham jewellery was an indispensable part of an actress's equipment. Bow Street abounded in shops stuffed with this spurious treasure. Even brass curtain rings and bosses could grace a queen, set off with false pearls. The plainest and dullest dresses could be made theatrically effective with a few stiff white satin rosettes. 'They give a dress character', explained Dolly, with a new authority. And if handsomer embellishment was needed, plenty of coloured glass bugles and a sheaf of artificial flowers would fill the bill.

Thus, with her basket of properties and word perfect in the part of Emilia (and of Ida in *Two Roses*, soon to be added to the repertory), she arrived at the stage door of the Metropole Theatre. The company were assembling on the stage under the cold unflattering light of the naked gas jets on a T piece suspended from the flies. She recognised Mr Henry Irving junior by his pale face and slightly disdainful expression. He was, she learned, to play Leontes. The rehearsal began. As Hermione's attendant, she had plenty of time to note the passion and fervour of the King of Sicilia's opening speeches. After his first scene in Act II he bided his time aloof and abstracted in the shadowy wings. Now for her scene—Scene II, a prison...enter a Gaoler with Emilia. She heard her cue.

> 'Dear Gentlewoman,
> How fares our gracious lady?'

Confidently Dolly delivered the few lines of her first professional part:

> 'As well as one so great and so forlorn
> May hold together: on her frights and griefs,—
> Which never tender lady hath borne greater,—
> She is something before her time deliver'd.'
> 'A boy?'
>   'A daughter; and a goodly babe,
> Lusty and like to live...'

It was strange that in her first speech as an actress she should report the

safe, if premature, delivery of a princess, for in the long run her voca-
tion for alleviating the cares and hazards of maternity for the under-
privileged would prove stronger than her present call for the life of a
player, clear and peremptory though it seemed. As she spoke, did the
sound of her voice arrest the drift of Harry Irving's brooding thoughts?
As he came forward to begin the next scene, had he subconsciously
come to the end of an inner solitude that was to be my beginning? Yet
I had begun when my two grandfathers, heedless of their relationship,
were so briefly acquainted across the footlights of the Theatre Royal,
Sunderland. It was they who had set the feet of their children on paths
leading them through twenty years to this encounter. Dolly, being a
woman, may have sensed intuitively the significance of this fated
moment. Harry would be slower to interpret the impact of her voice
upon his well insulated emotions. Nevertheless from that hour these two
young people, as yet strangers to each other, come as my father and
mother under the tender and affectionate observation of their son.

PART II

COUNTERFEIT PRESENTMENT

'Look here, upon this picture, and on this;
The counterfeit presentment of two brothers.'
Hamlet

I

IN THE EARLY HOURS of Sunday, November 26th, 1871, Florence
Irving, through the window of a hired brougham, watched her
husband stalk out of her life into the foggy void of Hyde Park
Corner. As the brougham continued its journey westward the
smouldering anger that had in part brought her to her present situation
was fanned by the bitter recollection of the injuries, real or imagined,
she had suffered at his hands, and of the night's acrimonies that had
ended so abruptly. But by the time she reached the little house in
West Brompton which they had shared for so short a time, the ashes of
her fury cooled. She had not reckoned the cost of provoking a temper as
stubborn as her own, but kept in such stern control that it could reach
flash point without the fair warning that would enable its tormentor to
calculate to a nicety the limits of its exasperation. As the intoxication of
her resentment evaporated, she found herself faced with three harsh
truths; that on one level of consciousness she still desired him; that on
another he repelled her; that these alternating affections would be a
continuing reproach to her latent puritanism, and to the fastidiousness
that should have curbed her infatuation with him before they were both
entrapped by their incompatibility.

She could not deceive herself into believing that he had given no
warning of his discontent. Only a few months had passed since he had
sought refuge from her sharp tongue and blunt perceptions in lodgings
where he could work without distraction to turn a long-sought professional opportunity to his advantage. Only too clearly and with
humiliation she remembered how she had begged him to return, his
almost boyish eagerness for reconciliation, and his resumption of their
life together without recriminations or reproaches.

The curious cab driver opened the door for his deserted passenger.
As she approached her front door she was startled by her sense of
isolation; as she closed it behind her she felt the surge of an instinct to
hold jealously to herself the baby boy asleep in the room upstairs, and
the unborn child of that brief reunion. She was only too well aware of

the extremes of love and malice that governed her nature. Henceforward all her capacity for love would be concentrated on her children.

The thoughts of my grandfather, Henry Irving,[1] as he walked
instinctively in the direction of Hezekiah Bateman's house in Kensington Gore must have been as sombre and confused as those of the wife
he had suddenly abandoned. That night had crowned his sixteen years
of struggle for recognition, even for survival, in the face of frustrations
and discouragements, with artistic and perhaps popular success; that
same night had brought the recognition that his wife had neither the
understanding nor the inclination to share this hard-won success.
Those lean years had proved to him the strength of his consuming
ambition as an actor, and the conviction that no human agency would
deflect him from fulfilling it. Yet, ready as he was to brush aside any
obstacle to his purpose, he had not foreseen that the most wounding
opposition would come from the very quarter to which he might look
for sympathetic encouragement. He realised that from the hour of his
betrothal to Florence O'Callaghan he had been wilfully blind to signals
warning him of dangers ahead. He had, no doubt, been flattered by the
admiration of a girl from a social background utterly different from his
own. He had ignored the possibility that she was unlikely, with all the
obstinacy she had shown in defying her parents' objection to their
engagement, to accept the unconventional way of life he was accustomed to and which, indeed, was essential to a theatrical artist.
After their marriage he had tried to tolerate her querulousness, to find
some physical excuse for her caustic contrariness, but, by her failure to
rise to this great occasion, and by parading her contemptuousness before
his friends rejoicing in his triumph, she had proved herself antipathetic
to his very motive for existence. He had hoped that family life and a
home where he could entertain his fellow players could fit into the
pattern of his destiny. So it might have done, had he not chosen a
partner who did not trouble to conceal her disapproval of his colleagues,
and was offended by convivialities that she regarded as debaucheries.

Now he knew that he must choose between the damaging sham of a
patched-up marriage to a wife forever chafing against the egocentricity
that, for better or worse, is characteristic of the artist, between the
crowded prison of empty social observances and the lonely liberty of
single-minded concentration on his career. When the Batemans opened

[1] I have written of these critical and troubled years of my grandfather's
life in *Henry Irving: The Actor and his World*

their door to him they may have been surprised by the hour but not by the cause of his appearance. They, like many of his friends, had long foreseen a disastrous end to such an obvious misalliance. They made him very welcome. Their affection for him and their artistic and financial interdependence imposed upon them a double responsibility for his well-being.

For on the Monday morning the newspapers were unanimous in their praise of Henry Irving. A great actor had come to town and the sooner the public were made aware of it the better. In a play, *The Bells*, that had been condemned by the critics and had failed in the hands of a lesser actor, he had given incontrovertible evidence of his genius. As Irving read the columns of eulogies he knew that the command of the English theatre was his for the taking; the way ahead looked less forbidding than it had during that long sad Sunday. When Florence read this confirmation of his success, she knew in her heart that he was beyond her reach, invulnerable to her taunts and deaf to any further pleas she might make for reconciliation. Failure might have restored to her a contrite and submissive husband; now his egotism would feed on this acclaim, and the adulation of the public would nourish his self-sufficiency.

The Batemans found cause for self-congratulation in the tone of the press. They had backed a winner who had rescued them from bankruptcy. Their faith in Irving as an artist had been genuine enough, but they had nearly come to grief through their failure to discern the nature of his genius. The play had been of his choosing, and, in producing it, he had demanded and was given a free hand. Exploitation of success was something that the American showman understood and revelled in. His leading actor must be persuaded to forget the past and to concentrate on the golden future.

So my paternal grandparents parted. They met again but once. I was present at this meeting. In the large ground-floor rooms of the house of the Baroness Burdett Coutts in Stratton Street, the body of Henry Irving lay in state before it was reduced to ashes convenient for his burial in Westminster Abbey. In a corner of those rooms through which mourners and his devoted public filed all day, Florence in widow's weeds held melancholy court to those who through the years had shown affection to them both, and to those enemies of Irving who had made her a willing ally in detracting him. Though she wept, her tears were bitter with self-pity. She never forgave nor recognised the causes of his desertion.

Her second boy was born just before Christmas in 1872. One of her causes for complaint may have been that though her marriage lines showed that she was married to John Henry Brodribb Irving, she knew that her husband had taken no steps to acquire a legal right to the name of Irving. He had adopted the name for stage purposes. Even as a youth his audience-sense had warned him that the impact of the name Brodribb on the ears and eyes of the public, phonetically and typographically, would be weak. Irving would be far more serviceable. But now, owing to his neglect, his sons were in law still Brodribbs—a situation pardonably exasperating to a mother in Florence's position. Her first-born was christened Henry Brodribb Irving; her second son was named Laurence Sidney after his godparents John Lawrence Toole, his father's dearest friend, and Sidney Bateman, the wife of the impresario to whom he owed the chance of fame. No hint of their mother's line went to their naming. Yet of the tributaries that mingled in their life-streams those emanating from maternal sources were richer in physical and intellectual content than those humbler springs that gave rise to the torrential genius of their extraordinary father.

II

IN A SOCIETY AS CONFINED as that in the United Kingdom, until the emigrations of the nineteenth century scattered its islanders all over the world, the hereditary transmissions of character and talent made a fascinating study. In 1850 you could be sure that the man or woman passing you in the street, or sitting opposite to you in a railway carriage, had in their blood a strain, however diluted, of abnormality —a fragment of the genius that one way or another had shaped our history. If John Aubrey's arch assertion that Shakespeare sired a child by his hostess on the London to Stratford road was true, by 1870, by the laws of average compound fertility, through that wayward line some 2,500 sparks of the poet's divine fire were smouldering in their unconscious hosts. There is hardly a family in England today that may not suddenly enrich the nation by some staggering reversion to type. Any biographer, therefore, must be pardoned for pursuing the characteristics of his heroes or heroines backwards through the winding lanes of lineage, in the hope of discerning the influences that moulded their appearance and governed their conduct.

Harry and Laurence Irving were at the receiving end of as bizarre a mixture of genes as could be found in any boys of predominantly Celtic origin. The Brodribbs for many generations past had been plain country folk working out their destinies on Somersetshire farms and having little impact on the world beyond their parish borders. All, that is, but one of them—the boys' grandfather Samuel, and he was innocent of any intent to leaven the worthy dullness of his clan. But by marrying Mary Behenna he fortified the rough full-bodied Brodribb vintage with a livelier and more refined spirit. For the mother of Mary Behenna and her two sisters had an improvident and complacent husband. In return for the payment of his recurring debts by a well-to-do neighbour Behenna did not look too closely into his wife's relations with his benefactor. How he had acquired a farm near Penzance and fathered three handsome and elegant girls was never satisfactorily explained, particularly as before very long he lost the property to a publican who encouraged him to drink it away on credit. Gossip fixed the paternity of the Behenna girls on a local landowner; closer conjecture led to the supposition that their father was a member of the Praed family of Trevethow, near St Ives—a family that at about this time, in its Devonshire branch, produced the poet Winthrop Mackworth Praed, who in 1830 stood unsuccessfully for the constituency of St Ives. Whether or not there was any truth in these rumours, it is a fact that two generations later there sprang from the earthy Brodribb stock, through Samuel, and later from a female cousin of his line, two sports—the actor Henry Irving and the poet W. H. Davies. Thus it seems likely that the Behenna girls grafted on to this Somersetshire briar the dominant bud of genius. So much for Harry and Laurence's paternal forebears.

While my rude Northumbrian ancestors were bridling under the harsh but efficient administration of King Canute, other Danes were ravaging western Ireland with the enthusiastic collaboration of Ceallachan, King of Cashel, called the Hard or the Just, according to the prejudices of contemporary chroniclers. From him sprang the multitudinous and once powerful family of O'Callaghans, now powerless though persistent. Later the O'Callaghans preferred to think of themselves as of Milesian or Anglo-Norman stock, a fancy that must have been hard to reconcile with their pride in their only kinsman to become an Irish peer, Baron Lismore, for he claimed to be of direct descent from the Royal House of Cashel.

For eight hundred years the O'Callaghans kept a precarious hold on their properties in Munster, surviving without particular distinction the violent changes of fortune that ever have been the lot of Irish landowners. When William of Orange landed at Torbay most of the old Irish families felt that in spite of James II's evident shortcomings their allegiance to him as a Catholic monarch was binding. 'If', as John Cornelius O'Callaghan wrote, 'the English and Scots as Protestants objected to James for their King, as a Catholic, and adopted William, as a Protestant, the Irish, as Catholics, did not see *why* they should not prefer James for their King as a Catholic, and reject William as a Protestant.' His argument, in terms of Irish logic, seems irrefutable. James's Irish champions would have preferred to fight for him in their homeland, where the unhappy natives were acclimatised to desolation. But the help they counted on from France was not forthcoming, assailed as she was on all her frontiers by Protestant forces welded uncomfortably together by the Edict of Nantes. So they fought three confused and losing campaigns against the vastly superior (at least in numbers and equipment) forces of the 'Usurper' before they accepted the hopelessness of their position, and were forced to choose between an ignoble peace or soldiering on abroad with the defenders of their faith in France and Spain. They had lost over a million acres of property to William's commissioners, but they consoled themselves that as their resistance had cost the English eighteen million pounds the price per acre was excessive. After the surrender of Limerick many of them sought service abroad. The majority, amounting to a military brigade of some 24,000 officers and men, joined the armies of Louis XIV. Others went to Spain, among them my ancestor Cornelius O'Callaghan. He entered the service of Philip V in 1750, took a Spanish wife and had two sons. The elder, Richard, returned to Ireland during a lull in her troubles to recover family property in County Clare; the younger, Thomas, remained in Spain and had thirteen sons; the eleventh, John, was Florence's grandfather.

Of John O'Callaghan little is known except that he was the first Catholic to be admitted to the Irish Bar as an attorney after the relaxation of the penal laws in 1793. If he was a successful advocate his looks as well as his law must have won him many clients. In appearance he may have favoured his Spanish grandmother, for his colouring and features would not be incongruous in a gallery of Goyas. His raven-black hair, his shrewd but candid regard, and, below a long upper lip, a firm mouth delicately carved to suggest a lurking impish humour were his legacy to his great-grandson, Harry.

By marrying Ann Donovan John introduced into the family another Irish strain, and with it a temperamental proclivity to extremes of religiosity and worldliness. His wife was the sister-in-law of his brother Peter. Peter's three children were long lived. His daughter Teresa died, at the age of ninety, as Mother Superior of the North Infirmary of Cork, after sixty-two years as a Sister of Charity; she served with Florence Nightingale in the Crimea and her habit, damaged by gunfire, is still a revered relic in Cork. His son Malachy was a Vincentian priest who at the age of seventy-four went round the world visiting the houses of his order. Such were the Donovans on the side of the angels.

John O'Callaghan had five children by his first wife Ann; three, weak in mind or body, died young. His surviving sons, John Cornelius and Daniel, were both remarkable for their staying power.

John Cornelius was in all things over life-size. His powerful physique was matched by a voice he was unable to modulate to the tones of polite conversation. His appearance, however, was that of a scholar. Beneath a high and bulging forehead accentuated by the recession of his black hair, his eyes below their dark brows peered through strong spectacles; he was very like his father and his slightly sharper features were framed by a full Newgate fringe. Like so many Irishmen, his emotions and his intellect were often in conflict. He was a poet of rebellion, a man of inflammatory letters and a diligent student of history. He was called to the Irish Bar in 1829 but soon gave up the law for journalism and historical research.

When in 1842 Charles Gavan Duffy enlisted a team of young Dublin writers to help him, as proprietor and editor, to found a weekly journal to voice the discontents of his distressed people, chief among them was the Protestant politician, Thomas Davis. Duffy, who regarded Davis as the most 'nobly gifted man' he had known, accepted his suggestion that the paper should be called *The Nation*. John Cornelius was persuaded by Davis to join the 'Young Irelanders' as the contributors to *The Nation* came to be called. For the first number he wrote 'The Exterminators' Song', a fiery ballad that itinerant agitators would soon hear sung all over Ireland. Later Davis, in an appraisal of the periodical, wrote of him that 'he put his name or his mark "Gracchus" to all things notable in it and they were few'.

In the summer following its publication John Cornelius was among the million supporters of O'Connell assembled on the Hill of Tara and, with his friend Hogan the sculptor, placed what has been described as a crown on the head of the Liberator. This episode led to republican misgivings and to suspicions that O'Connell might have Caesarian ambitions. The 'crown' was in fact the model of a cap designed by Duffy in the hope of substituting some sort of national headgear in place of the imported 'Glengarry hoof' popular at that time. The prototype was of rich velvet embroidered with 'artistic ornaments'. Though this cap was thought to have a certain antique dignity, when it was mass-produced for ordinary wear out of grey shoddy relieved only by a feeble wreath of shamrock, its resemblance to a night-cap discouraged the most ardent patriot from adopting it as a cap of liberty.

Thereafter John Cornelius did not figure much in the activities of the Young Irelanders. He seems to have played no part in the trial of O'Connell, and was not among the members of Duffy's staff arrested when *The Nation* was suppressed. He published *The Green Book of Gleanings from the Writing Desk of a Literary Agitator* in 1845, including in it his trite epigrammatic verses and some patriotic ballads set to popular airs. Soon he became absorbed in the past rather than in the future of his country. Duffy quoted him as saying that 'he loved not the entremets of literature but the strong meat of sedition', and that he 'made a daily meal on the smoked carcass of Irish History'. This was true enough but, though he had a hearty appetite for historical research, his powers to digest it were weak. His outstanding book, *The History of the Irish Brigades in France,* is crammed with fascinating military detail so incoherently assembled as to be almost unreadable. John Cornelius's uncompromising idealism and a passionate concern for justice were to be transmitted to his great-nephew Laurence.

Daniel O'Callaghan, ten years younger than his brother, was born in 1815, the year of the battle of Waterloo. If Mars was in the ascendant at his birth, some gentler planet may have influenced him to seek military service not as a combatant but as a medical officer. Handsome, strong and durable, he was qualified physically to be a formidable man of war; an over-plus of Donovan guile might have made him a subtle strategist. He had something of his brother's intellectual capacity, but, being naturally lazy in this respect, he seldom exercised it. When moved to express himself in print he did so with force and clarity. Reverting to his ancestral type, and sharing none of John Cornelius's passion to redress the grievances of his country, he offered his scalpel to its oppressors in return for the prospect of more colourful conflicts overseas. His philosophy was illustrated aptly in the crest that on occasion he sported—a mailed arm brandishing a sword encoiled by the Aesculapian serpent.

Having gained a rudimentary knowledge of medicine, he served first as a surgeon in the Royal Navy. In 1835 fighting afloat was hard to come by, and this happy state of affairs may have driven him to seek more active service with the Honourable East India Company. In 1842 he was posted to the Field Hospital of the Army of the Sutlej with the 49th and later with the 11th regiment of native infantry. Once settled in Bengal he married Elizabeth Walsh and established a home for her at Pudural. She brought him not only a measure of financial security but a tenuous influence in high places that enabled him to indulge his weakness for gambling and for insubordinate pamphleteering with comparative impunity.

Oddly enough the Walshes had been blessed with the same hint of legendary bastardy as the Brodribbs. Elizabeth's father, George Walsh of Tipperary, was an amiable, well-educated and attractive man with a flair for languages. He was half-brother to Robert Stewart, Viscount Castlereagh, though it was generally understood that their relationship was much closer. Certainly the excellent education Walsh received was in accord with the care that the second Marquis of Londonderry gave to that of his legitimate sons. The two half-brothers were devoted to each other. In 1809 Castlereagh became Secretary of State for War with power of appointment to the newly formed Corps of King's Messengers. This patronage, shared with the other two Secretaries of State, had resulted in a discrepancy between his colleagues' irresponsible exercise of privilege in finding billets for pensionable servants, and his own more realistic recruitment of gentlemen, preferably officers, with the enterprise and natural authority needed to carry out their secret and often dangerous missions. The Diplomatic Corps were quick to differentiate between the King's Messengers to be invited to dinner and those to be relegated to the servants' hall, though there was little to choose between the gentlemen and the pensioners in their devotion to duties that often cost them their lives.

On Castlereagh's nomination George Walsh was appointed King's Messenger. With Andrew Basilico and William Ross he became one of three most highly regarded and exceptional men in the service. He was, unlike the Stewarts, an ardent Catholic. His fearlessness and tact were at once exemplified when in reply to George III's reiterated: 'Walsh, are you a damned Papist?' he answered: 'Sir, I am ever your Majesty's obedient and humble servant.' He carried home the Duke of Wellington's dispatches from Waterloo. Seven years later Lord Castlereagh, after showing signs that the stresses of his turbulent political life had affected his mind, killed himself. Walsh, when he heard of this, was inconsolable and for several days shut himself up in his room. He retired in 1824 and died some ten years later, leaving a son, Thomas, and three daughters, Martha, Henrietta and Elizabeth.

When Daniel O'Callaghan married Elizabeth he found he had acquired an avuncular brother-in-law in Cornelius Donovan, his mother Ann Donovan's brother, who had complicated the relationship by marrying Elizabeth's sister Henrietta. Donovan was a natural rogue. He contrived the marriage of his brother-in-law Thomas to the daughter of a Jamaican sugar merchant; she was suspiciously dark and died of dipsomania. Happily this did not prejudice her husband's career at Court where he became Master-at-Arms to Queen Victoria, earned the nickname 'Handsome Walsh' and was no doubt the dispenser of those favours of privilege and influence that Elizabeth and her husband later enjoyed.

The Walsh girls had each inherited a modest fortune. Donovan soon ran through his wife's share and encouraged Daniel to run up gambling debts that Elizabeth patiently redeemed. My great-grand-mother was a handsome and intelligent girl, with an enquiring mind above the average of women of her class and time.

The Indian Mutiny came as no surprise to her husband. Though he did not agree with those who asserted later that a certain day and date had been assigned for the rising, he did not doubt that such a conspiracy was inevitable and certainly was not very far off at the beginning of May 1857. He was, however, convinced that the events he was about to witness precipitated matters, and drove the native army into premature revolt.

By that time Elizabeth had born him two daughters, Edith and Florence, and a son, Fred. A few months earlier he had taken the precaution of sending them home, or rather to Germany, where they lived for several years and the children were educated.

On May 1st Daniel O'Callaghan was marching with his regiment from Allahabad to Meerut. A week or so earlier ninety native troopers of the Meerut garrison had refused to handle cartridges greased with the fat of the cows they held sacred. D.O'C (as he was later referred to by his family) paraded with his regiment at the court martial of these offenders and heard them condemned to labour on the roads—'a fate literally more dreadful than death'. It was apparent to him that some sort of rebellion was imminent, and he chafed at the cautious dispositions made by his Divisional General, William Hewitt—'now', as he wrote later, 'seventy years of age...corpulent and disqualified for energetic action, a *bon vivant* fond of the pleasures of the table... hospitable, kind and an excellent private character'.

When a few hours after the court martial the cantonments were in flames and most of the European occupants massacred, he witnessed the noble and devoted offer of Captain Rosson of the Carabineers to lead his cavalry and a troop of artillery to head off and to contain the mutineers, who, exalted with their unopposed rioting, were rampaging down the road to Delhi. To his dismay the Brigadier, Wilson, refused Rosson's request, being reluctant to divide a force that, in D.O'C's opinion, was more than adequate to have dealt with the situation. Thus the mutiny spread through the plains of Hindustan—an infection that he believed could have been arrested by capable and ruthless surgery at Meerut. In the event, his regiment having joined the mutineers, he attached himself to the British Foot Artillery, and served with the distinction shared by all Lawrence's subordinates at the siege of Delhi.

Whether on account of the resentment of his seniors at his outspoken criticism of Hewitt's blunders, or because he realised that the days of the Company were numbered, he arranged for his transfer to the British forces in China. There is no further record of his military career other than a campaign medal with a clasp on its faded red and white ribbon—'Pekin 1860'. Evidently he ministered once again to an army relieving a beleaguered city, this time rescuing the Manchus from the rebellious Taepings.

When he returned in 1861 to Calcutta, he published a pamphlet on 'The Fatal Falter at Meerut'. Reading its yellowing pages today, his criticisms and conjectures seem reasonable enough. In Churchillian prose he debates the consequences of Hewitt's inaction and gives one of those authentic glimpses of a catastrophe that sets the dry tinder of history ablaze. This does not seem to have delayed his well-earned promotion. In a few years he was appointed Surgeon General in the new-style Indian Army.

With the prospect of her husband spending most of his time in India, Elizabeth O'Callaghan returned finally to England. Her eldest daughter, Edith, had married Edmund Morgan, a Calcutta banker. For some time past Morgan's family had been legal advisers to the East India Company. Another branch that had emigrated to America was about to celebrate the birth of an infant, John Pierpoint junior, and of an era when all bankers would defer to the name of Morgan. Edith and her family had a house in Roland Gardens; Gran O'Callaghan, as Elizabeth now became, took a house nearby and made her dispositions for bringing out her beautiful, wilful and unpredictable daughter Flo. She rarely spoke of her son Fred. He had been a handsome but irresponsible youth. His father found him a job in China. He was soon in trouble and on his way home in disgrace. Considerately he died and was buried at sea. When his effects reached his mother she found among them all the affectionate letters she had written to him—unopened.

Perhaps this grievous hurt and the waywardness of her husband inclined her to extreme feminism and to preoccupation with the then novel principles of free thought. She was, however, gregarious by nature, and found plenty of time to enjoy the social privileges she owed to her brother Thomas's position at Court, and to attend the Old Bailey in pursuit of her study of criminology. She allowed Flo to find her own friends, encouraging her theatre-going and her acquaintance with theatrical folk. Her broadminded tolerance was to be severely tested.

Daniel O'Callaghan was still abroad when he received news of Florence's infatuation with a young actor, Henry Irving, fresh from the provinces, scarcely known and with no prospects whatever. Indignantly he forbade any further communication between them. Though his letter travelled slowly round the world, by the time it reached South Kensington its message had lost none of its vehemence. Elizabeth, attractive as she found this strange young man, yet knowing that her daughter was quite unfitted for the life he had to offer her, endorsed her husband's disapproval. Florence, being a girl of spirit, became more obstinately determined to evade her parents' interdiction. Her father himself reached London soon afterwards, ready to play his stern unrelenting part. But to Elizabeth's dismay he quickly appreciated the situation and then went straight over to the enemy's camp.

John O'Callaghan's widow had remarried and now, widowed once again, was Mrs Franks. Her recreation was mischief-making. The furthering of Flo's clandestine love affair would make piquant mischief, and she found in her disreputable brother, Cornelius Donovan, a willing and equally mischievous ally eager to be revenged on Elizabeth for her unconcealed disapproval when he had set himself up as a phrenologist in Ludgate Circus. So between them these subversive matchmakers persuaded Daniel to meet Flo's adored actor, with the result that he found his prospective son-in-law so congenial that in a very short time his prejudices evaporated in cigar smoke and the steam of rum punch. Thus Elizabeth's objections were overruled and preparations put in hand for Florence's marriage which, if not made in any particular haste, after its brief distresses she would repent in bitter celibacy for sixty years of vigorous life.

D

III

M Y GRANDMOTHER'S SITUATION when she found herself left
to bring up her two children and dependent for her income
on an unreliable and now hostile husband was not desperate,
but infinitely galling to a woman of her pride. No doubt she could
count on help from her family in an emergency but it would have to
be extreme before she turned to them—she was as reluctant to ask
for money as she would be punctilious in repaying it. In her heart she
must have known that she had only her stubborn self to blame for her
present pass, and the fact that nobody had told her so can only have
aggravated her self-reproach. When Henry left her, her father was in
India where, on his retirement from active service, he had become
Deputy Inspector-General of Hospitals. From there he had written
incoherently to his daughter:

> *The reproach that that marriage was contracted in opposition to the
> wishes of your parents or to express it as justly in compliance with
> your own hopes and affection is one that could never now be thrown
> or even thought of against you except by mean and cruel people who
> pride themselves on their malignant sagacity...All that I have ever
> had has ever been and must always be cheerfully yours to have and
> to share.*

Flor would have found her father's gallant forbearance intolerable but
for her grim suspicion that the Donovans would see that he had little
to share, and for the certainty that he had seen the last of a son-in-law
in whom he found those habits most attractive that were to her most
odious. On the other hand her mother, though she made no bones
about Flo's wilful folly, could be trusted to lend a sympathetic ear
to her denunciations of men in general, and of her provoking husband
in particular. Thus Flo came to use Roland Gardens as a secure base
from which to skirmish with my grandfather's lawyers, and to confound
the well-meaning efforts of her friends to lure him home again or to
extract from him alimony commensurate with his income. His refusal

to return was categorical; he was less forthcoming about his income.
'I am informed,' wrote Flo's baffled solicitor, 'that Mr Irving has
indulged his employees with a banquet at the Freemasons' Tavern
the cost of which must have been something very considerable.'
Nevertheless the incorrigible host had so far made ample, if arbitrary,
provision for his family. My grandmother was careful with money
and a competent housewife. Two years of marriage to an actor with a
precarious salary of £10 a week had been a testing experience. The
rent of their little house in Wharfdale Road had been £50, regular
remittances to old Samuel Brodribb had amounted to £5 a month,
so that with household expenses and Henry's fares to the theatre
averaging £7 a week they had just managed to make both ends meet.
Henry's wanton hospitality had not made things any easier; but with
lobsters at 1s 6d, oysters at 2s 6d a 100, stout at 14s 6d a cask, and
whisky 3s 6d and port 1s 6d a bottle they had been able to do a certain
amount of entertaining. The fading Fechter and the evergreen Johnnie
Toole often came back with Henry to supper after the theatre. Indeed
it was on one such occasion that, after she had retired, supper had
degenerated into an 'orgy'—there was no other word for it, though
Henry never forgave her for using it. Now there would be no such
extravagances, and she should be able to live within her means unless
these proved to be as erratic as the resources and behaviour of her
husband.

My grandfather's position at this critical stage of his career was so
fraught with psychological and financial stresses as to jeopardise any
success he had gained. Bateman was now paying him a salary of £20
a week, but this would barely suffice to meet the cost of providing for
Flo and the children, of helping his old father, and of living himself
in the style expected of a rising star. For a time he continued to lodge
with the Batemans. Their care of him saved him from trying to resolve
his problems in drink—for there came a point when they feared that,
nearing the end of his tether, he might succumb to this professional
hazard. Not only had he lost his family, but now his friends, even
Toole, in their misguided attempts to reconcile him with his wife,
were becoming estranged. He had not yet forged the armour of
reserve that later would hide his vulnerable nature from the world.
   It was hard to make Flo understand that in his separation from her
and the children lay the hope of survival for them all. Beyond his art
life had little meaning, and on his success as an artist their future

depended. Had she realised this she would have been disturbed by a
letter she received from Manchester. Irving's old friend, Christopher
Bradshaw, had seen him there when he came on tour with *The Bells*.

> *I felt miserable to look at him* [he wrote to Flo]. *His appearance
> is so altered, you have no idea how shocked I felt. I would give a fair
> proportion of what I possess if I could take away his haggard look
> ...I am sure he isn't happy. No happy man ever looked like this.*

As Bradshaw's possessions included the railway guide that bore his
name, he must have been satisfied that Henry's ills were too deep
seated for financial remedy. But he had seen him at his nadir. By the
time Irving returned to London Mrs Bateman had found him rooms
of his own in Grafton Street. His success as Charles I strengthened
his hold on the public. Among his many admirers he found new
friends eager to welcome him to their homes. Gradually he recovered
his equilibrium and was once more on the rails of his predestination.

Gradually, too, Flo understood that his determination to live apart
from her was irrevocable and that, though he bore her no ill-will,
the subject as far as he was concerned was closed. 'I hope you will
wish me well as I wish you' were his last words to her. Had she done
so, her sons would have been spared tensions and trials that would
have been damaging to boys of lesser character.

If, then, my father and uncle during their childhood and adolescence
were to be dominated by a mother nursing an abiding grievance, and
were not handicapped by her perpetual airing of it, she must have had
qualities less apparent than the defects that had lost them a father.
It is hard to understand how a young woman bred to the acceptance
of Anglo-Indian and middle-class values and prejudices can for a
moment have imagined that she could find happiness by marrying an
uncouth young actor in character no less inscrutable than the Knight
from Nowhere of the legend he became. He was, no doubt, a romantic
figure and had a lean physical attraction. But their dissimilar backgrounds and ways of life were totally incompatible, and this was
apparent to all but themselves. As a friend remarked shortly after their
separation Flo was 'an active lady, fond of society and attention.
He was moody, reserved, absorbed in thought and even in private life
a very Hamlet'. Having made such a wild miscalculation of her capacity
as a wife, what reserves had she to call upon to meet the challenge of
mothering her two boys?

She was a tall and handsome young woman. Her head, with her

auburn hair parted in the middle and gathered in a low bun, would
have pleased Rossetti as much as the well-tapered neck on which it
was set proudly with a hint of arrogance. There can have been little
promise of compassion in her features. The regard of her wide-apart
eyes under almost manly brows was one of cool appraisal foreshadow-
ing an unfavourable verdict; her firmly-set lips indicated tenacity of
purpose. She may have imagined herself something of a bohemian.
Long before she met Henry she had become a keen playgoer. Her
mother had encouraged her friendships with stage folk. At the houses
of such respectable theatrical families as the Mathews and the Tooles
she had taken part in the kind of private theatricals that Dickens had
made popular. In that *galère* she had caught the eye of Clement Scott,
as yet a clerk in the War Office but soon to be the most courted dispenser of critical favours in the London Press. He was attracted by
her, and for a time wooed her with coy love lyrics. It was on their
way to one of his parties that she and Henry Irving accidentally met.
Scott may have welcomed the deflection of her attention to this young
actor as a neat denouement to their flirtation. That she met him
apparently at ease in the polite fringes of the theatrical world may have
aggravated her disillusion when she came to share with him the
impecunious and rather shabby existence of a young player preoccupied with the hatching of a genius apparent to no one but himself.

It would not have been surprising if this experience had turned
her love of the theatre into a hearty distaste of play-acting of any
kind. But not at all. As soon as she got her bearings again she recovered her delight in amateur theatricals and began to look forward
to promoting performances by her boys almost as soon as they could
walk. Equally contrarily, though she affected contempt for her husband's talents, she soon insisted on her right as his wife to a stage
box at his first nights, and of being placed on the free list of other
theatres—a courtesy that at that time members of the profession
extended to their colleagues and their families. Her presence at the
Lyceum cannot have been relished by her husband or by the Batemans
—for she was known to have blamed them in part for the way Henry
had treated her.

She had few interests, other than the theatre, beyond the busy
social round of South Kensington. Her family used to say that the
only book she read was Burke's *Peerage*. Yet her snobbishness was
not simply the innocent adulation of rank. Her intricate knowledge
of the nobility served primarily as a stimulus to her collection of

any news or gossip reporting its moral shortcomings or falls from grace. She clung firmly to the belief that there was no smoke without fire, and a whiff of it was to her the breath of life.

On the face of it she does not seem to have been very well equipped, practically or temperamentally, to bring up single-handed two sensitive boys—for with such a bizarre ancestry they were likely to be an eccentric pair. But paradoxically she not only created for them a placid and happy home but herself won their affection and trust to a degree that few mothers have been privileged to enjoy. Together they made a united trio, devoted to one another and as one reacting to any threat to their proud independence, and inclining to ridicule rather than to rancour in opposing it. In fact their attitude to life might have been inspired by one of Uncle John Cornelius's prolix epigrams:

> 'If we look,' says Racine, 'to the lives of the wise,
>   What opposite maxims we find!
>   Here sad Heracleitus despondingly cries,
>   While Democritus laughs at mankind!
>   Yet, as long as *my* stay in this planet extends,
>   To follow them *both* I propose—
>   With one,—may I weep for my suffering friends
>   With the other—I'll laugh at my foes.'

Unhappily the boys were taught to regard one foe as beyond the pale of this light-hearted philosophy—their father. He was not spared ridicule; but, being persuaded that he had injured their mother and was still a source of anxiety and offence to her, they came to regard him with a distrust and suspicion that to some extent warped their gay and generous natures.

IV

No. 10 GILSTON ROAD was on the left of the walled approach from the clattering Fulham Road to the secluded elegance of The Boltons. The house was set squarely in a generous plot of sour London soil. In summer it was pleasantly shaded by green leaves sprouting defiantly from the barren-looking branches of trees blackened by the continual precipitation of London grime. A visitor, having agitated a brass bell-pull set in the stucco wall, would wait expectantly until the garden door gave an admissive click in response to a remote signal from the house. A short flight of stone steps led steeply to the front door, and on each side of them the barred windows of the semi-basement peeped suspiciously through the sooty evergreens flanking the short drive. I have always visualised that house and its approach as the setting for the murder of Enoch Drebber in *A Study in Scarlet,* though its associations for me are by no means macabre, for at this distance Gilston Road reminds me only of brown sugar on brown bread-and-butter for tea, and summer games with my fanciful Uncle Laurence in its seemingly spacious garden.

Thither my grandmother brought her two boys in 1876. Geographically the move from their previous house was a short one; socially it was a far cry from the perimeter of Brompton Cemetery to the threshold of Roland Gardens. When in 1890 she bought the lease of the house, after protracted negotiations with her vacillating husband, she had so enlarged and improved it that she could claim with truth that her boys were much attached to it as their home. And well they might be, for she had been at pains to make it a happy one. This had been made easier by her discovery at an early age that they had an affinity of affection and interest as a rule found only in twins. Indeed, until they grew out of their uniform sailor suits, they might have been taken for twins. Their likeness to one another was most marked in their brown bird-like eyes set wide apart in their acorn-shaped faces—eyes bright with intelligence, and disconcerting when bent in critical appraisal on some suspect stranger. They shared,

too, a whimsical sense of humour that was expressed in terms of the
delightful nonsense that had been the legacy of Edward Lear to their
generation. My grandmother, though she had a caustic wit, lacked a
sense of humour; nevertheless she responded to their ridiculous chaff
and to their delight in mockery, being wise enough to know that this
deepened their love for her. They seem always to have been on nickname terms with one another. Harry was enduringly Bim or Bam;
Laurence grew from Wee to Lamb's Fry, or more waggishly Lord
Leek or The Welsh National Plant. Did they in calling their mother
'Malcho' detect at an early age her propensity for mischief-making?
That she accepted this and the kind of banter that inspired it was
proof of the strength of their alliance.

If her chief concern was for their health, their good manners and
their social aptitude, Gran and Flo's sister Edith could be relied upon
to improve their minds. A governess was installed at Roland Gardens
where, with their cousin Stella, they had a thorough grounding in
elementary subjects, supplemented by sporadic tutorials with their
grandmother that excited in them an intellectual curiosity far beyond
their years. When Harry was five years old, Mrs O'Callaghan attended
the trial for murder of the brothers Wainwright. No doubt she gave
him a vivid account of the proceedings that stood him in good stead
when forty years later he came to edit the volume dealing with that
case in Hodge's *Notable Trials*. Certainly she planted in his young
mind a love of accuracy and of the lucid arrangement of facts that in
time to come would make him an exemplary and entertaining crimino-
logist. And it was at her house that the boys met frequently a Russian
friend, the mother of one of Edith's contemporaries, who awakened
in eight-year-old Laurence an appetite for all things Russian that
would be keen throughout his life.

In the summer holidays both families would spend two or three
weeks together at one or other of the *plages* on the coast of northern
France and Belgium. Harry would remember the delights of sitting
with his mother outside the busy cafés sipping *crême de cacao* through
a smoother layer of delicious cream; from those happy excursions
Laurence would date his love of bathing and the excitement of trying
to talk to foreigners in their own language.

From Dunkirk in 1879 Harry wrote to his father:

*We enjoyed ourselves immensely at your benefit. I particularly
liked Charles 1 and want to know when The Corsican Brothers*

commences as mother has promised to take us both to London in time for the first night and I am looking forward to it. My brother and myself send you a souvenir of this place which we like very much. I had several birthday presents, mother opera glasses, Laurence a purse, auntie and uncle gave me a set of plays of all nations. We have a theatre here a small affair after yours and we go every other night to see plays. They don't act badly but in French. We also have balls and concerts. We bathe every day and Laurence swam a little today. We are so happy that I wish you were with us as you swim.

I am,

With love,

Your affectionate son,

Harry.

My grandfather's reaction to this letter must have been as confused as the thoughts of the boy who wrote it. It is hard to imagine how Harry and Laurence reconciled the contempt for their father instilled into them by his implacable wife and their growing appreciation of the advantages to be gained by keeping on good terms with him. Certainly their dilemma nourished in them a machiavellian subtlety that, being at odds with their natures, would in due course breed its own tensions. For their growing awareness of the problems of having estranged parents coincided with their father's emergence as un-disputed head of his profession and as the presiding genius of the Lyceum theatre.

One of the symptoms of my grandmother's dudgeon was to put the darkest interpretation on his relations with the women he worked with or who were known to be his close friends. Often these suspicions were ludicrous, and never more so that in the case of Isabel Bateman, his first leading lady, whose deep and unrequited affection for him was a contributory factor to the ending of his partnership with her mother. As this target drifted out of range, the fire of her jealousy was directed against the Baroness Burdett Coutts. At this critical time of Irving's entry into management he owed much to the friendship and advice of that cultivated philanthropist, and, by implication, to the collateral security her friendship gave him, though in fact he never asked her for financial help.

Flo urged a mutual friend to make her suspicions known to them.

I am continually hearing of the name of the Baroness Burdett Coutts coupled with that of my husband, Mr Henry Irving, in a manner

*which I am sure and hope neither of them would like. My friends
naturally remark 'Can she possibly know that he is a married man
with two children whom he has long since deserted?'*

It is unlikely that the most malign of her friends would have encouraged her in these oblique attacks on her husband. Anyhow the
Baroness was soon forgotten when Irving announced that his partner
at the Lyceum would be Ellen Terry. Such theatrical gossip as Flo
avidly collected would have persuaded her, if she needed persuasion,
that Irving would find the charms of this enchanting actress irresistible,
and that Miss Terry would be a formidable and lasting obstacle to their
reconciliation. Certainly this was the picture she drew for Harry and
Laurence of the Wench, as they called her. Yet the boys, though
thoroughly imbued with the idea that their father's association with
Ellen Terry was a gross and final insult to their wronged mother, were
naturally disposed to a measure of casuistry when it came to choosing
between their loyalty to their mother and denying themselves the
theatrical delights that their father's favour could afford them. Happily
when next they had to face this dilemma the occasion strained their
allegiances less than usual.

On the evening of September 18th, 1880, the foyer of the Lyceum
theatre was crammed with starched and flounced notables for the first
night of *The Corsican Brothers*. It was the opening of Henry Irving's
third London season, and to be seen at his first nights was to be of the
socially elect. It was more to Irving's purpose that many pre-eminent
in the other arts were there to pay homage to his own. All those
scrimmaging in its vestibules were on the Lyceum 'list'. To be on the
'list', as the box office manager called it, was a coveted privilege. Those
listed constituted a sort of club that met twice a year at the opening
of the winter and summer seasons. The entrance fee was Irving's
goodwill; there were no subscriptions, for few had paid for their seats
—the patrons of the drama on those occasions enjoying the patronage
of its most admired exponent. The list ran to social extremes from
the Prince and Princess of Wales in the Royal Box to some old actor
friend of my grandfather's stock company days, more comfortably
disposed in the dress or upper circle.

In the stalls shirt fronts crackled and lorgnettes flashed like helio-
graphs as the habitués strained and craned to identify and greet each
other, making sure that their presence was noted by the press—

unaware that Irving's manager, Bram Stoker, had already seen to this. Scattered among them were the critics, little pockets of resistance to the seething enthusiasm that Irving's subtle sense of occasion had promoted. Programmes ('the Bill of the Play will in every part of the House be supplied without charge. No Fees of any kind are permitted...') were fluttered as the parts allotted to old favourites in the company were noted and the splendours forecast in the synopsis of scenes assessed. Some would remark with regret that Ellen Terry was not appearing; the knowledgeable would remind each other that she was touring the provinces with her husband, Charles Kelly. Here and there elderly playgoers would be boring their neighbours with their recollections of Charles Kean's production of the play. The house lights were lowered; the decorous hubbub was stilled. The curtain rose on the first piece. Most of the audience regarded this as a tiresome interruption of the social prelude to the evening's business.

Flo, flanked by her boys immaculate in Eton suits, swept through the portico where broughams and hackney cabs were discharging their cargoes. In the foyer Bram Stoker, now Irving's deputy as front-of-the-house host, greeted familiar patrons and eased the passage of the more important by directing attendants to see them to their places. As soon as he recognised the tall commanding figure of my grandmother and her young escorts, he disengaged himself and advanced to receive her, his resignation masked by an unconvincing affectation of pleasure. The boys would notice her brusque acceptance of his courtesies as he conducted them to their box; their bright little eyes exchanged mischievous signals as he made much of them and arranged to take them behind the scenes after the second act. For their mother had not concealed from them her dislike of Stoker and of his accomplice, L. F. Austin, Irving's gentle secretary, whom she regarded as conspirators bent on preventing her direct communication with her husband. In fact my grandfather was, as his friend Toole said, such 'a Turk' at letter writing that but for them she might have had no communication with him at all. As it was she attributed any of his sins of omission or commission to their unctuous influence.

They had arrived as the lights went up after the curtain-raiser. The amusing little comedy had served its purpose to sustain suspense and to cover the arrival of late-comers. The boys cannot have failed to observe the kaleidoscopic change of the scene below them as the dark heads in the stalls bowed in conversation became white faces uplifted as they scanned the box and identified Irving's family in confidential asides. A round of applause greeted the musical director, Mr Hamilton Clarke, as he emerged (down to the waist and lit from below) from the orchestra pit. At the end of the overture, as the lights were dimmed and the orchestra played the anticipatory bars that hushed the audience, the boys leaned forward with their elbows on the velvet rim of the box, cupping their faces, pale with expectancy, in their hands. They were already enthralled as the strip of light beneath the curtain expanded to reveal—Corsica, the Hall and Terrace Dei Franchi at Cullacaro.

Dumas's tale of the ill-fated twin brothers Franchi was very much to their taste, providing as it did a measure of fraternal self- identification, spectacular scenes (the first was seventy feet deep and the last a snow-bound forest glittering in the moonlight), a *bal masqué* at the Paris Opera House, a duel and a hair-raising apparition. The finer points of the play and of the acting may have eluded them, but they relished the performance no less than the most sophisticated members of the audience. It was in the provision of entertainment acceptable to the young and to the old, to those with and without intellectual pretensions, that their father excelled.

In due course Stoker collected them. They reached the stage in time to see the opera house scene being dismantled, and for Stoker to point out its ingenious false perspectives that necessitated children impersonating adult revellers far up-stage to enhance the impression of its depth. They were introduced to William Terriss; the cheerful banter of this big, jolly, handsome man contrasted oddly with his sinister make-up as the villainous M. de Château Renaud. With him was a younger actor, comparatively short and unprepossessing in appearance. Earlier he had had an unnerving experience when, playing a minor role, he had entered from the deep extremity of the first scene. As he had advanced slowly down stage the audience, mistaking him for Irving, applauded rapturously; the applause dissolved in laughter as they realised their mistake, thereby dispelling momentarily the romantic illusion that Irving, as *metteur-en-scène*, had striven painfully to create. The embarrassed actor would have been more disconcerted had he not had other preoccupations.

He had been a member of Irving's company for several years. By then it must have been apparent to him that he was not intended by nature to be an actor. But his purpose in persisting was to master stage technique in order to perfect himself as a dramatist. That night's curtain raiser, *Bygones*, was the second of his one-act plays that Irving had bought and produced. This encouragement had sharpened his ambition. His name was Arthur Wing Pinero.

While this kindly man was chatting to the boys, another actor, Matthison, joined them. He was dressed as their father's double for the coming scene when the ghost of one brother (Irving was playing both parts) had to appear to the other. Matthison was an actor who had suffered much misfortune; he had, no doubt, been engaged on compassionate grounds. The boys must have been tickled by the sight of their counterfeit father. Laurence, probably over-excited by Terriss's breezy familiarities, cheeked poor Matthison in words Pinero knew would be wounding. Pinero, with Harry's help, persuaded him to apologise. He and the boys could not have guessed that this embarrassing incident would be a lasting bond between them.

Suddenly Irving appeared among them. Pinero watched the brief constrained meeting between him and his sons. There and then he vowed to do all in his power to bring them together by gaining their trust and helping them to understand one another. He survived them all and lived to fulfil his vow. He was rewarded by the lifelong regard they felt for a friend who did so much to heal the scars of their estrangement.

If the boys were ill at ease with their father, it may have been due to their bewilderment at the contrast between the austere and commanding figure of the actor-manager and the image of the vain and irresponsible player their mother so frequently evoked. They would have been still less at ease had they known that he was fully aware of Flo's persistent denigration of him. Only recently he had been warned by a friend of the effect this might have on his sons. His remonstrance was so severe that it alarmed Flo into prevarication.

> ...the wicked [she protested] *have parted us and are still to keep us apart or rather to feed your dislike of me. Indiscreet I have been in this instance but wicked never. I have not once reproached you with the cruel past and still believe that you will one day make some reparation. In the meantime pray disabuse your mind of the idea that your children are trained not to care for you. From the moment they could lisp their prayers I have taught them nightly to invoke God's blessing on your head.*

He cannot have derived much comfort from these assurances or from the thought of his children being taught by an aggrieved mother to pray for their wayward father. Once roused, he made up his mind to remedy the situation. He warned her that if she did or said anything hurtful to Ellen Terry she could look to him to fulfil no more than his legal obligations to her. This, he hoped, would protect him from frivolous divorce proceedings that might damage their theatrical partnership At the same time he decided to concern himself in the education of his sons. What he probably regarded as an attempt by their mother to exploit their theatrical talents had not escaped his notice. It was high time that they disabused themselves of any idea of going on the stage. His first step in that direction would be to send them to boarding school, and so detach them from the petticoat influences of Gilston Road and Roland Gardens.

Whether he liked it or not, the boys by this time were salted actors and much in demand for children's performances got up by their mother's friends in support of local charities. At three Harry already was the pride of his dancing master, the famous D'Aubon, and had danced a hornpipe on the stage of the Haymarket Theatre. Later, at the house of his mother's friends, the Routledges, he had played Captain Corcoran in *HMS Pinafore* with a cast that included little Maximilian Beerbohm. Harry, probably owing to a show of indolent condescension, was relieved of the part during early rehearsals; later he had the intense satisfaction of having to be persuaded to resume it, as no child could be found to take his place. Well padded, for he was a weedy child, he appeared as Master Bardell in a private performance of *Pickwick* at the St George's Hall. Soon he and Laurence were to appear in public for the first time in *The School for Scandal,* played in Knightsbridge Barracks by hale children in aid of ailing ones in Chelsea Hospital. Harry was cast for Joseph and Laurence for Charles Surface—a fair indication of their respective bents. They were coached by Mrs Chippendale, whose husband had played Polonius to Edmund Kean's Hamlet, and had himself instructed their father in Kean's methods, when, as a young actor in Manchester, the latter had played Hamlet for his benefit.

Yet in spite of all this, and of the gushing adulation it must have won them, the boys had not developed those odious conceits that are the badge of infant prodigies. They remained grave and serious-minded boys with sufficient sense of fun to keep their heads squarely on their shoulders, and their values remarkably well adjusted for their years.

My grandfather's education had begun in the tiny village school of Halsetown, a cluster of stone cottages perched bleakly on the moors above Penzance. There he learned to write and to read the Bible, *Don Quixote* and a collection of ballads, all the books available in the house of his aunt Sarah Penberthy, the wife of the mining captain with whom he spent his childhood. As far as he remembered, this simple schooling had stood him in good stead when he came to compete with London schoolboys of his own age. He had, therefore, been puzzled by the calls made upon him to contribute to the salary of his sons' governess—in his view disproportionate to the amount of knowledge she could possibly impart to such little boys. Evidently his ideas on education were old-fashioned. So, with his instinct for seeking expert opinion, he asked his old friend, Dr Edward Pinches, to advise him on their future schooling.

He had good reason to trust the judgment of this wise and kindly man. When he came to London with his parents he attended the City Commercial School near Lombard Street. The headmaster was Dr Pinches. Parents, observing that the black gown and broadcloth of his academic uniform was set off by the Byronic flamboyance of his neckwear, were not surprised to hear that he considered elocution so important a part of the curriculum that he taught it himself. He had been quick to detect a seed of talent in this rather ungainly West Country boy with a slight impediment of speech. Soon he was coaching him to play a leading part in the speech-day recitals at Sussex Hall. When the boy told him that he wished to be an actor, he did what he could to overcome Mrs Brodribb's prejudices. Failing in this, he introduced Johnnie Brodribb to the old actor William Creswick, who later helped the lad to get his first engagement with the Sunderland Stock Company. Small wonder that my grandfather's respect and affection for his benefactor were deep and lasting.

As a start Dr Pinches recommended a small preparatory school in Hereford Square. There the boys could be gently hardened off for a year or so before going to Linton House School in Holland Park Avenue, where they could be prepared for entry to a public school. Any misgivings their mother may have had about these decisions must have been soothed at the end of their first term at Hereford Square.

There can be no question [wrote Mr Simpson the headmaster] *that both boys have attainments far above the average. Harry is a perfect model of a boy. His bright face, his quickness of perception and the intelligent comprehension which he shows all that is told him make it a pleasure to teach him. A better hearted boy I'm sure never existed. Laurence possesses very many of Harry's noble qualities. He is a charming little boy and continues to be the idol of his schoolfellows and the darling of his masters. He may not be so sharp as Harry is but certainly he has more perseverance.*

Making every allowance for the hyperbole expected of an usher by a doting parent, as an estimate of the relative qualities of the boys it was not wide of the mark.

At Linton House too they soon made themselves as popular with the masters and the boys. They were beginning now to show divergences of character and appearance. Harry was inclined to be sceptical and cool in sentiment unless his quick temper was aroused by anything smacking of injustice—particularly in matters affecting his mother and his brother. Laurence appeared to be more sensitive. He was certainly more vulnerable. He was not at pains, like Harry, to conceal his light-heartedness, and was inclined to take too sanguine a view of the essential goodness of his fellow creatures. Harry was fastidious in his habits and in his dress—very conscious of the cut and style of the Eton suits that were in keeping with his gravity of bearing. Laurence was indifferent to his appearance and incorrigibly untidy—tweeds were as complementary to his dishevelment as cloth to the precocious elegance of his brother. Both were industrious, but easily distracted by curiosity in subjects beyond the range of required study.

At both these schools the fact that their father was an actor and that they themselves enjoyed playacting added, if anything, to their popularity. The theatricals they organised and led were encouraged by the masters and welcomed as a diversion by their schoolmates. Yet Linton House, while ensuring that they would take entrance exams in their stride, failed to condition them for the spartan life that lay ahead.

Their uncle, Edmund Morgan, had a nomination for Marlborough College, and he agreed with Dr Pinches that this should be turned to account. Though Edmund Kean had managed to get his son Charles into Eton, the old prejudices against theatrical folk were still deepseated. The boys were entered for the Christmas term in 1882. Their mother needed all her courage to face this first loosening of the bonds that held her sons so closely to her and to accept the growing influence that their father would exert upon them. Had she seen the letter that Mr Hardy, the headmaster of Linton House, had written to their future housemaster, and had she appreciated the physical rigours of the system to which she was committing her ewe lambs, her parting from them would have been doubly agonised.

Mr Irving has requested me to write to you regarding his sons who are to join you at Marlborough after the Midsummer Holidays.

Harry and Laurence have been my pupils for three years. They are boys of good ability, very gentlemanly and very tractable. Both are perfectly truthful and otherwise singularly free from moral faults, more or less common among boys. I should like to see both display more energy in work. That they do not do so is due I think to want of physical strength and also in Laurence's case to an over-playfulness which however is hardly a bad feature in a boy of 10.

They both shrink from games which involve effort or violent exercise of any kind. I hardly know to what extent football and other games are compulsory at Marlborough but think especially Harry ought not at first at any rate to be made to join in these except to a very limited extent. It seems to me that to drag the boys into the usual amount of public schoolboys' vigorous exercise now might be fatal to them. They have not the necessary physique. I do not mean that they ought not to play at all, far from that, physical exercise is the very thing they want but it must be under wise control.

I am writing you thus frankly for I assume you will be anxious to know as much as possible about the boys especially as, if I understand Mr Irving rightly, they are to reside in your own house...

A less propitious introduction could not have preceded them. Only an enlightened housemaster would respond favourably to the prospect of accepting such peculiar charges. In the material flowing through Dr Arnold's production lines—the pattern to which all public schools now conformed—two flaws were unacceptable, physical infirmity and eccentricity; and the more intolerable of these was eccentricity.

V

A HEAVY COLD IN THE HEAD prevented my grandmother seeing off her sons to their public school. It was as well. For, however determined they may have been to put a brave face on this dreaded separation, her distress, sharpened perhaps by glimpses of their more loutish and unattractive future schoolmates, might have unmanned them. So Gran O'Callaghan, fond but less emotional, bundled them wistful but dry-eyed into a carriage full of boys enviably familiar to each other and, at any rate until the train started, polite enough to the little newcomers committed to their charge. For Harry, a rather delicate twelve-year-old, and Laurence, only a slightly sturdier ten, were plainly tender novices to be submitted to the climatically harsh and physically rigorous conditions for which Marlborough College was notorious. Gran, when their train was lost to sight in the murky exits from Paddington Station, drove back to Gilston Road, where she gave Flo a consoling report of their manly farewells.

On the journey to Marlborough the boys must have realised the awful finality of their commitment. It was one thing to be at boarding school a few yards from home among London boys ready to be impressed by their theatrical background and sympathetic to their unconventional interests; it may not have occurred to them that the prospect of being invited for the jolly teas and half-holiday outings that the Irvings' mater dispensed ensured them cupboard popularity of a kind. It was quite another thing to be pitchforked into an utterly strange institution unlikely to indulge their foibles or to tolerate any attempt to evade the stringencies of its code. The chances were, moreover, that the less they said about their father's profession the better. Though, as it turned out, such fears were more or less ground-less, they could not have known that they were heading for a school less like Tom Brown's than most of its kind.

The authorities at Marlborough College made a humane practice of allowing very young boys to spend an acclimatising year in a

small house, The Priory, at that time under the benign supervision
of Mr W. Mansell. While otherwise entering fully into the school
life they had a refuge during those out-of-school hours so dear to
tormenting bullies, though considering that the College was much
frequented by the sons of clergy (who had a reputation for working
off the heavenly restraints at home by creating merry hell for their
juniors at school) there seems at that time to have been virtually no
bullying at all. Certainly this sensible arrangement made life easier
for the new bugs, as they were called. Laurence's immediate report
on their situation was calculated to reassure their mother.

> *Dear Malcho,*
>   *I know you will be glad to hear that we are very happy but of
> course nothing like as happy as if we were with you. Here all the
> boys are very nice. There are only 14 boys. I sleep all alone in a very
> nice little room. Harry sleeps with a few other boys and says it's very
> nice as long as you tell the boys stories they are very nice to you...
> One of the nicest boys is a South American fellow who showed me a
> lot of things amongst which was a bottled up snake...Here we see the
> Daily Papers. A fellow told me you pay about 30£ extra for being in
> a master's house...*

This buoyant letter veiled the despair of two most un-blithe spirits.
For ever since they had arrived they appeared to Mr Mansell to be
stunned with home-sickness. All his kindly efforts to cheer them up
and to distract them from their melancholy preoccupation were of no
avail. They seemed unwilling or unable to accept their situation, or
to resign themselves to making the best of it. Whenever they showed
signs of responding to his encouragement, a letter would arrive
from their mother, plunging them once more into brooding despondency. That they were clearly boys of above average intelligence,
and unusually good-natured, only added to his puzzlement. Never
before had he failed to gain the confidence and co-operation of two
such little boys.

   To his dismay the term was only three days old when Mrs Irving
appeared in Marlborough. He could not prevent her seeing her sons,
and the effect of her doing so was exactly what he expected. Not only
did it leave them more home-sick than ever, but it landed him with a
distressed and now hostile parent, more fearful than ever for her sons'
welfare. She left them, as she noted in her diary, 'very sad'. But at
least Mr Mansell was now aware of the disruptive influence he had to

deal with. Convinced that the future education of these promising boys was at stake, he consulted his colleague Mr Beesley, to whose house, Summerfield, they would go in a year's time if their mother could be persuaded to see reason.

Two days later a scene occurred worthy of the pen of Wilkie Collins. The brothers, taking advantage of the freedom Marlburians enjoyed in their spare time, went for a walk in Savernake Forest. Harry, perhaps, was pumping Laurence for ideas for stories that he must be ready to tell to save his skin. Happily he had discovered that Edgar Allen Poe was unknown to his audience and that his rendering of the macabre was much to their taste. The dejected boys were sitting on a stile when through the autumnal wood a man approached them. As he came nearer they saw that he was wearing a bowler hat and London attire. The russet woods were matched by the colour of his close-trimmed beard. He addressed them rather severely by name.

> *Who should it be* [wrote Harry to his mother] *but that blackguard Stoker. His intention was to find out whether we would like to remain here or go* home. *We received him as coldly as possible but we were thoroughly taken by surprise. We persisted in a wish to consult you, but he was going directly to telegraph to H.I. He saw Mr Beesley and they had a long conversation...This is a terrible mar to our happiness and we are rather wretched. I don't know what to do. I was getting on so much better before this cad came.*

Stoker had been momentarily non-plussed by Harry's spirited refusal to discuss the matter with him. After telling them sternly that he would report the conversation to their father he turned and was soon lost to sight, leaving the boys to their anger and resentment at this intrusion into a matter that solely concerned themselves and their mother. Laurence in his report of what he described as 'a curious coincidence' added 'when he had gone Harry began crying...there is an Irish boy here and he says he's heard that Bram Stoker drinks. We are jogging along very nicely...' He was the more easily appeased by this unwarranted assurance of Stoker's inebriety; a touch of melodrama had at least alleviated the boredom that animated his longing for home. Harry, responsible as he felt for them both, was shocked and humiliated by the implications of this mysterious visit.

Stoker's dramatic appearance had been the result of agitated exchanges that followed Flo's return to London. She had poured out her anxieties to her brother-in-law Edmund Morgan. He would have been more inclined to see the situation from the point of view of the schoolmasters than of the too-fond mother, accustomed as he was to coping with her temperamental obsessions. Realising that the time had come for immediate remedial action, he wrote at once to Irving reminding him that he was now responsible for the boys' education, and that this did not begin and end with paying school fees, but called for the exercise of authority and the sound advice that only a father could give. Unless he intervened, the boys' lives might be ruined by their father's default and their mother's indulgence.

Irving reacted characteristically. In a telegram to Morgan he accepted his responsibility and undertook to act on his advice. Stoker was sent to Marlborough on reconnaissance, while Dr Pinches called on Flo and explained to her the dangers of the situation and how they could be overcome with a little co-operation on her part. The following day Morgan went to Grafton Street to hear the reports of Irving's agents. Evidently they agreed that the boys should be left at Marlborough to work out their own salvation, and that in future Flo would defer in all matters concerning their education to her husband.

For the boys that encounter in the forest had been the moment of truth. Together they came suddenly to their senses. They realised that had not their mother's visit suggested that there was still a loop-hole for escape and distressed them by her own unhappiness, they were becoming reconciled to their fate. Now, if only to spite their father, they would cast home-sickness aside and resist any attempt to send them home in shame to Gilston Road. Later that afternoon Mr Mansell knew that his troubles were over and that he had in his care two biddable and promising boys. He had good reason to congratulate himself on a diagnosis that had led to such a speedy and, he hoped, permanent cure.

That night Harry may have learnt for the first time the ruthless theatrical convention that the show must go on however despondent the player. He would, like Sheherazade, have to buy his own and his brother's immunity from ragging by spinning a well-turned yarn. However dispirited, he would have to give a spirited performance. A plot that recently he had jotted down might suit the occasion and his mood.

THE VAMPIRE ON THE COMMON

A traveller was once benighted on a common in the North of Scotland and being far from any habitation he feared he would have to remain there all night. He suddenly spied a blue light, and thinking it came from a cottage advanced towards it. As soon as he moved forward the light did the same until it got quite close to him. He then saw it was a large bat which took the form of a most hideous man. Jumping on the throat of the traveller and making a hole in his arm it began sucking the wretched man's blood. The figure after remaining in this occupation for about five minutes left him. On a coach that was passing the gentleman inside seeing the traveller on the ground took him to his house. When he related his adventure to the gentleman he was [told] *that this vampire was the spirit of a murderer who had been hanged and buried on this common.*

All this could not have happened at a more inconvenient time for my grandfather. He was in the thick of the final rehearsals of *Much Ado About Nothing*. It was to be his most ambitious production, and he had pledged most of his resources to mount it handsomely. But he found time to give his assurances to Mr Beesley that the boys should remain at Marlborough, and that he could expect them to be in a more reasonable frame of mind. He followed this up by writing a stern but timely letter to Harry pointing out that his purpose in sending them to Marlborough was that they should equip themselves to earn their living in any other profession but his own. If they had any thought of going on the stage they should abandon it, for, regardless of whether or not they had any talent for acting, the fact that they were his sons would be, if anything, a disadvantage if they did so. His motives for writing this may have been mixed, but it was likely that the still fresh memories of all he had endured in the twenty years it had taken him to reach his present position urged him to deflect them from a course that might be hazardous and unrewarding. He was only a little older than they were when the great Samuel Phelps had warned him that 'acting was an unrequiting profession'; such success as he had had was too recent to convince him that Phelps had been wrong.

What a beastly letter that is of Irving's [Harry commented in sending it on to his mother]. *It was written because he was in a bait about the row caused by the College muddle. But now let us talk about more pleasant subjects. You asked what position we each took in the school. Laurence is in the Second which is the lowest in the College. But you would naturally expect the youngest boy in the school to be there. I am in the Lower Third and there are two forms below me...We went to tea with Mr Beesley and enjoyed ourselves*

*enormously...I am getting now into the ways of the school. There is
a fellow named Tate who is a relation to the Archbishop...he is my
best friend and we often buy grub and go up to the forest together.
I find my lessons pretty easy especially the Greek. There seems to
be very little going on now, Egypt is so quiet. I wonder what they'll
do with Arabi.*

A few days later the first knot of the apron string was unravelled.

*The boys have begun to humbug us somewhat because I get so many
letters. I should think one nice one to both of us a week would be very
jolly...I am sure you have a quite good reason for sending so many
letters considering you haven't (as most mothers have) a husband
to be with you it is natural all your love should be given to your
children...Talking of your husband he has sent us an immense cake
from Buzzards which is almost as big as a playbox. There was no
letter just a little note—'to Harry and Laurence from their father.
This is not much ado about Nothing'.*

Harry's devotion to his mother was not at all diminished by recent
stresses. For the rest of his schooldays he would write to her at least
twice a week. She would have to accept the withdrawn self-possession
that now would be his characteristic. She would be his confidant in
all things, but in none his keeper. He realised he would now have to
reckon with his father, and that independence from him could only be
won by making the most of the education he was providing. Between
these parental extremes he would have to find his own way. By hard
work he could repay the tremendous debt he owed to his mother, and
might force his father to accept his self-determination. He knew he
had the brains and industry to do both.

Laurence marked his brother's change of heart, and was prepared
to accept what he found acceptable. He was by nature more easy-going.
And after all no father could be wholly bad who could provide such a
magnificent cake.

Did either of them note the sly innuendo on the card?

As the year closed the tensions of the last months began to relax.
Flo sought consolation in the exacting social routines of South Kensington—dinner parties at Roland Gardens, amateur theatricals,
drives in the Morgans' brougham and visits to the theatre as enjoyable
as those to the Central Criminal Court. Sometimes she was escorted
by her father. He had now returned from India for good, and was

settling down to a bachelor existence based on the United Services
Club and on such hospitalities as his wife and daughter offered him.
When the boys came home for the Christmas holidays, their spirits
and their reports confirmed their qualified reconciliation to school life.

My grandmother noted in her diary 'Boxing Day. Boys began
holiday lessons with Mr Sickert.' They must have found their tutor
distractingly entertaining—his vulpine good looks set off by the
Third Empire effect of his long frock coat and four-in-hand cravat.
For it seems more than likely that he was 23-year-old Walter Richard
Sickert. He had been for some time a 'utility member' of the Lyceum
company, and only the year before had abandoned acting to devote
himself wholly to painting. He had been with Irving long enough
to become the friend of Ellen Terry, and through her of Edward
Godwin, who had taken him to see Poel's production of the first
quarto *Hamlet*. His friend and fellow-painter, Johnston Forbes-
Robertson, had conversely, when he joined the cast of Irving's *Much
Ado*, committed himself irrevocably to the stage. It was not unlikely
that my grandfather may have asked Ellen Terry (for by now he
trusted her judgment in most things) to help him find a tutor for his
sons, and she, perhaps out of curiosity about the ménage at Gilston
Road, may have reminded him of the striking if not very talented
young actor, fluent in French and German, who would now be glad
of a little extra work to help him to pay his way through the Slade
School. Forbes-Robertson would have endorsed her suggestion. So,
perhaps, young Sickert spent those mornings teaching the Chief's
sons, with frequent interruptions to answer questions about their
father and to give encores of lively but reverent imitations of his acting.
Later he may have regaled Ellen Terry with his impressions of Irving's
obdurate wife, and of her acute boys who had begun to make their
presence felt in the Lyceum enclave. So he may have been the first to
erase the outlines of the crude caricature that Harry and Laurence
had come to accept as a portrait of their father, and to sketch in for
them a more authentic likeness, for he was deeply impressed with
Irving's personality and to his dying day reflected something of it
in his own.

Tickets for *Much Ado About Nothing* were waiting for the boys
on their return to Gilston Road. These were rejected in favour of a
visit to Toole's Theatre, where they saw their friend Mr Pinero's
first full-length play, *Girls and Boys*. Toole would not have hesitated
to rally Irving on the wisdom of his sons' choice. If my grandfather

felt this to be a calculated slight he kept it to himself. The next day
he took them to the pantomime, *Dick Whittington*, at the Avenue
Theatre. The holidays began to assume the pattern they would conform
to during the next five years—theatres every other night, parties at
home for school friends, and theatricals that now had the added charm
of defiant conspiracy. If love of home and the felicities provided
by their mother made absence from her hard to bear, it was on the
whole worth it. When there was a lull in the round of entertainments,
Harry and Laurence, in their separate snug rooms, each with its rapidly
growing and essentially individual library, charged themselves, like
the accumulators they were, with reserves of curious and stimulating
information that kept their fancies flickering during the prosaic intervals
reluctantly but now resignedly spent at school.

On the last day of those holidays they lunched with their father at
Grafton Street. His flat was crammed with fascinating bric-à-brac
that provided plenty of red herrings to divert conversation, if it
scented of confidences they were not yet prepared to share with him.
Together they pored over large volumes on costume and armour,
and explored the portfolios of engravings that littered the room.
Everything in it had some bearing on the profession they were forbidden to follow. While Irving talked to them he toyed with the
swords and sticks stacked beside the long mirror that had reflected his
patient self-rehearsings. Before they left they had made a friend and
ally of his dapper little valet, Walter Collinson. If later they told
their mother of Walter's recent marriage to May Holland, Ellen
Terry's dresser, a grim nod and pursing of her lips would accept this
as further evidence of a scandalous union.

With the summer came the end of a triumphant season at the
Lyceum. My grandfather's career was at its zenith, and his situation
altogether propitious for his long-planned expedition to the United
States. The Queen had commanded him to play *Much Ado* at Sandring-
ham. He had dined at Marlborough House and the Prince of Wales
had reciprocated by supping on the stage of the Lyceum. The Lord
Chief Justice, Coleridge, had presided over a farewell banquet given
in his honour at the St James's Hall. Gladstone's admiration of him
was well known. There were rumours that he might be knighted.

It looks as though you're going to be Lady Irving, doesn't it? [wrote
Harry to his mother]. *There seems to be such a lot of knighting
going about now…We have not yet had H.I's hamper. We only got*

a newspaper from him. It was the Daily Telegraph and was full of
gush about his Mathias. There was also a leading article about the
banquet full of gush about it would be proper for him to have some
high honour conferred on him. Of course it meant knighthood. I will
send it to you...if you like but it's awful rot.

Flo must have been in two minds about the rottenness of it. Entry
into the pages of Debrett was a pleasing prospect, however vile her
titular escort. Her feelings would have been even more mixed had she
known that when Gladstone's wishes were conveyed to her husband
he had declined the honour. 'There is a fellowship', he had written,
'among actors or a company that might be impaired by any elevation
of one member above another.' Even when present hopes faded, the
possibility that one day she might share his title was an undreamed-of
compensation. But for the time being she did not rest from provoking
the boys to disdain their father. Any gossip hinting at his inebriety,
any reports of divorce cases from which a moral might be drawn to
his disadvantage were sent off to Marlborough with dispatch. At
about this time the scandal sheets led her to believe that Charles Kelly
was to bring divorce proceedings against his wife. Enquiries to her
solicitor brought, alas, only a sharp rebuke and a warning to pay no
attention to such unfounded nonsense—though too late to prevent
her on this account working Harry up to righteous indignation.
'How dreadful it would be,' he protested, 'if that about Irving and
Ellen Terry was to come about in the divorce court. What a cad he
is to bring all this disgrace on himself.'

Gradually, however, the responses of her sons to such goads began
to lose conviction. For H.I.'s hampers when they did turn up were
bumper ones; and after repeated and wearisome demands he did supply
them with the autographs so coveted by their chums, and very occasionally a six-page, almost illegible letter broke his long silences—all
these things cumulatively curbed their criticism of him. So when he
left for America communication with his sons, though tenuous and
fragile, was sufficiently established for him to hope that when he
returned he would find them readier to judge him for themselves on
his merits, which, after all, were in the eyes of almost everyone but
their mother considerable.

It was much to the credit of the staff and the boys at Marlborough
College that these two aberrant lads were absorbed so painlessly into

its system. They were not dragooned into even pretending to care for games or into suppressing their eccentric interests. Neither was a born scholar, but both worked their way steadily up the school with an adult approach to learning that made it a pleasure to teach them. At a time when at least one old Marlburian was 'struck by the marvellous untidiness and want of uniformity in the boys' attire' and parents were declaring it a great pity that they looked so slovenly and dirty, Harry's oddity must have been made more conspicuous by the dandyish cut of his Eton jacket and his generally immaculate appearance. Laurence, on the other hand, fitted well into his dishevelled surroundings. 'He is well and happy,' Harry reported, 'but is as untidy and dirty as ever. The cold water gives him a fine excuse for not washing.'

Two afflictions they found hard to bear—monotony and chilblains. Harry made no bones about his boredom with school life. Thanks to Gran O'Callaghan he took a passionate interest in the world's news. Though his mother fed him with political and criminal intelligence and the major scandals of the divorce courts, his companions, other than Laurence, seemed as bored with such affairs as he was with the small change of school life. This was the harder to bear at a time when London was agog with the Phoenix Park murders and the Parnell affair. ('What a oner for Parnell Forster's speech was. I wonder if he did have anything to do with those murders in prison. He didn't seem to defend himself very well, did he? I do wish I was at home it would be so jolly...') Laurence was readier to come to terms with life as it was, and in his good nature was prepared at least to appear to enjoy it if by doing so he could give others pleasure. He could make a 'splendid joke' of most things from sowing vegetable seeds in his housemaster's flower garden to slanted reports of his father's failure at the Lyceum.

Both stubbornly refused to take the slightest interest in games. They were short-sighted and wore glasses. Their myopic attempts to play football and cricket earned them the derision of their fellow players and from the less patient encouraging kicks. 'I went to football,' Laurence wrote during his second term, 'it was horrid the boys hit us because we didn't know what to do and it was just spitting you wear nothing but your jersey I have heard that when it's terribly cold we have to play. Already I've got a cold from it.'

To which a term or two later Harry added: 'I don't care what Billy (his housemaster) says about us not going in for College sports and games. I'm not going to for all that. They are simply beastly.'

But the bounds were wide, and in time, as their ineptitude was recognised and tolerated, they were allowed to take their exercise on long walks together in the surrounding country.

It was not until the summer of 1886 that they began to figure as notables in the pages of the *Marlburian*. By that time they were leading a less harassed life in the Upper School. Harry, mildly protesting to his father that he had been ill-advised to go on the classical side, seemed disinclined to exert himself to the limits of his capacity, and he may have surprised his tutors by winning in June of that year the Congreve Prize. Laurence, on the modern side, was indulging his passion for languages. He was able to take Italian as an extra. Russian was not in the curriculum, but this did not prevent him from studying it. His letters to his mother were not the usual fourteen-year-old appeals for tuck and pocket-money but for books on Russian grammar and history. When hard pressed he had no hesitation in inviting his father to make his contribution—'I have asked him to send me *Die Geschichte Russische* —the price is pretty stiff...I am sure that if he didn't spend his £2 19s on that he would spend it on something not half so worthy.' Irving probably did so gladly if it was a sign that at least one of his sons had no wish to be an actor. In fact Laurence at that time was thinking it would be very jolly to be a military engineer, so much so that he had surprised his brother by enlisting in the Cadet Corps. 'Yesterday,' reported Harry to his mother, 'Laurence donned his uniform and looked a very dapper little soldier; the last thing I saw of him as the "troops" marched out of the court he was making frantic efforts to keep in step.'

Laurence would hardly ever again be described as dapper, and if he managed to get into step that afternoon he soon fell out of it for life.

Earlier that year the Sixth Form Debating Society moved 'that in the opinion of this House the stage as a profession is in no way derogatory to gentlemen'. Irving, H. B., though in the Remove, was invited by the proposer to support the motion.

I got an enthusiastic reception when I rose and when I sat down— and urged on by the excitement of the moment and by the cause I was pleading I flatter myself I made an eloquent speech. The opposition utterly broke down, the House was all for us and our side gained a great victory. Oh, I feel so glad that at last I have had a chance of publicly defending the stage.

Debates proved so popular that membership of the Society ceased to be confined to the Sixth. Harry, having found a field of endeavour where short sight was no handicap, and where he could exercise his gifts fully and even elegantly clad, joined the Society and rarely missed a meeting. Evidently he was a persuasive orator, for he succeeded in the course of his remaining years at Marlborough in convincing the majority of the House that superannuation was desirable, that horse-racing was pernicious, that temperance movements were to be encouraged and that a belief in ghosts was unworthy of the enlightenment of the nineteenth century. In this last debate the motion for the ghosts, as it were, was led by E. F. Benson, the son of the Archbishop of Canterbury. Happily his belief in ghosts was as unshaken as his affection for the leader of the opposition. 'He is a great friend of mind,' wrote Harry. 'He is a prefect, intensely amusing, fond of acting and the Old Bailey, and recommends himself to me.' Benson's athleticism, for he was captain of the rugger team, did not lessen his regard for his professedly unsporting friend. More than once they celebrated the first day of the holidays by lunching at Lambeth Palace and spending the afternoon at the Central Criminal Court. As a rule Laurence supported his brother in these debates. Upon only one issue were they divided—that suicide should not be considered a crime. Harry spoke against the motion and carried the House with him. There would come a time when he would be sharply reminded of Laurence's defeat on this occasion.

Penny Readings, once a popular college entertainment, had fallen into decline owing to the alleged apathy of the organisers. The gentle miscellany of duets, glees and piano pieces that were the rule were not very skilfully performed, were poorly attended and coolly received. Some complained that the songs were not as comic as they might be; others that the choice of music was not likely to educate the taste of the school. But in November 1886 a newcomer was to take the stage and word went round (spread no doubt by his claque in Somerville House) that his performance should not be missed. As a result the Bradleian Hall was so crammed with an eager and expectant audience that the programme was delayed by difficulties in seating it. It was a Saturday, and the choral singers opening the concert, whose vocal resources had been weakened by cheering lustily throughout the afternoon's football match, began shakily but recovered enough to win a lukewarm call for an encore. 'Then came H. B. Irving's recitation "Sheltered". Irving recited this melodramatic piece with great feeling. His dramatic genius called into life-like being the murderer

Anderson as he lay crouching on the cottage floor bespattered with mire, hiding from his pursuers. The audience was spellbound, the encore vociferous, and Irving in response gave a reading from Artemus Ward's *Charles F. Brown's Agricultural Experiences*, in which he brought out every point making each more pointed with his humorous intonation.' Thus Harry scored a tragic left and a comic right with an accomplished ease that later enabled him to 'infuse plenty of go' into Haydn's Toy Symphony under the baton of his friend Benson. The following term he won equal applause with an Ingoldsby Legend, and, with Laurence ('though a rising light...not as good as his brother') played a scene between Brutus and Cassius from *Julius Caesar*. In the summer of 1887, before an audience in Upper School that included an unusual number of visitors, he threw down the filial gauntlet by reciting Hood's *Dream of Eugene Aram*—a piece that his father had made his own and that had led to his engagement by Bateman at the Lyceum. Again he delighted those impervious to his 'dramatic force and thrilling effect' with the gentle humour of Calverly's *Gemini and Virgo*—a manifestation of a rarer gift that he was prone to undervalue. In the holidays he repeated his performance before a large audience in Tottenham to raise funds for the Marlborough Mission Hall in that Borough.

At his last appearance at the Penny Reading he overreached himself —or such was the opinion of his less impressionable schoolmates. He may have been led by Laurence's radical persuasion to choose a turgid piece by George R. Sims that expressed the execrations of a wronged pauper in a work-house.

> *...though we have nothing but praise for the dramatic style in which it was delivered, we must enter a protest against the subject. Surely Upper School is not to be made the field of a crusade against Bumbledom. If one's hair is to be made to stand on end and our blood to be chilled let it be done with some fine stirring lines like 'The Dream of Eugene Aram' and not by Mr Sims's sickly sentiment and revolting socialism...We were sorry to see many of the simple minded evidently sympathising with a polemical ballad of a mischievous sort.*

This may have caused his housemaster to endorse Harry's end of term report—'I hope he is not getting spoiled by popularity.' Mr Beesley had given up his house, yet he continued to be the confidant of Harry and his parents. After this Penny Reading he had taken the boy to task, somewhat equivocally, torn as he must have been between his liking for him, his duty to his father, and sympathy for his mother.

'When I came back,' Harry reported, 'Beesley said to me, "I don't think I should let you do such a thing again, because I don't think it's very good for you and it's very difficult for me to judge how to act in the matter." At the same time he said he should like to repeat that we do them very well and that we always recited in a most un-affected manner—a fact that seemed to give him great satisfaction.' Mr Beesley may have been justifiably alarmed lest this popular success might undo all the patient efforts he had made to set Harry's feet firmly on the road to Oxford.

Applause, whether on the football field or in Upper School, can be intoxicating; though the ring of it in E. F. Benson's bruised ears did not tempt him to become a professional footballer, in Harry's it spurred his resentment against his father's refusal to let him become an actor. For on this score Irving was adamant and communicative. Over the years he had proved a poor correspondent. The boys wrote dutifully to him but he replied tersely and infrequently. Harry complained to his mother than when he did write his letters were 'the most infantile and stupidest I should think a father ever wrote to his son...more like a meteorological report than an epistle'. Laurence, too, explained to his father: 'We would have written to you more in America only we got no answer we found it rather *uninteresting*', and went on to compare him unfavourably as a letter-writer with their friend the American actor, Lawrence Barrett. But, when need be, my grandfather expressed himself forcefully and explicitly.

My letter this week [Harry wrote to his mother in the summer of 1884] *will be devoted to the substance of a letter to Gussy[1] received yesterday. You must say nothing of what I tell you to Gussy because he did not want me to tell you yet...that evening I am summoned by Gussy who relates me the principal substance of H.I.'s letter which is this (the letter was written by Austen I can well see), 'I should rather Harry did not go on the stage. If however he means to he had better not go to Oxford (blow for Gussy) but remain at Marlborough for some time. Let him remember that on the stage his name will prove a drawback (I couldn't see this quite) and both must work for their own living.' Then he said something about conforming with wishes. Gussy couldn't understand this...said he thought apart from all relationship and duty we should obey Irving more for our* own

[1] A. H. Beesley was known to the boys of his House as Gloomy Gus.

interests after first duly repaying the great love and affection for us which he had seen in our mother's conduct. [He] is much afraid that you may think him siding with H.I. so does not want to tell you yet ...He is still excited about Oxford and in two days I am to give my answer whether I shall go there or not. I shall, of course, say I will not go—no matter what anyone says. The stage is what I like... and to nothing else will I give my full power and attention. It may be wrong but it is what I like and wish for and nothing will deter me from it. How I wish I could say all this verbally but try and gather as much as you can from this scrawl.

It was asking much of a boy of fourteen to make such a decision. Beesley handled the situation with persuasive tact. He had a shrewd idea of Harry's intellectual capacity and was determined he should go to Oxford. So, turning Irving's argument to his own purpose, he prevailed on Harry to give up any idea of going on the stage for the time being, and to work hard to prepare himself for the University—thus rewarding his mother and setting his father's qualms at rest.

As time went on Harry became reconciled to this plan. Not surprisingly, a year or so later he began to favour the idea of going to the Bar as an alternative profession.

...masters to whom I've confided the Bar scheme (no connection with the Public House) have taken great interest in it. Mr Thompson, one of the cleverest of our staff, was telling me today that a Mr Haldane, M.P., a leading Barrister, à propos of me said that never as now was there such a chance for a young man to get on at the Bar, that let him only apply himself hard at first to the preliminary work and then all the more showy qualities he may possess...as oratory or impudence or wit will help to work him on about his fellows. Not a bad prospect, I think.

When in the Debating Society he found he had the gift of rhetoric and persuasive reasoning the prospect pleased him the more. Yet in capitulating to his father's demands he did not give his parole. The clear call to be an artist was more compelling than the insidious assurances of 'getting on'. In the holidays he took lessons from the old actor Herman Vezin, who had created the part of Dr Primrose in *The Vicar of Wakefield*—the play that Irving for Ellen Terry's sake was about to revive at the Lyceum. Vezin was a powerful tragedian and, as *The Times* recorded, had 'no equal on our stage as a declaimer of English'. So he imparted to his eager pupil those traditional techniques of acting on which Irving himself had superimposed his own original style. The measure of Harry's response to this instruction had been the applause in the Bradleian Hall at his first reading. If his success in debate had tempted him to waver in his original intention, his first taste of power to excite and hold an audience reawakened his repressed ambitions.

Irving went to Marlborough only once to see his boys. Having subscribed handsomely towards the rebuilding of the chapel, he took Toole down for the day to view the results and to take the boys for a drive through Savernake Forest. He was shrewd enough to appreciate the situation now that the boys' schooldays were drawing to a close. Laurence, the more amenable, was already dreaming of diplomacy, and of studying in foreign capitals the languages that would gain him entry into the Foreign Service. With affairs so prosperous at the Lyceum, his father saw no difficulty in subsidising his welcome choice of profession. But it is unlikely that Irving was not flattered with praise of Harry's talents, and that he did not sense Harry's grudging acquiescence to his wishes. In May 1886 he made a tactical error in referring publicly and deprecatingly to his son's desire to go on the stage. Harry reacted sharply:

> *I feel I must immediately send you the enclosed cutting* [he wrote to his mother]. *There at last is a deliberate attempt to bully me out of my determination concerning my future by making a private family matter a public and readable to all paragraph. He thinks to frighten me out of it by putting forward ridiculous arguments to which I have not the power to publicly reply or else I would. He seems utterly to forget there exist in the theatrical world other managers besides his mighty self who would be willing to give me an engagement...I will defeat his statement if I possibly can and prove to him that there are others who can act quite as well if not better than the invincible Henry Irving.*

News of Harry's kindled defiance must have reached his father, for shortly after this Irving wrote a long and carefully composed letter warning him of the difficulties of making a career on the stage, and of these being aggravated rather than alleviated by bearing his father's name.[1] It was a frank and well argued appeal to the boy's reason;

[1] See *Henry Irving: The Actor and his World.*

E

that it was the first of the kind Harry had ever received was the more regrettable. It reached him when, for his last year, he came under the influence of M. H. Gould, one of those eccentric and unsung schoolmasters who through the lives of predestined boys that have passed through their hands have left their mark on English history. Gould was quick to see the promise of his pupil; he called him a 'sharp' boy; Harry found in Gould an urbane citizen of the world beyond the school boundaries. In the holidays that remained Gould was a frequent guest at Gilston Road and at theatre parties organised by Harry. Between them, he and Beesley shepherded Harry through this crisis in his life and brought him safely to the threshold of Oxford. Both these schoolmasters recognised my grandfather's genius and appreciated the position he now held as a man and as an artist in public esteem; both were aware of the inculcated antagonism of this sensitive boy to a father who, whatever his faults, was concerned for his sons' future. Neither could have conceived the extremity of Harry's rancour that wrung from him in protest:

> *How often, by how many inconveniences, by how many unkind speeches am I made to feel the villainy of the creature who calls himself my father.*

What spiritual and philosophical reserves had Harry to draw upon to meet these continuing emotional tensions? Marlborough, founded as it was for the education of the sons of clergy, did all it could to induce in its boys a Christian frame of mind and habits of worship. The young Irvings were not alone in finding the long hours in chapel tedious, and the constant repetition of the liturgy irrelevant to the Gospel it was striving to promote. Yet their scepticism was more thoughtful than that of most boys of their age. Between Gran's free-thinking humanism and their mother's perfunctory churchgoing as a social exercise they had arrived at an easy-going pragmatism, on which the incantations of orthodoxy made very little impression. Thus Harry, though impatient of cant and sentimental exhortations from the pulpit, enjoyed a well-reasoned and well-delivered sermon. The causes he espoused in the Debating Society showed that his inclination was to take a humane and even puritanical stand on most issues.

Nearly all schoolboys sooner or later are faced with moral problems that, for the most part, they have to grapple with in irksome solitude. In those days they were exaggerated by the conspiracy of silence at home and among masters as to their causes, by veiled yet horrific warnings of their physical consequences and by the assumption that any boy expelled for succumbing to them was ruined for life. In few homes was the existence of these dangers ever discussed, so that the sense of guilt and failure in a boy enmeshed in them was the more acute. Harry and Laurence managed to fit all this into their objective interest in human weakness. Expulsions would be reported briefly to their mother with promise of further details when they returned home. For my grandmother had awakened in the boys a precocious curiosity in matters of sex that now paid off handsomely by sparing them the sense of isolation felt by boys debarred from telling their parents the facts of school life. Her boys were not immune to the attentions that any good-looking schoolboy then and now is likely to attract, or to the temptations they offered in terms of privilege and protection. But frank discussion of the subject at home made it easier when the time came to cope with the situation. After one of them had had such an experience his Aunt Edith wrote: 'I am so glad you are quit, my dear Harry, of those horrid companions—the road of life is broad enough for the virtuous and the vicious to go their different ways. Do not be angry if I did worry you on these unpleasant subjects but I was so fearfully anxious for your welfare that I couldn't help myself.'

So, if at Gilston Road and Roland Gardens spades were called spades and Irving's frailties vices, the boys were nevertheless fortunate in having a background in which, unlike that of more conventional homes, plain-spokenness precluded duplicity and the harassment of shame.

All this, while in no way curbing their irrepressible sense of fun, inclined Harry and Laurence to a gravity of mind beyond their years. Yet in matters of religion the uncompromising Harry showed a surprising pliancy. If martyrdom was his last resort, it would be as a recusant against football rather than as a professor of faith. When the time came to submit himself to the routine preparation for confirmation, he managed to conceal from his pastor his disbelief in most of the avowals he was called upon to make. Inwardly he resisted any attempt to instil in him fear of eternal punishment or hope of apparently uncongenial consolations after death. In due course, however, he knelt before the visiting Bishop and later made his first communion with sceptical resignation. Had the Bishop felt under his hand the bristling agnosticism of the candidate, the shock would have been less had he seen a letter the boy had written to his mother on the previous Sunday.

An epidemic has been through the school and that epidemic is Theft. *Two boys to my knowledge have been sent away for it this term— two boys have returned to sorrowing homes disgraced and ruined for future life. You can picture your feelings if one of us came home in this miserable state. Think of the parents. One of the boys was Bishop A—'s son, a fellow I knew well.*

The other boy named S— I would have sworn was honest yet last Monday I hear that he is gone. I ask 'Why?' 'For stealing!' was the answer, and I have come to the conclusion that boys are living lies. It may seem strange but four years of Public School life have taught it me. And yet I ask 'Can it be these boys have been kept short of money by their elder brothers?' It is a curious coincidence that each of these boys have brothers, 4 or 5 years older than themselves, both brothers seem to take but little notice of their younger brothers; and may not the older ones have had all the money and the younger ones left with very little...The older one grows forgetful nay callous to the younger and fast brotherly love vanishes. A—'s elder brother said on hearing of his expulsion: 'Well, I shall never speak to him again.'

Is this common charity? Is this brotherly feeling? No, no this is heartlessness. Perhaps I have moralised too much; but it is my way: I am thoughtful by nature and events of this sort make me think; it is my nature.

This was the first expression of Harry's lifelong preoccupation with the mystery of human motive. If such was his nature he was unlikely to derive much more benefit from school life. Neither Laurence nor he (though he had won the Congreve Prize for the second time) reached the sixth form; neither were made prefects. Yet such influence as Harry had on his fellows (and in his headmaster's view it was considerable) he used wisely. So 'one of the red letter days of our lives and perhaps the only one' drew near, for the summer term 1887 would see the end of monotony and chilblains, though applause and anointing with glycerine had ameliorated those persistent afflictions, and at Gilston Road my grandmother's eye ranged proudly along her sons' bookshelves, where a dozen volumes, calf-bound, embossed in gold with the College arms and inscribed by Dr Bell, were tangible proofs of her doting yet astute motherhood.

Untidy Laurence had survived an interview with Mr Eric Barrington at the Foreign Office; luckily he could not have known that it was the idiosyncrasy of this Under Secretary to judge candidates for the Foreign Service by their boots. His road to diplomacy would lie through Paris and St Petersburg after spending the rest of the summer studying Russian with a tutor, Eugénie Dolbuschoff. Harry would have to cram for his matriculation to New College with pleasant interludes of amateur theatricals in the country homes of his friends. When Harry delayed his final return home to fulfil a promise to recite in Cheltenham my grandmother must have realised that the close-knit life she had shared with her sons was nearly at an end. Harry, too, felt something of the kind.

...Somehow it makes one look and think of the long years of a mother's love which has passed undying from year to year working and toiling in sorrow and gladness for the welfare of those who I fear sometimes forget the great measure of their obligation. Alas it is not in youth that we best remember such things; but it is well to do so for with age the recollection will show us no mercy.

His devotion to his mother and his resentful suspicion of his father were, perhaps, greater than either of them deserved. My grandmother had marvellously mitigated the handicaps of a broken home. Both boys would have to bear the scars of her bitterness towards their father; but these would be superficial. Harry's would be the slower to heal. He had inherited much of his father's forceful and stubborn character. His mother, for all her cross-grained Irishness, had steered his passionate disposition in the right direction. She could be confident that from the volatile and incompatible elements of his ancestry there was distilled in him an essence of probity that, whatever the future might hold for him, would mark his occupations.

VI

IT WAS ON THE ARM OF DR JOWETT that Thespis entered demurely the precincts of Oxford University. Her charms had been long apparent to its undergraduates. Until the Vice-Chancellor vouched for her respectability, the instinct of his fellows was to refuse admittance to a Muse, however classical, whose reputation was as shady as scholars of the Restoration were glad to reaffirm. There was no temple waiting to receive her. She would, moreover, have to live down the disrepute of her poor relation at the 'Vic', the 'drab and reeking hall where half boozed mummers roared a glee'. This squalid though licensed flea-pit was the stamping ground of rowdies and a fruitful source of revenue to the Proctors. If the impact of Thespis on Oxford proved to be as disruptive as Zuleika Dobson's, her sponsor could plead that he had been persuaded to chaperone her under false pretences. For, though Jowett deserves the credit for having restored drama to Oxford, making it as worthy an object of study as divinity, and play-acting as admirable a recreation as football, he was at all stages prompted and persuaded to do so by William Leonard Courtney, fellow and tutor of New College.

Courtney, though he failed to win a scholarship to Balliol, later as a member of University College had taken a first in 'Greats' and been elected to a fellowship at Merton. When marriage forced him to resign his fellowship, he became at the age of twenty-three the headmaster of his old school, Somersetshire College. Three years later, when celibacy was no longer a condition for fellowship, he returned to Oxford as a tutor at New College.

Unlike many academics of his day whose lives as dons or ushers seem to have been an innocent extension of their schooldays, Courtney was a determined man of the literary and theatrical world of London. He was tall and grave of bearing, adept at the kind of sagacious wit that went down well with the port at high tables. Yet he and his wife were never happier than when promoting amateur theatricals. His own performances were earnest rather than convincing, due in part to the heavy dragoon moustache that he was not prepared to sacrifice on the altar of art; it fell like a waterfall breaking on his strong chin, so defeating disguise that his favourite impersonations of Bassanio and Malvolio were partially screened from his audiences.

Courtney was a pliant Christian, a plain-spoken Platonist, a tolerant Proctor and an energetic elder of the Boat Club. All these qualities won him the regard and trust of the Vice-Chancellor. Exploiting this advantage, he had little difficulty in encouraging Jowett to believe that a liberal attitude towards the drama would bestow lasting benefits on the University. As a keen theatre-goer he was among my grandfather's devotees, and a short paper he had written on the Lyceum production of *Faust* had brought them together. It was at his house that Jowett and Irving first became aware of each other's 'fine reserve'. Over his dinner-table plans were made for Irving's lecture in the Schools at which the Vice-Chancellor took the Chair.

This occasion won for Jowett the support of all but his most bigoted colleagues. Thus Courtney came to be, as it were, the architect of the New Theatre and in consequence the master of all subsequent revels that its existence in Oxford made possible. It seems likely, too, that his subtle mind contrived the suppression of the Vic, not by proctorial action that might have excited controversy, but by the simpler expedient of having it condemned as a fire risk.

It was, then, no more surprising that Irving was glad to put his son Harry into the hands of such an enlightened champion of his art than that Courtney welcomed a promising pupil who would strengthen his ties with the profession. But if my grandfather imagined that at New College his son would come to his senses and, under his tutor's guidance, work earnestly to equip himself for a more stable career, he was much deceived. For, thanks very largely to Courtney, the climate of Oxford was becoming more favourable to stage-struck young gentlemen than anywhere else in England.

Before Harry went up to Oxford in the autumn of 1888, he spent a last rather lonely term at Marlborough. He was cheered at intervals by Laurence's letters from Paris where, as a boarder with a crammer favoured by the Foreign Office, he was studying French and Russian. Before he left England Eugénie Dolbuschoff had piloted her sixteen-year-old pupil through the complete works of Gogol and Lermontov. He gave his host in the Rue Concordet no cause to complain of his lack of industry.

I must commence by telling you [he wrote to Harry] *my deep thanks for the Masson*[1] *which I received last night. How kind and noble of you to get it for me. It is so jolly. Thank you again and again. I find that you can buy here Puschkin's plays translated into French, Boris Godounov, etc. They must be jolly. I should like them more just now as I am reading Le Faux Dimitri de Prosper Merrimée. I am sure you will like it. Boris is such a good villain...Would you like the Causes Célèbres at Marlborough fortnightly but I must warn you that some of the cases are very French, that is very broad. Still you need not give them to be read. In the Russian Causes there are only two cases but so good and so light. There is a case of abortion (quite your sort) and the other murder. Both splendid. Germany, Belgium and England have come out so far. The English cases are The Kiss of Colonel Baker and the Claim of Mr Tichborne. You'll see the general trend.*

I am so glad you liked the portraits. You can make your room a sort of Pantheon of the French Revolution and Nap and Peter the Great.

Visits to the Comédie-Française did not lessen his admiration for his native dramatists, which he suspected his host, M. Caken, did not share.

I'm not sure he does not despise Shakespeare, little fool! Last night he got Vladimir [a fellow student] *to read some of Corneille's Horace. Ah, how I wish you could be here to read some fine old Shakespeare in your fine old way—much better than Corneille and Racine put together.*

A word from his father won him the enviable favour of Sarah Bernhardt. 'I have just received two seats from Bernhardt,' he reported to Harry. 'They will make me "Boss" here. They regard her as a sort of goddess.' Yet he hastened to assure his mother that he was not to be suborned by such indulgences.

I see...that Irving intends bringing out Macbeth with the wench as Lady Macbeth. What a combination. I also read...that Terry does not tour with Irving but goes on the Continent, being replaced by Marian. Irving cannot be without one of the weird sisters. The Weekly Times tells me further that Ilsa [sic] *Craig has appeared at the Lyceum and that that loving and devoted lady Ellen Terry*

[1] Charles Masson: *Mémoires Secrets sur La Russie.*

finding no one ready to play her part as a servant, to the great sur-
prise and horror of the audience took it upon herself to play the part.
I almost dropped a tear...at reading such a pathetic story.

By now he saw himself as the heroic young Dmitri rebelling against
the Tsar of the Lyceum; not that he wished his father the same fate
as Boris—anyhow, he wasn't half so good a villain.

He was now impatient for Russia. Nothing he had seen in Paris had
impressed him so much as a performance of Tolstoy's tragedy *La
Puissance des Ténèbres* at a third-rate theatre that had doubled its usual
price of three francs for a seat in the dress circle in honour of the
dramatist. 'The acting was really very good for such a theatre...just
as good as you see at first-rate theatres.' There, for the first time, he
felt the force of an influence that increasingly would govern his
thoughts and actions.

In September, escorted by his mother, he arrived in St Petersburg,
where he was to lodge with Professor Turner, a lecturer in English
at the University. Flo must have been relieved to find the Turner's
home an outpost of Kensington and her host as keen on amateur
theatricals as herself.

I have seen but little of St Petersburg [Laurence reported to
Harry]. *Mother arrived with a slight cold and is keeping indoors.
I stay with her. Yesterday I went out for about half an hour's walk
up the Nevski Prospect. It being Sunday some of the shops were shut
but not all, about the same percentage as in Paris. The streets were
very crowded and almost every other man was a soldier—or rather*
[wore] *a uniform which is not the same thing.*

*I saw statues of B. de Tolly and Kutusoff both very merry looking
old fellows with French marshal looking uniforms. I have also seen
at a distance the St Isaac Cathedral and the statue of Nicholas,
beside a real live Grand Duke driving along in a five horse droshki
quite unattended...There seems to be a general edging away from the
secret police who parade the streets armed with daggers and dirks.*

Flo parted from him with some misgiving. It had been a courageous
sortie and she was at least assured that he would be in good hands—
but, still barely seventeen, he was so impulsive and vulnerable, and
so lacked the cool scepticism that gave Harry a defensive poise. As
for Laurence, high as his hopes and extravagant as his dreams of
Russia and its capital had been, he suffered no disillusion. He was soon

immersed in the warm hospitable life of an elegant society familiar to him through the Karenins, and in the reeking neighbourhood of the Cyennaza he discovered the violent contrasts that had disgusted the sensitive and fastidious Raskolnikoff. Fourteen Russian lessons a week, dancing classes, play-readings with the Turners and soirées were the order of his days and nights.

It was not long before he found life at the Turners oppressively English, and Turner was bound to admit the advantages of his living in a Russian ménage.

> *...of course the most important to me just now is my new home. Turner has thro' a friend been recommended a certain M. Groozdyeff and it seems I am to be with a young married couple, relations of his daughter...My lessons are all in full swing and with the exception of a day for Russian they are the same lot as before, all very agreeable.*
>
> *My new Russian teacher is long and tall and wears a horrible poke bonnet being about 25 years of age but I think I shall learn well from her as she is, I believe, a well read and scholastic person. She had some difficulty in surmounting her scruples to give lessons to a young man but here she is and none the worse for it.*
>
> *I saw in the English paper about the latest Whitechapel horrors.[1] The incapacity of Scotland Yard is becoming more and more apparent. Something should be done to ensure at least a respectable percentage of the number of crimes committed and convicted. The strikes have also collapsed so London must at this moment be in a very tragical state.*

Comparatively and at such a distance St Petersburg seemed a model city, as architecturally well ordered as it was free from crime and industrial strife. It had not as yet dawned upon Laurence that the secret police were there to suppress homicide and human liberty with impartial severity.

When Harry returned to New College for the Lent Term of 1889 he and his fellow undergraduates, after mutually unfavourable first appraisals, took a more lenient view of each other.

As a rule eccentricity of manner or dress was tolerated, indeed welcomed, as a contribution to the Oxford scene. Dons and their pupils conspicuous by their appearance or behaviour on the High and the Broad were valued as sources of anecdote or models for caricature.

[1] The Jack-the-Ripper murders.

The entry, therefore, upon this scene the previous term of a freshman at New College wearing a white billycock hat, with a touch of the baroque in its voluptuously curving brim, would normally have been greeted with a tolerant amusement. Harry, whatever may have induced him to acquire such a provocative and vulnerable hat (for in the air of Oxford its whiteness would be as fugitive as that of London snow), must have been surprised, pained and finally angered by the hostility it aroused in his fellows. He and his hat became victims first of passive ridicule and then of physical assault. His illusions of Oxford as a haven for uninhibited individualists were shattered. The offending and now sullied bowler went into retirement while Harry, wearing another of conventional black, pursued his way unmolested but sadly puzzled.

And well he might be. Perhaps such bizarre headgear would have been acceptable on the head of some raffish member of the Bullingdon Club or of one known to be hospitably sowing his wild oats; but perched above a pair of penetrating eyes and a grave judicial countenance that intimated six months without the option of a fine, it seemed, to those conscious of young Irving's stern regard, a paradox that could only be resolved by direct action. Harry, in fact, had overstepped the interminate bounds between eccentricity and 'side'.

This disconcerting episode encouraged him to indulge his tendency to a superior aloofness that was the protective shield of a nature sensitive to criticism. In bowing to popular disapproval he did not seek popularity. Indeed, not long afterwards, he risked unpopularity again, not this time for a hat but for a principle. Courtney, as Senior Proctor, had taken disciplinary measures that had aroused general indignation against him. Harry, satisfied that his tutor's action had been just, when occasion served publicly defended him. 'I am bad at showing gratitude,' wrote Courtney the next day, 'but I must write a line to tell you how much I valued and appreciated your affectionate loyalty last night.' So Harry made few friends at Oxford until he came to discover kindred spirits at the Union and in the O.U.D.S.

The Oxford University Dramatic Society was planning its fifth production since, in 1883, it had as it were taken over the Oxford Philothespians who, sponsored by Dr Jowett and led by Frank Benson, had dented the crusted hostility of the senior common rooms to play-acting. So young was the Society that several founder members were to be in the cast of *Julius Caesar*. Arthur Bouchier, Past President and the most zealous actor of them all, had gone down but was creating a not entirely welcome precedent by returning to

Oxford to play Brutus; another graduate, W. J. Morris, was to play Mark Antony. To Harry, as no doubt to other members of the society, these lingering stage-struck graduates were an intrusion into what should be an entirely undergraduate affair. He was, moreover, dissatisfied with the small part he had been offered of Decius Brutus. He felt, with some justification, that if the plum parts were to be usurped by post-graduates, the dramatic range of resident members would be limited. Courtney, whose wife was to play Portia, wisely advised him to accept the part and make the best he could of it. Soon his discontent was forgotten in the bustle of rehearsals.

On the day of the production he wrote to his mother:

> *...my letter will reach you just as we are playing tonight for the first time and then all your thoughts will be for your old Bim. Mr Courter* [Courtney] *told me Irving was not coming to my great relief, he is such an incubus. I suppose he must have written to Courter and left unanswered his son's letter: rude hound! Really it's beginning to go too far. A letter asking him if he's coming down and no answer! Let us leave him!*
>
> *When shall you come? I believe Friday afternoon will be the time when most of the Londoners will be coming down. Also George Lewis, Alma Tadema and others come on Saturday night...my dress is a crimson toga which suits my dark hair well; and an old nightgown affair underneath. Clarkson says he shall make me up just enough for stage purposes and curl my hair a bit...*

Harry had no need to worry about the size of his part; as he might have foreseen, his performance attracted disproportionate attention. The critics, aware no doubt of local feeling, were cool about Bourchier and Morris—Bourchier, *facile princeps,* had been seen in parts better suited to his talents; Morris was earnest enough but did not look at all like Antony. The presence of 'Mr Henry Irving junr.' in the cast really gave them something to write about. They noted 'peculiarities of form, voice and gait which had so long been associated with his distinguished father'. One critic rated him 'the best of the actors and he certainly influenced the cast very considerably. His face, figure and especially his walk are more or less those of his great father...whether it is that Irvingism is infectious or that Mr Irving is wilfully imitated at Oxford, the comic idea suggests itself at the crisis of the play that an Irving was being killed by a dozen other Irvings, which was a pity.'

Harry, as he read these inevitable comparisons, felt the weight of his absent incubus; the latter, if he read them, had the sardonic satisfaction of seeing his prophecies fulfilled, unaware that he had once more offended his son at a moment when this might have grave consequences.

But Harry must have realised that this kind of comment was to be expected; as was the appearance of Arthur Waugh in his burlesque of *Julius Seesawcer* at the Holywell Music Room as Decius Brutus wearing a white bowler hat above his toga. Less expected was the visit from an envoy of Mrs Langtry offering him the part of Orlando in her coming production of *As You Like It* at the St James's Theatre.

Lily Langtry had already played Rosalind with some success in America. Ellen Terry thought her a much better actress than most critics, suspicious of her equivocal position as a society beauty and professional player, cared to admit. She had neither conceit nor false modesty. 'I bundled through my part somehow last night,' she wrote to Ellen Terry after her first performance as Rosalind. 'Oh, what an impudent wretch you must think me to attempt such a part...' On the other hand she described herself in a book of reference as 'probably the best known lady owner of the turf'. She was certainly no mischief-maker. In trying to lure Harry from Oxford she can have had no idea that she was acting as an *agent provocateur*. Though Irving and Ellen Terry were her friends it was unlikely that either of them would have told her of the efforts being made to discourage him from going on the stage.

> *The great visit has come off* [Harry reported] *and was in a way of note. He came to see me principally to make me an offer if I wished by any chance still to go on the stage to go and play jeune premier parts with Mrs Langtry when she comes to the St James's at probably £12 a week. I told him that unless anything unforseen happened to H.I., I had no present intention of taking such a step. Mrs L. appears very keen to get me and he asked me for my photo to show her and he said it was a grand chance for me if I cared to take it—and so it is but cannot be. He also paid me many compliments—said that à propos J.C., people were saying that I had all H.I.'s powers without his mannerisms, etc., etc.*

But Harry was not vulnerable to flattery of this kind. With Courtney's steadying hand on his shoulder he was by now shrewd enough to realise that, in view of his inexperience, Mrs Langtry anticipated the value of publicity to be gained by his engagement rather than that of any lustre his performance might add to her production. Her offer was declined. The fact was that Harry was becoming increasingly absorbed in his work. He attended lectures regularly. He found the eighteenth century congenial study, even if he pecked at the dry fare of constitutional history in order to gorge himself on the human dramas with which the period abounded.

He had been lucky in his friends. Very soon after Mrs Langtry's invitation had set the seal upon his commitment to Oxford his mentor, Courtney, was himself lured to London by Edward Lawson the proprietor of the *Daily Telegraph*. His was almost the first defection of the Oxford don to Fleet Street. Perhaps his colleagues were not surprised that the University could not contain so genial a fellow, whose interests, social, literary and theatrical, were as wide as his circle of friends eminent in the world of art and letters. But the members of an enclave that regarded *The Times* as its parish magazine may have been shocked by his destination. As far as this story goes Courtney had played his part, good boatman that he was, in steering Harry through the rapids of his discontent; now that he had piloted him into the placid reaches of reconciliation to Oxford, he left him confidently to paddle his own canoe. From his Fleet Street desk he would keep a benevolent eye on his young friend's future.

During the long vacation Harry and Laurence, on holiday from Russia, were reunited. Much of their time was spent with a company of pastoral players organised by Alan Mackinnon, all but Laurence being members of the O.U.D.S. Performances of *Romeo and Juliet* and of *Love's Labour's Lost* were given in the summer-proud gardens of Copped Hall, Birling, and Cranmer's Palace in Maidstone. Harry was an elegant Boyet; Laurence, no doubt, clothed Sir Nathaniel in his own eccentricities; and it was in these parts that they happened to catch the eye of William Archer, then dramatic critic of *The World*, who reported that, while sharing the handicap of youth, both spoke 'with good discretion'.

In July, at the invitation of the Master of Marlborough, Harry enlisted a number of his Oxford friends to play scenes from *As You Like It* on the terrace of the Master's garden. This was to be the chief attraction of An Old English Fancy Fair in aid of the College Mission in Tottenham. Among the undergraduates they recruited was a history scholar and captain of the University Soccer team,

Thomas Pellatt of Trinity College. His visit to Marlborough would change the course of his life—as indeed it would indirectly affect my own. One of the stall-holders at the Fair was Mrs Thomas, the widow of the late Bursar. The beauty and charm of her three step-daughters had for several terms gladdened (and occasionally broken) the hearts of susceptible boys in the Upper School. The eldest, Eleanor, as gay and spirited as she was handsome, was quite ruthlessly exercising her charms on customers at her step-mother's stall. During the afternoon Pellatt played Oliver to Harry's Jaques and Laurence's Touchstone. The play was followed by a concert in College. The leader of the orchestra was Eleanor's younger sister, Betha. No doubt Eleanor had taken time off to see the play in the afternoon and had rewarded the players with rallying compliments. Consequently, when Mr T. Pellatt rose to sing a baritone solo, 'I Arise from Dreams of Thee', his dreams were of the vivacious girl who had said such nice things about his earlier performance. She seems, moreover, to have enchanted him into accepting, in the autumn, an appointment as history master at the College. In due course he wooed and won her. Together, with great courage but with very limited resources, they started a preparatory school for boys at Langton Matravers, near Swanage. Their way with the boys and with parents was unconventional and utterly free of the unctuous pomposity that in those days was affected by most schoolmasters. In fact they and the Lynams at Oxford were pioneers in an entirely new approach to preparatory school education.

Though Tom Pellatt was not a member of the O.U.D.S., his friendship with my father, thus begun and continued through the years, was rooted in his passion for the theatre. So, when the time came, my father sent me to his school at Durnford House. For this reason I have never ceased to bless the encounters of that summer's afternoon at Marlborough.

By the time Harry began his second year at Oxford he was a notable figure and popular with the limited circle of friends who had penetrated his constraint, and through shared enthusiasms had touched the hidden spring of his cordiality. He spent more time in his rooms than most undergraduates, reading and entertaining those who could be relied upon for good conversation and had a taste for criminology as keen as his own. Study came naturally to him; it would not have occurred to him to divide the hours into periods for work or recreation. His spontaneous essays were, according to his friend W. J. Morris, 'tense, arresting and thoughtful', providing his tutors with a welcome change from the laboured or perfunctory submissions of the average pupil. Debates at the Union were the livelier for the explicit logic of his arguments and for the dry humour of his repartee; he had been elected to its committee, and was marked as a likely candidate for the Presidency. He had succeeded Claud Nugent as secretary of the O.U.D.S.

Harry's year of office began in some confusion, but, for him at any rate, it ended to the sweet sound of applause. The Society now felt fairly secure. Having breached, under cover of Euripides and Shakespeare, the defences of entrenched opposition to drama in the University, its members were tempted naturally to exploit their success. The nation suddenly had become aware of her disregard for one of her brilliant but disreputable sons. Christopher Marlowe had been dead 400 years and officially his memory was still unhonoured. There could, alas, be no question of reviving his plays. Shakespeare, it is true, was given to indelicate passages, but these could be omitted without detriment to his plots or characters. Marlowe was so liberal with his improprieties that if they were expurgated the plays became incoherent. So plans were under way to placate his shade by setting up a memorial to him in his native city, Canterbury. Perhaps he would have preferred it to be outside the Precincts; anyhow, standing in the middle of the Butter Market it could not possibly give offence. My grandfather had been invited to unveil it in the coming year. To the Society this seemed an opportunity not to be missed to persuade the Vice-Chancellor, Dr Bellamy, to extend the range of permissible drama.

Courtney, before he left Oxford, had prepared a sterilised version of *The Jew of Malta*; the still turgid play, bound up with a commendatory preface by Swinburne, was ready for submission. At that moment Robert Browning died—a bereavement that for the time being outweighed the nation's tardy concern for Marlowe. Though Harry was already word-perfect in the part of Barabas (as were most of those who had rooms within earshot of his declamations), Alan Mackinnon, a devotee of Browning, had no difficulty in persuading him and the rest of the committee that nothing could be more appropriate to the occasion than a revival of the poet's early play *Strafford*. Courtney once more obliged by preparing an acting version of that unwieldy verse drama. Dr Bellamy agreed that in the sad circumstances the play justified a relaxation of his predecessor's rule, though he insisted that this must not be taken as a precedent. The Master of Balliol was now too ill to voice an opinion. A cynical don predicted that if Browning was acceptable, the field would soon be open to Meredith and George R. Sims. Harry had no doubt about the wisdom of the choice; he had been offered the part of Strafford. At last he saw a chance of proving to himself and to influential men of the theatre attracted to Oxford his capacity as an actor.

The part of Thomas Wentworth, Earl of Strafford, would be a long and testing one, for the structure, such as it was, of the whole play rested on it. Browning was twenty-four years old when Macready, with some courage, suggested he should write a play for him. When the young poet told him his theme, the actor felt he could hardly have chosen a better one. But a year later, when the play was finished, Macready was disappointed and confided to his diary that he feared it would fail—'it is *not* good'. When it was put into rehearsal, he found that much of it was 'feeble rant—neither power nor nature nor healthful fancy'. Soon, however, he worked himself up into a state of mind dear to actors that, though the play was poor, his performance might pull it through. *Strafford* was presented at Covent Garden in May 1837, with Helen Faucit in the ill-defined and unrewarding part of Lady Carlisle. It was played only five times. Browning was enraptured by it. The critics on the whole were kind. But Macready, knowing his public, dropped it from his repertoire. Since then, this would be its first revival of any account.

Browning's dramatic idiom would be found more acceptable today. Ignoring the unities, and dispensing with a plot, he used his characters to personify the political and personal conflicts of which, rather obscurely, Strafford became the victim. As *The Times* said, the play was a 'maze of historical allusions and influences'—a puzzle, in fact, that was more likely to be solved by an academic Oxford audience than any other. In spite of Courtney's judicious excisions the cast soon realised that the play would be heavy going. Nevertheless they tackled it with spirit. During rehearsals an influenza epidemic struck the town. Five successive King Charleses were laid low. At last the part fell to Alan Mackinnon, a professed Royalist who must have embarrassed his performance by trying to mitigate the poet's unfavourable view of the unhappy monarch. On the first night he, in turn, was stricken by an evidently Puritan virus, and had to surrender the crown to Mr Carew Hunt of Merton, who for one night only did justice to Browning's republican sentiments.

Harry, normally very susceptible to such infections, held his own. At the first performance the view from the stage was depressing. The sparsely filled house threw into relief the forbidding rows of academics sitting in judgment on the concession of their Vice-Chancellor. Harry knew what he was up against. When he asked the Warden of his College for permission to appear in the play, the latter expressed his disapproval of the theatre. Harry asked if he'd ever been to it. 'Yes, once,' replied Dr Spooner. 'What did you go to see?' 'Pepper's Performing Horses,' was the Warden's answer.

The ranks of dons, who would certainly forbear to cheer, may have intimidated him during the earlier scenes, in which his rather monotonous delivery alternated with attempts to force effects the poet had not intended. As the play went on he gained confidence and stability—'which enabled him to do justice to his idea of Strafford, his pride and tenderness, his dignity and tragic devotion with a power very rare in so young a player'. At the fall of the curtain, an ovation surprised him as much as the maturity of his performance had surprised many of his audience. In the papers next day there was a notable absence of comparison with his father, and general agreement that his success had been won by careful and thoughtful study of the part, interpreted with a grace and manner all his own. If he needed further reassurance he got it from W. H. Hutton, a lecturer in History at St John's College who, since Courtney's departure, had become his mentor and friend.

St John's College, Oxford.
Feb. 14. 1890

Dear Mr Irving,

I think you may care to have a word or two from one who studied your performance very carefully on the first night. It must be a word of sincere congratulation. The difficulties of the part are very great and you overcame them with remarkable success. I was much struck with the sympathy and tact and skill that you displayed— and with the genuine power of the last scene. The last two acts seemed to be especially fine—and the acting was throughout leading up to a climax without any failure or lack of strength. This was the more interesting as the unavoidable laughter of the audience at the comic figure of the king in the last act must have much disturbed you.

I thought you played the first act too slowly on Wednesday.

I don't think it is effective enough to be taken slowly but this is the opinion of an outsider. The last first night I saw before this was that of 'The Dead Heart'.

Yours sincerely,

W. Hutton[1]

With the rest of the cast falling around him like ninepins, and the nervous strain of rehearsing his last and most critical scene with six different kings, Harry can have had little time to attend to his duties as secretary and manager of the company. Perhaps it was as well. For his highly developed theatrical *amour propre* must have been offended by his small-part fellow actors who, when not on the stage, lounged and chattered in the gangways of the auditorium and, between the acts, usurped vacant seats and seemed affronted when these were claimed by their rightful owners. Certainly it must have struck him that if the gentlemen aspired to be players they could learn with advantage from the players how to behave in the theatre like gentlemen.

[1] William Holden Hutton, historian and later Dean of Winchester. *The Dead Heart* was produced by Henry Irving at the Lyceum on September 28th, 1889.

VII

MEANWHILE LAURENCE WAS NOT IMMUNE from the promptings of hereditary tendencies. Yet by the spring of 1890 he had become so ardent a Russophile that it looked as though nothing would deflect him from his diplomatic course.

Among his English friends in St Petersburg was Marie Page, the daughter of a resident Anglican clergyman. The Pages were attracted to their warm-hearted, rather uncouth, compatriot. They introduced him to their Russian friends, many of whom played a lively part in the artistic life of the capital. Marie Page watched Laurence taking on the colour of his surroundings with affectionate amusement. As a disciple of Tolstoy he was now an avowed vegetarian; he had grown a tentative moustache which took courage as it merged into a braver beard; and, like many Russians in the summer, he had had his dark curls closely cropped. She was shrewd enough to warn him against doubtful acquaintances. Of one of these Laurence had told Harry: '...M—is 34 years of age—Civil Service commissioner—awfully clever; had a most brilliant career. He and I great friends—raggers of Turner, we laugh at him awfully. M— has a really humorous vein about him. He has proposed I should give an honorary Shakespeare reading at the University. Do you think I'm equal to it? It would be a joke and would make Turner jealous...'

Marie Page, instinctively sizing up M—, confided to her sister:

...he is a fellow of Oxford, very gentlemanly, very clever and cold-hearted, does not believe in anything good or anybody. A horrid kind of man. L— knows I don't admire M— but he knows how clever the boy is...They in a way enjoyed each other's company. Although M— is twice as old as the boy he used to talk to him as he would to a clever college fellow of his own age.

Evidently Laurence heeded her warning. Nevertheless she was glad when, at the end of August, the time came to see him off on a trip through southern Russia—well beyond the influence of his sophisticated friend. From Tiflis Laurence wrote to his mother:

> *I have traversed the Caucasus and am now in a roundabout way returning to St Petersburg. From Astrakhan to Tiflis I had a travelling companion in the shape of a middle-aged American—a barrister, a very original person. He did not speak a word of Russian —beyond his native yankee he only pronounced a little bad German. Whilst we were together I acted as interpreter and he was a difficult one to interpret for. He lived by principles. He drank by principles —that is to say he drank no spirituous liquors because, as he said, he had once been too largely addicted to the same—then he put down his foot and resolved to drink no more. With the best intentions in the world he became rather a bore—since I have a confession to make —through his worrying I have lost my beautiful opera glasses and my old watch—Bim's cast-off, the latter of small importance. The American did not like officers on principle. So we were obliged to change carriages at one station and in the brave pursuit of imported food I think the loss must have been consummated...*
>
> *...In the whole of Astrakhan there was not a decent eating house. I was obliged to go and feed on the steamers that were in the port. I have only caught one bug in two nights which is good considering the appalling dirt of the hotels...It is astonishing I have not caught every existing epidemic.*

It was indeed, for at that time typhus was one of them. But he, in contrast to Harry, had a tough constitution and seemed to have inherited the combined stamina of Brodribbs and O'Callaghans. In Tiflis he bought for his father '...a dagger of the country costing the convenient little sum of 15 roubles—silver inlaid with gold. He seems to have a liking for weapons as I remember that when we used to go there many years ago he used to play with different swords and daggers.'

Laurence was back in St Petersburg for Christmas. The theatrical season was in full swing. It had been a bumper year, beginning with the production of Tchaikovsky's ballet *The Sleeping Beauty* and ending with the first performance of his opera *Pique-Dame* at the Marinsky theatre, where rehearsals had now begun of *Prince Igor*, that Rimsky-Korsakov and Glazounov together had arranged and orchestrated from the fragmentary piano score that Borodin had left behind him.

The theatre had, of course, been seldom absent from Laurence's thoughts. Play-readings at the Turners' and news of Harry's activities at Oxford kept it ever in his mind. He had begun to write a play pitched in the low key of his own Tolstoyan introspection.

> *My tender old Lamb* [he had written to Harry before the O.U.D.S. had decided on *Strafford*]. *If the watchman has been tardy to send his report and inspection register, at least it shall not suffer in length or sufficiency. Day and night I have been high up in my tower. I have seen and heard many new things.*
>
> *You cannot think how glad I am that at last you are really going to have a show, for I suppose whether they give The Jew of Malta or The Jew of Venice or every other Jew, Christian or Pagan the chiefest part will fall to Lamb's paramount deserts. As soon as I have finished my play I will send it to Oxford and order that you take the chief part in it. About the interior or even exterior of my play I shall tell you nothing as you are a wretched scoffer at such sacred things...*

Laurence was, therefore, fatally receptive to a proposal that reached him through Marie Page. It had been suggested to her that she might persuade members of the English colony to give a performance to raise funds for the poor students of the Conservatoire. *The Bells* seemed to be an appropriate play, with young Laurence Irving available to direct it and to play Mathias; but technical difficulties and Laurence's reluctance, perhaps, to challenge comparison with his fathers famous interpretation led to the choice of *David Garrick* as an alternative. This play had been written by Robertson for E. A. Sothern and in it the comedian, who had made his name as Lord Dundreary in *Our American Cousin*, had proved his versatility as a tragedian. Later Charles Wyndham had made it the corner-stone of his repertoire, and had indeed played it in St Petersburg three years earlier. This did not daunt Laurence. The part recommended itself to him, for the second act called for extravagant drunkenness followed by bitter remorse.

Anton Rubinstein, the director of the Conservatoire, welcomed the proposal and invited Laurence to meet his noble patronesses, who gave the project their enthusiastic approval. Soon after the New Year Laurence was in the thick of preparations for a gala performance of *David Garrick*.

He was confident that if he could get together a fairly large cast, the play would be a great success. 'I pay not one penny for acting D.G. as you see that between Russia and England there is no copy-

right. If only we can get the actors we shall wake up this old Petersburg.'
When he had first arrived there, Laurence had been introduced by
Sir Eric Barrington to the British Ambassador, Sir Robert Morier,
so that now he was able to recruit some of the Chancellery staff to
his company. They and the members of the English colony taking
part were to play incognito. Only Laurence was to appear under his
own name, that was calculated to be a draw.

The Duchess Katarina Mikhailovna, the daughter of Grand Duke
Michael, lent the little theatre in her Palace on the Krestovsky Ostrov
for the occasion. Prince Beloselski consented to be patron of the
performance and gave Laurence the run of the scene-dock of his own
private theatre. The stoutest republican can turn the perquisites of
privilege to his account with a clear conscience; Laurence had no
difficulty in squaring his principles with the acceptance of any means
to such a commendable and jolly end. It was harder for art's sake to
surrender his seedling moustache and soft young beard to the barber;
his cropped head would, however, be perfectly in period under a
powdered wig.

The short midwinter days, after his morning lessons, were spent
conferring with costumiers, choosing scenery and collecting properties; the long evenings in rehearsals. Such time as he had left he
gave to studying his part. He had no intention of appearing as a pale
ghost of Wyndham.

*I wish to give it a more serious tone—more the idea of what one
imagines a great tragic actor to be. I want particularly to bring out
all through the piece the man's strict sense of honour, because on that
the whole intrigue and character seem to turn. The chaff with Ada
[Ingot] in Act 1, I shall try to give a more serious tone than Wyndham and in such a way it becomes harder to know whether he is really
in earnest. It keeps up the dignity, and dryness, I think, always
adds to the humour.*

*Tell me what you think of my reading of the part? I shall always
try to reserve much repose when on the stage as I find nothing makes
the important points tell so much, as amateurs are always apt to
fall into the mistake of over-acting—better, I think, be a little on the
other side. I have given this the most serious study. I am sure this is
the only way to secure success. Next Saturday D.G. I really think
it will be a very good performance. I must say thanks to me. I have
drilled conductor and stage manager. The weakest is Mrs Turner*

(Ada Ingot), I think; she is not quite up to so dramatic a part but she will look very pretty and that is half the battle.

His nineteenth birthday passed unheeded in the flurry of production. Rarely can so young a man have been called upon to harness a spirited team of princes, duchesses, diplomats, professors, musicians, carpenters, painters and dress-makers and to coax them bilingually to meet their individual crises in a theatrical performance. That he brought them to the post and got them off to a punctual start was in itself a feat that must have left him a little breathless for his title role.

At last Garrick has come off...successfully I think. Better than ever anticipated. I am altogether discontented with myself and kick myself for not doing as well as I ought...and disgusted with the rest for their base ingratitude prompted, I suppose, by the meanest jealousy. If the play was successful they had me to thank: no one of them thanked me. The room was full—650 people in all. The stage was small but not badly got up. I got two re-calls in the middle of the play: one after the scene in the first act with Ingot and one after the drunken scene. I was the only person who received any personal applause. Everybody seems to have been delighted with my performance of which, by the way, there will be no criticisms by reason of being a private performance. Certainly in Petersburg my playing has gone well.

The chagrin of the unrequited producer was soon appeased by flattering appreciation of the player. Laurence could have wished for no greater compliment than to be begged by Rubinstein to repeat the performance in the Zal Pavlova during Lent when all the Russian theatres would be closed.

We are going to give a second performance of D.G. in the Little Theatre, not so called in relevance to its size as it cannot be much smaller than the Lyceum. We can get the theatre for nothing and shall act for charity—an English charity. We shall try to get the patronage of the English Ambassador. It might go off well if only the cold will not break.

It went off well enough for *The Times* correspondent to mention it in his despatches.

Laurence found that the dresses his father lent him fitted him very well. As Garrick, he wore the cut-steel-buttoned brocaded finery in which Irving, as Doricourt in *The Belle's Stratagem*, had first forced himself on the attention of London's playgoers at the St James's Theatre in 1866. My grandfather feared, with some justification, that if his mantle fell on his sons it might envelop them and hamper their progress; by lending them lesser items from his wardrobe he was encouraging them to believe that there was no harm in trying it on.

Laurence returned to England when the providentially delayed thaw set in. Before he left St Petersburg he played a leading part in a tribute to Turner by members of their play-reading coterie. Dr Anton Chekhov in Moscow had not as yet had much success as a dramatist, yet with affectionate irony he could have written the brief comedy that was played that evening.

The company were assembled in the drawing-room of the Turners' apartment, speculating on what was hidden behind the draperies that for the occasion divided it from the bedroom beyond. Conversation faded away as Laurence rose to read verses he had written in honour of their host. At their conclusion the curtains parted to reveal a bust of Shakespeare crowned with laurel upon an improvised plinth, and at the foot of it another wreath. Beckoning the blushful Turner to stand with him beside the Bard, he then declaimed the 38th Sonnet:

> How can my Muse want subject to invent
> While thou dost breath...

As he finished the sonnet Laurence picked up the wreath and to the lines:

> If my slight Muse do please these curious days
> The pain be mine, but thine shall be the praise.

laid it on Turner's brow. Applause, laughter, eyelids abrim with tears, pince-nez unpinched and polished furiously to mask emotion brought the ceremony to a close.

The Slavs and the Celts have much in common, particularly an ingenuous bonhomie ever at odds with a barbaric belligerence. The Irishman in Laurence had responded warmly to his Russian environment. The hurts of *David Garrick* were forgotten in the childlike simplicity and sincerity of farewells. His days in Russia had been curious and sometimes painful, but now it all seemed to have been so jolly—so very jolly.

As the applause for his performance of Strafford and the congratulations on his success faded away, Harry settled down to the hard work he would have to do if he was to get the degree his tutors expected of him. Though urged by his friends to stand for the Presidency of the Union, he refused to do so. The only distractions he allowed himself were a tentative start on a biography of Judge Jeffreys and entertaining his friends. Actors like William Terriss, whom he knew or who were his father's friends, if they came to play in Oxford would breakfast with him—although it was not a meal at which actors usually felt their best. The vacations he spent with reading parties. He saw less and less of his mother at Gilston Road.

He was, in fact, making the most of his time before the autumn, when his duties as President of the O.U.D.S. would claim more of it than he could properly spare. The success of *Strafford* had promoted the Society almost to the status of a faculty of the University. Mackinnon, before he had gone down, had received a formal vote of thanks from the Committee of the University Extension Lectures. Harry had discussed the next production with him; they had agreed that *King John* would be an appropriate reversion to Shakespeare. Few were alive who could remember Macready's spectacular production of the play at Drury Lane in 1842, or Charles Kean's farewell performance in it at the Princess's Theatre in 1858, when Ellen Terry had, at the age of ten, played Arthur. It was therefore overdue for revival. The part of the King appealed to Harry as a fitting farewell to his hopes of becoming an actor. It would not be easy, however, to find enough undergraduates to fill so large a cast. There would be plenty of athletic volunteers to enjoy the lark of walking on as soldiers or clerics, but owing to the pressure of Schools several seeded players in the Society had failed him, leaving him short of capable actors for the principal parts. Forgetting his own impatience with the persistent Bourchier, he appealed to Mackinnon, Holman Clark and Lechmere Stuart, all of whom had gone down, to return to Oxford to support him.

Shortly before Christmas he received a letter which assured him of an additional attraction to his programme.

> *Longford Castle,*
> *Salisbury.*
> *Dec. 14. 90.*

My dear Mr Irving,
> *You know what powers of persuasion the great 'Mack' possesses —but I must confess to a feeling of the greatest astonishment(!)*

*when I realise that I have actually written to him to say that I am
prepared to take some twenty or thirty of my Band to do orchestra
for your performance of King John. I really am quite alarmed now to
think of it...all I can say is that you will have to be very nice to us if
we do come...How do you like the prospects of King John? I shall
like immensely to see you do it.*

I am,

yrs,

Helen R.

Helen, Countess of Radnor, was the talented and energetic daughter
of the Rev. Chaplin, Vicar of Ryhill. She had married Lord Folkestone,
the grandson of the Earl of Radnor, on whose death her husband
had inherited the title and Longford Castle. Her mission in life was,
it seemed, to shed a radiance of culture upon the landed but un-
enlightened gentry. That this was a worthy field of endeavour was
proved by Lord Salisbury who, three years later, had welcomed to
Hatfield his future daughter-in-law, Violet Maxse (evidently suspiciously artistic and 'advanced'), by saying: 'I must warn you, my dear,
that you are now in the headquarters of Philistia'.

Until she could set to work rehanging and cataloguing the splendid
but ill-cared-for collection of pictures at Longford, music had seemed
the best way to demonstrate that patronage and performance were
not incompatible. So, from among her peers, she recruited a string
band and, having raised its performance to a professional standard,
was rewarded by the large and appreciative audiences that attended
her concerts in London. In due course, to the delight of the members
of the O.U.D.S., if to the dismay of the 'University ladies' with
eligible daughters, she arrived in Oxford with her bevy of young ladies
and her youngest son, the Hon S. Pleydell Bouverie, who was to play
Prince Henry.

King John was produced by Mackinnon. 'Your father,' he told
Harry, 'is kindly lending thirty suits of real chain mail and if six
principals I have named send their measures, boots will be made to
fit them.' Irving had also advised him that armour was most effective
seen against a background of massed browns.

A larger first-night audience than usual applauded Lady Radnor
as, maternally magnificent in a dark velvet gown frothing with lace
and fichus, she mounted the podium and drew from her maidenly
orchestra the first bars of the overture; their white dresses were

relieved by coloured ribbons on their shoulders that dipped and bobbed rhythmically to their bowing. Harry struggled to give expression to the weeks of study he had devoted to the part, but he lacked the technique to realise the subtle characterisation he attempted. His task was not made easier by the ribald encouragement shouted by hearties in the audience to their friends on the stage. In the middle of the potentially strong scene of the quarrel between the French and English Kings, he and his friend, Willie Goschen, in their chain mail, became inextricably enmeshed and had to leave the stage vituperatively entwined. Later, when the combined armies of France and England were due to enter to the strains of a wedding march composed by Claud Nugent, the drawbridge—their only axis of advance —stuck half-way down, so that the music had ended by the time the first soldier staggered across it. Mackinnon, left alone upon the stage, had to declaim the Bastard's line 'Mad world, mad kings, mad composition!'—an opinion heartily endorsed by irreverent members of the audience.

Things had gone better for Harry at the dress rehearsal, which his mother attended, and were improved by the time a contingent of theatricals from London came to the Monday matinée, among them the Bancrofts, George Alexander and Charles Hawtrey. The critics praised Harry's intention, but were critical of his execution; the notices were shorter, for the novelty of young Irving's appearance had worn off. Hutton could be counted on for an unbiased summing-up.

...I need not say that I most hearily congratulate you on a triumph over very great difficulties and on a really sterling result. Your coadjutors as a rule were distinctly inferior to last year's men— which made it all the harder for you...and moreover all the difficulties of the first night. And I really think you conquered them all. What I thought best was Act IV and Act V in all of which I most cordially accept your reading of the part and rejoice in the success with which you carried it out. The bit with the Prophet was excellent; so was the whole scene with the Lords and then the interview with Hubert really splendid—and in the last scenes you showed such perfect taste —no fuss, nothing over done but all most powerful and convincing...

May I say that I don't quite agree with your conception of the temptation of Hubert scene...Why do you knight Falconbridge with an air of profound melancholy and deep depression? I have no doubt you have a real meaning for it. Please tell me what it is.

The whole play goes very well I think. But why o why those ridiculous and immense and voiceless cardinals in obvious 17th cent: costumes and ridiculous mitres? And why does Pandulf wear the vestments of a Greek priest...and I wish Mr Lechmere Stuart would not quite unnecessarily and I think profanely be always making the sign of the cross?

As Harry read these kindly comments he may have wondered if the time and trouble he had spent on the play had been worth while. The result, through no fault of his, had been in many ways ridiculous. He knew that it might have cost him the first in Greats that was well within his reach. Perhaps at that moment he was readier than ever before to renounce his theatrical ambitions and to put his whole heart and mind, if not his soul, into making a career at the Bar.

He surrendered his presidency of the O.U.D.S. amid a storm of controversy. The Rev. Mr Chandler, Vice-Principal of Brasenose College, wrote an angry letter to the *Oxford Magazine* protesting that the University was being transformed into a third-rate histrionic company, and asking if 'the great sacrifice of time and expenditure and trouble was justified in order to win the qualified admiration which Dr Johnson accorded to the dancing bear?' He admitted he had never attended any of the plays and never proposed to do so. But there was, as Harry knew, some truth in his contention that the performances were not good and could not be good with the limited time available for rehearsal. Obliquely Chandler attacked the late Vice-Chancellor and the departed Senior Proctor for their un-principled patronage in bringing the O.U.D.S. into being. Harry did not reply to the letter. There were plenty of people for and against Mr Chandler eager to do so. As it turned out, this was the last assault of the faction that opposed acting in Oxford, and it failed.

On the credit side Harry was indebted to the Society for the many friends it had brought him. E. Holman Clark (Cassius, Pym and Hubert de Burgh), now a professional actor, would be his right-hand man during his last years as an actor-manager. When the time came for me to be coached for Responsions, W. J. Morris (Mark Antony), by then a parson with the voice and manner of a heavy tragedian, undertook the thankless task for old time's sake. One friendship that had grown out of *King John* was particularly oppor-tune. Evidently Lady Radnor was attracted by Harry's earnestness and by his mischievous humour that helped him to endure exaspera-

tion and frustration. Before the end of the Lent Term she invited
him to visit her in London—'...don't come and leave a card as you
know I shall be out, 2 o'clock lunch or 5 o'clock tea will be a sure find.
There will be a piano there and operas of sorts, as I love playing to
those who care to listen; if you don't hear enough operatic music
the fault will be yours entirely.'

Thereafter hardly a week passed without a letter from her. She
introduced him to opera from her box at Covent Garden, finding
him an apt initiate to the art she loved the most. He escorted her to
the Lyceum and, finding her an astute critic of acting, was able to
discuss with her his father's performances without prejudice or
reservation. She admired Irving; after seeing *Ravenswood* she wrote:
'...Shall I confess that I was so wrought up by his acting that I did
—what never in my life has happened before—I cried in the carriage
on the way home.' She was cool about Ellen Terry, finding that she
seldom lost herself in her part. In her Harry was lucky enough to find
a sensible and practical confidant willing to consider his own problems
with detachment. And on his most pressing one she commented:

> *...I wonder whether you did go to the Assizes and fancy yrself a
> Judge—'and a good judge too' in embryo? I think you must take to
> that (if circumstances permit) for a bit at any rate, it is so easy to
> turn to the other later; but so long as yr father is still at the zenith
> of his fame I am certain (that if you succeed which I think you
> would) it would produce friction that you would like to avoid—but
> there—why do I ramble on—these sorts of thing every man settles
> for himself—whatever his friends say or think.*

By the end of his last term Harry had done so. None of his friends
was surprised or doubted the wisdom of his choice. He seemed cast
by nature for the judiciary. Not long before he went down he was
invited by his friend, George Bancroft, to breakfast in his lodgings.
George was the son of Squire Bancroft and Marie Wilton who, by
improving the amenities of their theatre and consequently the manners
of theatre-goers, helped to create a climate favourable to the emergence
of my grandfather as the leader and champion of his profession.
George was very much his father's son. He had already acquired a
grave, profound but always kindly manner that in years to come
would make him fair game for the mockery of his mischievous contemporaries. He was not destined to excel at anything in particular.
But by inviting young Max Beerbohm to meet Harry Irving at break-

fast, he exploded momentarily with the brilliance of a flash-bulb, and by doing so illuminated for all time an instantaneous exposure of my father in the setting of that morning encounter. Sixty years later I and Max's devoted radio public were given a glimpse of Harry Irving's manner and appearance at this juncture of his life, in such sharp focus that it will, I hope, confirm the sum of characteristics I have tried to convey—characteristics that in their persistence must be accepted as the basic tonality of a portrait to which touches and accents will be added as the years go by.

All too rarely a man of letters is able with percipience and skill to recall the experiences of his youth with vision undimmed by the astigmatism of hind-sight, and with his hearing unimpaired by the confusing echoes of a critical faculty later acquired. Max Beerbohm had this gift of preserving intact the impressions of his youth until in the fulness of time he discovered he had the power (if such a word can be used of so gentle a raconteur) of communicating to us his memories in a style that, however crafty, never permitted the sophistication of his maturity to intrude upon the innocence of his early observations.

And I, like a navigator not too sure of his position, find relief, having checked my dead reckoning against Max's accurate sights, that they coincide in the identification of my father at his point of departure from Oxford.[1]

[1] See Appendix

VIII

M Y GRANDFATHER, as reports reached him of his son's successes, though he did not overrate them, must have felt the prodding of the horns of his dilemma. He had kept a benevolent eye on what appeared to be Laurence's innocent enterprise, encouraging him with telegrams and the use of the Lyceum wardrobe. Yet he must have known in his heart that the cub of such a tiger as himself, having tasted the hot blood of the theatre, would have less appetite for the cold meat of diplomacy. Apparently Harry's performances at Oxford had not turned his head; his degree was a token of his obedient intentions. At the same time, Irving began to realise that he was not in a position to insist that his sons must earn their livings in professions that would call for considerable subsidies from him before they could do so.

What *The Times*, much to his annoyance, had called the 'non-success' of *Ravenswood* had contributed to his loss of £4,000 at the close of that theatrical year. Though his private ledgers showed that £58,000 had flowed through the box office, this deficit warned him that the equilibrium of profit and loss was precariously balanced. He had been at pains to conceal the finances of the Lyceum from the public. His sons, like everyone else, must imagine that his princely dispensations in his theatre indicated a princely income. The time had come to disabuse them. He chose a curious way to do this.

My grandmother received a letter from her husband explaining in guarded terms his financial situation and telling her that, all things considered, it might be best for Harry and Laurence, as he was given to understand that they had some talent for acting, to enter his profession. He added that he would like both of them to join the Lyceum company. It was a *coup de théâtre* that left his audience gasping.

Flo sent the letter to Harry. 'This last act of Mr Irving's,' she commented, 'seems to have opened all this matter again...I am certainly not going to submit to this sort of thing any longer. If he is going

Dorothea Baird as Rosalind in *As You Like It*.

Dorothea Baird as Trilby.

As Trilby, with H. Beerbohm Tree as Svengali.

to act in this defiant spirit...I don't think it is possible that you can remain even if you go to the Lyceum.'

Though she may not have realised that her sons' futures were no longer in her hands, she knew that the offence to her contained in Irving's offer was felt as keenly by them as by herself. For so many years Ellen Terry, as the scarlet woman of the Lyceum, had been made the obstacle to any understanding with their father that his invitation seemed a calculated insult to their mother. But this was no time for my grandfather to take sardonic revenge—nor was it in his nature to do so. Such passion as he and Ellen had felt for each other was long spent. She had, as she told Shaw later, not seen him alone for some years. To him she was still his indispensable partner on the stage and his congenial companion on the journeyings this entailed. Society had accepted their relationship; it was inconceivable to him that his wife's bitterness had outlived the long dead and never genuine cause of it.

Harry took the news calmly. Certainly it released him from any further obligation to meet his father's wishes. Unexpectedly and inopportunely he was faced with a difficult choice. Pinero, whose advice he sought, pointed out that his histrionic gifts, if he had any, allied to his educational advantages could be as much value to him at the Bar as on the stage. His father's position might help him as a barrister but would inevitably overshadow him an actor. He reminded him very wisely that a barrister at fifty is still young, whereas a romantic actor of fifty is a veteran. Pinero's sensible advice might have prevailed had not the Bancrofts intervened. Marie Bancroft had been much impressed by Harry's King John. Soon afterwards she heard that John Hare was having difficulty in casting the part of Lord Beaufroy in the production of Robertson's *School* that he planned for the autumn. At her suggestion Hare offered the part to Harry, and Harry in his mood of indecision accepted it. Whatever doubts he may have had, the prospect of being a cadet at the Lyceum was not one of them.

News of his father's proposal reached Laurence while he was making preparations for the performance at the Zal Pavlova. His reactions, with his immediate concern for his brother, were characteristic.

This of our father's is indeed a momentous and far-reaching proposal. If Harry (I will speak afterwards of myself) is to go on the

F

*stage I do not well see how he can do other, as the offer is made, than
appear at the Lyceum—were he now to appear at any other theatre
the Lyceum would assume the role of martyrdom and the rankest
animosity would be attributed to us by its hired scribes and fawning
chroniclers Scott, Hatton etc. At the same time to us the thought
of appearing on the same stage with that Serpent must be most
repugnant and disgusting—to have to treat her with anything but
the scorn and contempt she merits.*

*That in the end good might come of it, you must not forget it
might be the means of ousting her from the place of infamy she fills
and of reuniting your lives, if ever you find so much magnanimity in
your heart to forgive the wrongs and insults that he has heaped
upon you.*

*There is another thing to be taken into consideration, granted for a
moment that these things were to come about. Could Irving with his
selfish and egotistical nature stand the presence of a young and gifted
actor just as he has at length after a hard struggle had to renounce
the cherished sweets of public adulation as a juvenile lead. Would
not the alliance, if it came about, end in bitter strife and contemptible
horrid envy from father to son? Would not Irving, perhaps not at the
out-start, try to chide Bim as he did if you remember Bellew by
giving him no good parts and keeping him at it.*

*We must keep in view with whom we have to deal but at the same
time these are reasons which should not deter. The opening is there
—the opening, the right thing (granted these were the only objections)
has been done and disruptions will be the father's fault. The objection
is the* Wench. *That is the objection.*

*To come to myself I feel certain that whatever I may be destined
to do the stage has attractions for me that I cannot resist. You will
laugh, darling, when I say that I regard the actor's as a great art
worthy of adornment and only too much in need of it—the adornment
of an educated man is what the stage most lacks. The spirit is stirring
within us. I must act.*

*The diplomatic to the dogs! It is a mere hollow service of lips, a mere
of platitudes and stupidities overrun with the worthless sprouts of
aristocracy in which I see little room for any actor's son be he whom
he may.*

My grandmother was troubled not only by Laurence's eagerness to
abandon the goal that he had worked for so hard and so long, but

by his readiness to turn his father's offer to his account. The absurd idea that it would be the means of bringing his estranged parents together would, in anyone less quixotic, have seemed the grossest humbug. Harry soothed his mother as best he could.

I don't think that at present there is any need for anxiety beyond the fact that his future in general is uncertain. Irving is not likely to write to him on the subject and the matter will remain as it is 'till his return at Easter when...Laurence can talk the question out with him.

I am not at all sure that Laurence is himself keen on the D[iplomatic] S[ervice]; he is young and very uncertain in his tastes and wishes...we'll talk it over when you come down and may 'God send us good deliverance' as they say to the prisoners.

In the event their different responses to their father's change of heart were equally disastrous.

In September Harry made his début with Hare at the Garrick Theatre. As Lord Beaufroy he was succeeding two popular actors, Montague and Conway, whose performances in the past were still remembered. In comparison, his inadequacies were obvious to critics no longer prepared to indulge undergraduate frolics. It was easy to see that he had not mastered the rudiments of professional acting. His delivery was monotonous, his manner stilted and 'ultra priggish'. His love-making lacked even the pretence of ardour. His name did not inspire critical leniency. He improved during the run of the play, and in *A Fool's Paradise,* that followed it, he made something of the part of a deceived husband. The critics gave him his due, but he had no offers of further employment. So, at the end of the season, he retired to his rooms in the Temple, to eating his dinners at the Inner Temple, and to extenuating the abominable memory of an earlier member of his Inn, George Jeffreys. His first essay as an actor had ended, if not with a whimper, with a tacit acknowledgment of his father's prescience; Laurence's, on the other hand, ended with a bang.

There is no record of Laurence's interview with his father when he returned from Russia. Perhaps when it came to the point Irving, piqued by Harry's rejection of the olive branch, shrank from having an antipathetic prince at the court of the Lyceum. He knew his company well enough to foresee that his son would be a prey to the factions that so large an organisation bred. He took the wind out of

Laurence's swelling sails by withdrawing his offer. Instead, he wrote in September to Frank Benson:

> *Dear Benson,*
>
> *If you have the opportunity I am sure you will give Laurence any chance that may rise for a display of the 'spirited and graceful' attributes which he may possess.*
>
> *An understudy perhaps or something in a new cast.*
>
> *I hope all is thriving and going well with you.*
>
> > *Sincerely yours,*
> >
> > *H. Irving.*

Benson was indeed thriving, though not as Irving would have understood it. After coming down from Oxford he had served a brief apprenticeship in the Lyceum company, where he learned at least how much as an actor he had to learn. His reasons for going on the stage were largely altruistic; his love of acting was free of vanity and personal ambition. He saw himself as a champion of drama leading a company of young men of education skilled in athletics that now were so much part of it and carrying the banner of Shakespeare to communities bereft of him as the old stock companies withered away. One thing he had learnt from Irving was the exercise of command; if he never ranked as a great actor, he proved himself through half a century to be an inspiring leader. By 1891 his company had been on the road twelve years. Now it had its veteran players and a loyal following in the provincial towns it visited.

Benson was glad to be of service to his old Chief. He engaged Laurence to join the company at Dundee. It was agreed that he should appear as 'Mr Lawrence'.

> *I was glad to learn* [wrote Laurence in answer to a letter from his mother] *what satisfaction my first criticism had earned at home…not withstanding the fact of my being criticised under the name of Irving. I appeared and was inserted in the programme as Lawrence. It's not much good.*
>
> *I see no immediate prospect of my getting good parts. You see Benson has already a certain staff of senior actors over whose heads I cannot very well be thrust and I shall have to bide my time and go up with the next form at the end of term. It's rather galling to see persons playing big parts feeling how much better I could do it, still I suppose it's part of the* [regimen] *that Irving has prepared for me.*

I expect...he told Benson to give me small parts. Of course, as is quite proper, Benson treats me just as the rest of the company...he said last night he was very pleased with my performances.

Though Laurence, with his shortsightedness and athletic ineptitude, could not share the robust and lighthearted attitude of his colleagues towards the art he took so seriously, he soon settled down and seemed content with the small parts that came his way—Nym, Snug, Boyet and Hortensio.

You can well imagine [he wrote later] *that I am satiated of Snug the Joiner by this time although it is to be I expect one of my biggest parts. I think I told you that Benson complimented me on my performance... The 'boys'—Benson boys—of the company are really a very decent set of their sort. There is one, Brydone by name, who is a most exemplary young man; he is very religious, sober and industrious, never uses bad language and is most devoted to his mother; it was he who said to me that he found the greatest drawback in the profession was that it kept one away from home.*

For the rest there is a low comedian called L— whose brother was at Marlborough, himself at Malvern, a very nice fellow named V— who enlisted in the 16th Lancers and saw service in India...besides being a relative of the manager of the theatre at Weymouth. George Weir, a respectable fellow of the old school, humble of origin but a very sound comedian, the prop and stay of the company amongst so much sportive youth. A man called Ross and a man called Roberts. I would refrain from criticising these gentlemen as actors for I fear they would not bear scrutiny.

I cannot say I was astonished at Irving being at Malvern with Terry. I might have been had he been there without Terry. We are cutting ourselves adrift from the old hulk and very soon we shall not need to fear his hatred or win his love. That he could not take us into his company was true whilst he is stuffing the goose with bastards of the fell Terry breed.

A month later he wrote:

I wished so much to write before but I have had so much rehearsing to do, for you must know that it is the rule of the company that all the actors double in minor parts and indeed some of them are obliged to stand on in other scenes as supers, I have to stand on, to do dances and heaven knows what so that I have to stick close to the rehearsals.

I was very much tickled by that notice. Nym has to be played as a low class skulking cut-throat bully of the most infamous kind, hence the dropping of the jaw and perhaps a certain slow insidious walk of the Irvingesque kind. One would have thought I dropped my jaw in all the parts I played. Benson is well pleased with me in The Taming of the Shrew. I play a juvenile, Hortensio—not a low part. I got through it after four days study—200 lines without a hitch and won golden opinions from Benson and Mrs. I dare say I shall soon have a good part in some production or other. I wonder if I shall get any London offers. The fault of the repertoire system is that I think it inclines one to be slipshod in one's acting.

I shall certainly stay with the company much longer than you contemplate. I want to get thoroughly grounded and, as they say, to go through the mill. I rub along excellently well with all the company. I am in peace and goodwill with all men and women.

But at heart he felt the mill ground all too slowly, and that the parts he was given were too exceeding small. Nor was he at peace with himself. Rightly or wrongly, he believed he was capable of more than he was doing, and was aggrieved to see actors of less serious purpose given roles he longed to play. Though his time with the company turned out to be brief, this earnest, gentle, erudite recruit made more impression on his master and on his fellow players than he would have believed. Those today who study the Bensonian Memorial window at Stratford-upon-Avon will be arrested by the wistful regard of a handsome Iago that is, in fact, a life-like portrait of my uncle, smiling ruefully at his promotion in stained glass to a part that, as a Bensonian, he never played.

His father, even if no longer feared or loved, could be depended upon to subsidise the pittance that was Laurence's wage as an apprentice; he also understood and encouraged his son's impatience.

I enclose the £10 for October [he wrote], *that is one month in advance. I should like you to drop me a line the week before the 1st of every month and tell me where to send remittance.*

Benson told me how well you had got on as Hortensio. I wish you could get more to do now. You must take it quietly for a while but it would be better soon if you had more important characters.

Harry has done well I am sure and has improved much since the first night but whether it was wise to launch him with such temerity I can hardly say. It might have been better had he played a less

important part—but what was done was thought for the best and all
will be well.

I wonder shall we be near one another at all. Drop me a line more
frequently. Harry by the way has not written since his first night. I
have generally 30 or 40 letters a day to get through but can always
spare a moment.

God bless you, my dear Laurence,
affectionately,
H. Irving.

In November the orbits of the Lyceum and the Benson companies
intersected at Manchester. From Newcastle his father had written
again:

I agree with you certainly that you must now be doing something
better. The difficulty just now is how *but I am thinking it over and*
shall be able to decide upon something to your advantage. There is no
chance I suppose of your playing better parts with Benson because if
you got practice that would be something. Have you ever spoken to
him on the subject…?

By now Laurence was becoming exasperated by the evasive answers
and vague promises he was getting from Benson and his father. His
mood when he reached Manchester was one of smouldering rebellion.

Well, I arrived in Manchester at 4.30 and went straight to the
Queen's Hotel, learnt Irving was timed to arrive at 6.30, met the
train at the station, saw Irving, bowed to the Creature at Irving's
'You remember Laurence?' Terry went to the Grand Hotel. That
evening Bradshaw and Stoker dined at Irving's invitation. I saw no
evidence of a rupture between H.I. and E.T. It cannot be true, if so it
has been smoothed down.

I told him that all he (Benson) offers me is a little part in Richard
III and the probability of Paris in Romeo and Juliet and that I should
like to take farewell of him on my return from Ireland—when Irving
remembered and alluded to the fact of your relations there and spoke
very highly of John O'Callaghan.

Irving was very dull. He was so icy and obnoxious. I was glad to
leave him to himself…

He arrived in Dublin, after a choppy crossing, to find the advance agent
had taken for him rooms so dirty, dreary and ill-fitted that he sought

others at £2 for the week at the Central Hotel. He was struggling against an attack of influenza. Again he pleaded with Benson to be given more to do. In spite of renewed promises, when *Othello* was cast he was disgusted to find himself allotted two parts, a messenger and a gentleman with twelve lines between them.

> *After our conversation this looks almost an intentional insult* [he wrote in despair to his mother]. *I have written to Irving but have had no answer. In Othello even Ludovico would be better. I am very sick, darling, too sick to visit anyone. Of course we cannot rely on Irving for anything. What care he what happens to any of us...at Manchester he was so icy and cold. One cannot say of him what the Queen said of John Brown.*
>   *Here an end!*
>   *Your affectionate*
>   *Laurence.*

The company moved on to Belfast. By now Laurence's friends were aware of his deep depression. On January 6th, after rehearsal, he and George Hippisley, to whom he was much attached, walked in the bleak dusk through the granite-grey city to the lodgings they shared in Upper Arthur Street. Each went to his room to study until tea-time. Soon afterwards, Hippisley was startled to hear a loud report. He ran into Laurence's room and saw his friend stretched across the bed; he was bleeding from a wound in his chest; a revolver lay upon the floor.

As though the pistol shot had been a signal for action, the dreary street became dramatically alive. Neighbours peeped through their drawn curtains to identify in the fading light the comings and goings at No. 55. Hippisley kept his head and sent for a doctor; the landlady lost hers and sent for the police. Laurence was unconscious, and his condition appeared to be grave. Benson, as soon as he heard of it, called in the best available medical men of Belfast. What at first appeared to be a flesh wound in fact marked the entry of a bullet that pierced the lung and lodged in the muscles of the back. When Laurence regained consciousness two nurses were attending him, and next day the distinguished surgeon, Lawson Tait, arrived from England to make his report to Irving. He complimented the Irish doctors on their work.

The police, who found themselves investigating a case of the illegal possession of firearms, said enough to the crowding journalists to give the rumour of attempted suicide a start that set denials in hot pursuit.

As the doctor's visits became less frequent and Laurence's condition less critical, Benson wrote to Irving:

> *Thanks for your wire. This is just a line to express my deep sympathy. All that is possible is being done...he is progressing favourably. The doctors seem to me much more hopeful than they will allow me to state in wiring. So far he hasn't had much pain, is quite conscious, may be read to a little. The account enclosed is drawn up and signed by the doctors and sent to the papers.*

Galland, the business manager, reported to Harry:

> *We are still quite in the dark as to how it can have happened and as the doctors wish to keep Laurence as quiet as possible he has not been allowed to talk more than is absolutely necessary. We surmise he was probably rehearsing in his room and unconsciously took up the pistol and discharged it before he knew even what he was handling... You shall be kept fully posted of every change for better or worse but I think there is little fear that he will not pull through bravely.*

Harry was unlikely to be impressed by Galland's discreet conjecture. He may not have known that Laurence had brought back a pistol from Russia; but he knew well enough that the rehearsal of small Shakespearean parts did not call for such a property.

My grandmother was soon at Laurence's bedside. Letters of condolence were pouring in; these and newspaper reports seemed to give her a morbid gratification.

> *Poor darling* [she wrote to Harry], *he has indeed suddenly become most celebrated and the press are clamouring at this house constantly for news...I trust it was only* accident. *No one has questioned him on the matter and think it better not at any rate for some time... He has been* sleeping *a good deal today but is doing well in every respect; he is, as always, patient and good. Benson has been a perfect father to him...*

Later she added:

> *I have just had a very satisfactory little chat, the first about this sad affair with the dear boy, which proves that it was all pure accident and he tried to explain to me as far as he could without having a pistol in his hand how it occurred. So that sets all doubts at rest and forever—and my heart is much relieved because it broke my heart to*

*think so good and noble a nature should be driven by any disappoint-
ment or distress to commit such an act. Please convey this intelligence
to your father and to all who impute any sinister motives to our
darling.*

Gradually all concerned would persuade themselves that it had been an
accident. Laurence, to be at peace with them, would be a willing
accessory to the fiction. As time went on the facts of the case were
distorted to fit into this comfortable reconstruction. Many years later
Austin Brereton, in writing a biographical sketch of Laurence, was
persuaded by my grandmother that he had been shot accidentally
during rehearsals in the theatre. Yet all the evidence, factual and
psychological led to the conclusion that Laurence had tried to put an
end to his short life. From the cradle his gentle nature had been
subjected to influences that induced in him a precocious sensitivity.
For love of his mother he assumed an unnatural bitterness against
the father whose affection and encouragement he craved. These
tensions were tolerable as long as he could find security and example in
the companionship of Harry, and self-sufficiency in the independence
of his years abroad. But when he came home to find himself once more
and more acutely the victim of insoluble dissensions, and prone again
to harbouring suspicions he knew in his heart were unworthy, when he
found the path of his fulfilment as an artist blocked by hereditary
obstacles, his natural optimism was vitiated by slavonic alternations of
hope and despair. It only needed the despondency of influenza to
destroy his will to live.

Perhaps, in their anxiety to conceal this from the world and from
each other, those who had brought him to this situation betrayed
their sense of guilt. If this young man of good will attempted suicide
his motives were not sinister; they were pitiable as the ultimate protest
of an idealist with faith in his self-development against the insensate
follies of his tormentors.

IX

CATASTROPHE GAVE WAY to self-conscious calm. The Bensonians soldiered on, leaving their casualty convalescing, their team spirit a little dampened by this morbid precipitation of their latest recruit; somehow or other young Irving had let the side down. Laurence, when his wounds had healed, returned to Gilston Road, but not to the old uninhibited affinity with his mother. Her nagging doubt and his acquiescence in concealing his intention constrained their habitual intimacy. Nor could he and his beloved brother Bim recover the light-hearted frankness of their indispensability to each other, for now they shared one secret too many. Both must have remembered the debate at Marlborough four years ago when, on the only occasion in which they were in opposition, Harry had led the house in defeating Laurence's defence of the motion that suicide should not be considered a crime. Harry, who alone may have been convinced of the truth of what had happened in Belfast, kept his counsel; but the keeping of it sowed seeds of mutual suspicion that would henceforth bedevil their indestructible love for each other.

My grandfather received the news of Laurence's predicament immediately after the first night of *Henry VIII* at the Lyceum. It had been his last great and successful theatrical gamble—a sumptuous production that won him three times his stake of its cost—£12,000. His interpretation of Cardinal Wolsey had been acclaimed. He had just written to Ellen Terry congratulating her on her son Ted's performance as Cromwell. This may have sharpened the shock of what he had every reason to suspect might have been the consequence of denying his son the stage of his own theatre. He was not gullible enough to accept the laboured assurances of an 'accident'; at the same time he was prompted by self-interest to subscribe to the discouragement of darker conjectures. He was, however, quick to take the steps that, to Laurence's almost fatal misfortune, had hitherto been prevented by quite irrelevant and accidental circumstances.

Over the years, on all personal matters, Irving had sought the

171

advice of his old friend Toole—ever since their friendship had begun thirty-four years ago when, as an apprentice juvenile in the Edinburgh stock company, he had first played with that already popular comedian. Only his broken marriage had proved too stubborn a calamity for Toole to mend. By unhappy chance, when he needed his friend's advice as to how best he could further his sons' careers, Toole was on a prolonged tour of Australia. The battered old droll, whose comicality caused physicians throughout Great Britain to prescribe a dose of 'Dr Toole' for their depressed patients, heard of Laurence's accident when he returned to England early in the New Year. Having suffered recently the loss of his wife and children, he was ready to do all he could to help his godson and to win his confidence and affection. So he invited Laurence, as soon as he had recovered, to join his company for the coming season at Toole's Theatre,[1] which would open with a new comic play in three acts that Irving had recommended to him—*Walker, London*, the first dramatic work by a young Scottish journalist, James Barrie. Laurence was to play Augustus Cadell in the curtain raiser *Daisy's Escape*—a part created by the author, Pinero, when this, his first play, was produced at the Lyceum. In contrast to the surly Cadell he would find comic relief in a small part in *Walker, London*. His first appearance in London led to no invidious comparisons with his father. He fitted quietly and unobtrusively into the ensemble, to everybody's satisfaction, not least to his own. By the time the London season ended and the company set out for a long provincial tour he had fully recovered his health and his confidence in his capacity as an actor.

He was sorry to leave behind him in London the most likeable of his fellow players—Edward Seymour Hicks, a gay young spark from Jersey who had come to London to seek his fortune on the stage and was already well on the way to making, if not a fortune, his mark upon the theatrical scene that would be indelible in the memories of those who saw him on or off the stage. He and Laurence were the same age. They shared only a love of the theatre and a keen sense of fun; otherwise they were sufficiently unalike to become devoted friends, as dissimilar in tastes as in appearance; for while Hicks, however impecunious, was immaculate in top hat, frock-coat and cloth-top boots, my uncle, however prosperous, contrived to make any clothes he wore look as though he had slept the night in them.

Hicks had a passionate curiosity about the theatrical past, and his

[1] Then on the present site of the Charing Cross Hospital.

appetite for anecdotes endeared him to his seniors glad enough to have an appreciative audience for the kind of retrospection that is the player's dearest indulgence. So it was that Irving and Toole came to adopt this genial young man as their attendant jester, and that he in turn, marking the contrast between Irving's sly majesty and Toole's plebeian exuberance, in his own maturity (he never knew old age) was able to convey their essence to later generations. Hicks lived in a constant state of infatuation. His heart was not worn on his sleeve, but was ready to hand to be offered to the latest object of his adoration. At this time he imagined himself deeply in love with Violet Vanbrugh, a young actress in the Lyceum company. She and her sister Irene, who was in Toole's company, were the daughters of the Prebendary of Exeter Cathedral and were among the vanguard of emancipated young ladies taking to the boards that angels, thanks to my grandfather's elevation of the stage, no longer feared to tread. Every night after their performances, the love-lorn Hicks took the Vanbrugh girls home to Earls Court Road where he had lodgings near by— the gallantry of their escort in no way diminished if now and then they had to pool their meagre resources to pay the fare.

So for Laurence, in London and on tour through the provinces, the year passed happily enough. He felt he was really making headway as an actor with a company that knew its business, particularly as on tour he was allowed to take over Hicks's part as Andrew McPhail in *Walker, London*, thereby having an opportunity to prove himself as a light comedian. Hicks, who knew that the actor's bread could be more thickly buttered by remaining in the capital, had shifted his gay pennant to the Court Theatre. They met again when Toole's company came back to London for what proved to be his last season. To Irving's grief his old friend had returned from Australia with evident symptoms of the spinal disease that was making his performances progressively painful for himself and for his loyal public.

Shortly before Christmas Laurence would be celebrating his twenty-first birthday. Toole suggested to Hicks that the occasion might be opportune for a reconciliation between Irving and his son—for since their encounter at Manchester there had been little communication between them. So, on December 1st, Hicks took his reluctant friend to Grafton Street and discreetly left father and son alone together. From Laurence's halting account of the interview Hicks gathered that his father had embraced him and had tried inarticulately to convey how eagerly he longed for his sons' affection and for an opportunity to redress past grievances. On parting he gave Laurence a gold watch, which was proudly shown to Hicks as an outward and visible sign of his change of heart. A fortnight later Irving gave a similar watch to Ted Craig on his birthday 'with love and remembrance' —a memento of past amities rather than a token of good intention, for so far Ellen Terry's children had shown him more trust and affection than his own. Two gold watches—the one that at his bedside ticked out the life of the ancient and venerable Craig; the other silent, full fathom five beneath the Gulf of St Lawrence, its hands forever set at 2.30, the morning hour of its owner's untimely end.

Whatever was said during that long overdue meeting, it was the beginning of a new relationship between Laurence and his father, of a companionship that was not to be vitiated by suspicions engendered by mischief-makers. Laurence would always regard his father with a kind of quizzical pity; Irving, on the other hand, was henceforward ready to indulge his son's eccentric foibles in return for the affection he craved. And, in due course, it was Laurence who overcame Harry's deep-seated prejudices, and persuaded him to share in this too long delayed amnesty that was to be the comfort of their father's declination. So the kindly work begun by Pinero was completed by young Hicks. My grandmother had, by now, perhaps lost heart in her implacability, and was happy enough to find that her sons' love and concern for her was not at all diminished by their discovery of their father.

Harry had spent the summer working in the Temple, and during the vacation visiting his now wide circle of friends in the country. At Longford he had found Lady Radnor supervising the despatch of three of the finest pictures in the collection to London; her husband had been forced to sell them to provide for his grandfather's generous legacies. He happened to see one of the packers knock a hole through the face of Velasquez's Admiral, and was later asked to keep this to himself, as the officials of the National Gallery said it was of no account and the damage could be easily repaired.

At Oxford Alma Tadema, during the run of *Strafford*, had introduced Harry to George Meredith's daughter Marie. Later he had invited her to go with him to the Lyceum, and at her suggestion her chaperone Mrs Walter Palmer had been included in the party. The ubiquitous American hostess was now showing signs of fatigue in her frantic pursuit of notable persons and occasions; but she had been only too glad when the great novelist had asked her to introduce his daughter in society. In due course Harry was invited to a weekend party at her house near Sevenoaks, Ightham Mote. There old Meredith gave him a description of his father's performance as *Hamlet*, and told him how much more he had thought of it after Irving had patiently listened to his criticisms. In contrast he had described the Lyceum *Romeo and Juliet* as ceasing to present a sorrowful story but becoming a pageant with a quaint figure ranting about. Harry may have been glad to escape from this ancient, and to hang on the words of a livelier member of the party, Oscar Wilde. Although the clouds were gathering that in a short time would extinguish Wilde's radiance, Harry was charmed and fascinated by him. Thereafter there was always a place for him and for Laurence at Wilde's convivial luncheon parties at the Café Royal. Though their host's features were now sullied by unsuspected dissipations, his young guests were conscious only of eyes that challenged a dull return to his volleying wit and of a generous gaiety that persuaded his guests of their own transitory brilliance. Like a jovial confessor he would encourage his enchanted young penitents to talk freely of their artistic hopes and ambitions, giving them absolution of their aesthetic follies and loading them with indulgencies paid for by their laughter at his kindly and whimsical criticisms. There Harry met Alfred (A.E.W.) Mason, who was accepting defeat as an actor and now, encouraged and inspired by Wilde, was at work on his first novel. There, too, he discussed his book on Judge Jeffreys with William Heinemann, and gave the publisher first refusal of it when it was finished. Round that table youth was served not only with carefully chosen food and wine but with a serious attention, with no trace of patronage, that was Wilde's unique gift, his most admirable contribution and the source of the only true happiness he enjoyed. Harry's analytical perception may have detected flaws in his idol—the hint of a perilous vanity and the hand that masked the decaying teeth behind the flaccid tell-tale lips, muting the taut aphorisms they effused. Laurence saw him only as a lighthearted philosopher who translated his own moral introspections into the language of self-expression in art.

At one of their now rarer meetings Harry had read passages of his book to Laurence, who responded with all the old fraternal devotion:

Most glad of all I was to hear that your work was progressing. Yes, you were quite right in being pleased with what you read to me.

*I thought it was most admirable—quite exceptional in fact—at last
you have now taken to something worthy of your steel and now you
are launched on the high seas of literature there's no knowing what
time and trouble may not get out of you. I should awfully like to
read some more of your work.*

    *For the moment I'm working all round and at all kinds of subjects.
The 2nd act of Silas is completed. Today we are to meet and talk
over the 3rd...I am mapping the whole play out before commencing.
I think I should have persisted in the past had I been less precipitate.
I think Silas will be successful if produced.*

He was in fact dramatising that masterpiece of tales of suspense,
Uncle Silas by Sheridan LeFanu. The story cast a traumatic spell on
two generations of Irvings that I was driven finally to exorcise by a
prodigious waste of my time and other people's money. My uncle's
infatuation with it proved less exhausting and expensive, though it
cost him dear enough.

While on tour in the summer with Toole he heard that his great-
aunt, Martha Walsh, had died leaving him a legacy of £100. He was
the only member of the family who did not regard her passing as
characteristically tiresome. The rest of her money went to charities,
her collection of miniatures to the Victoria and Albert Museum, and
her old clothes to her finally affronted sister Elizabeth—Gran
O'Callaghan. When Hicks heard of Laurence's good fortune, he
suggested that it could not be used to better purpose than to finance
their collaboration in writing and producing a dramatisation of
LeFanu's novel—a project they had often discussed without much
hope of fulfilling it. Laurence was easily persuaded, and by the end
of the year they had finished the script. It was a mannered and rather
incoherent adaptation in the Erckmann-Chatrian style, ending with a
long soliloquy by Silas before he takes poison, and the off-stage
beating on the bolted door by his abused and agonised niece. Evidently
The Bells had been much in the authors' minds, and perhaps the
making of a second Irving with the opportunities it would offer to
an actor of genius. They even managed to persuade themselves that
it was an improvement on an earlier version by the experienced
playwright, John Douglass.

The Shaftesbury Theatre was taken for the afternoon of February
13th, 1893; it had to be a matinée performance, for most of the cast
would be playing elsewhere in the evening. Haviland, a heavy duty

actor from the Lyceum, agreed to play the wicked uncle; for Madame de la Rougierre, Silas's fiendish accomplice, the young impresarios engaged Florence Cowell, the youngest of the famous theatrical family but an experienced and popular actress, whose daughter, Sidney Fairbrother, had just made her début with the Kendals. Laurence cast himself for Silas's virtuous brother Austin; Hicks disguised his natural elegance as Silas's oafish son, Dudley, content with having persuaded the stately Violet Vanbrugh to play Austin's daughter, Maud, who must have looked like Alice after she'd eaten the growing cake. Laurence, in spite of his euphoric mood of reconciliation, must have flinched when she suggested that she should bring along Ted Craig to play one of Silas's 'sporting friends'. As it happened she and Craig, to augment their modest Lyceum wages, were partnering each other in duologues at public and private entertainments. Perhaps, on closer acquaintance, Laurence found the Terry breed less 'fell' than he had imagined. The rest of the cast was drawn from the Irving and Toole companies—Violet's sister Irene, Harry's Oxford friend Holman Clark, and Tom Reynolds, soon to be one of Irving's most trusted table legs (as Craig called the Lyceum veterans) and already playing Fouinard to his Chief's Dubosc in *The Lyons Mail,* their last scene being perhaps, in its perfection of business and timing, one of the most skilfully contrived pieces of acting the stage has seen. There remained a newcomer to the profession, Tom Heslewood, a stage-struck wood engraver who about that time was sitting to Weedon Grossmith for his studies for Burwen Fosselton, Mr Pooter's friend in *The Diary of a Nobody,* who gave imitations of Irving. The authors had a promising cast for their first venture.

The Press, for the most part, discreetly ignored it. *The Era,* as the faithful keeper of the theatrical record, gave it two columns. It began by reproving the crowded audience—'the remembrance of well-known faces that were to be seen in all parts of the house, faces that are associated with distinction in art and letters, compels us to question its honesty, for a friendly feeling for the young authors and the actors led it to applaud vigorously and even enthusiastically a work which we are quite sure its judgment would not approve'.

There followed a scene by scene synopsis of the play, comparing it unfavourably with the earlier version, relying as it did 'entirely on horrors which happily...proved so outrageously horrible that they became laughable'.

Haviland evidently did his powerful best for his young friends and was commended at least for the 'energy' of his performance. 'If he was not convincing, and if many of the impartial listeners smiled the smile of derision and had to stretch their courtesy to keep themselves from roaring right out, the fault was certainly not with the actor. Mr Laurence Irving with awful solemnity and sententiousness represented Austin Ruthyn in the first act, was complimented with applause and then was seen no more.' Seymour Hicks was credited more as actor than as author with a clever character study. The Vanbrugh girls were praised for their charm and artistry but Florence Cowell earned equivocal mention for playing her 'repulsive part...with quite terrible earnestness'. The authors were warned that though, at the end of the piece, they 'were cordially cheered, they would be wise if they regard the cheering in the light of encouragement to further efforts than as a token of approval of their latest work'.[1]

---

[1] Since this was written, two of my grandfather's letters have come to light that contrast his paternal and managerial attitudes. To Laurence, who had sent him the first act of *Uncle Silas*, he wrote:

LYCEUM THEATRE

My dear Laurence,

Bravo! Bravissimo! You have both got on splendidly—you young dramatic authors!

The dialogue is splendid and seems to be full of promise!

I am anxious to see the whole play. Damns have had their day and like Bob Acres you should introduce a little more genteel swearing—but that is a trifle.

It has been a great pleasure to me to read the act and tell young Hicks so with my kind remembrances.

The situation at the end is very good indeed.

Ever affectionately yours,
H. Irving

12 July 1892.

He gave a sterner answer to the audacious Seymour Hicks who, perhaps with Laurence's connivance, had asked him to finance the commercial production of the play:

LYCEUM THEATRE

Dear Mr Hicks,

You must pardon my not answering your letter before—but I have been so pressed with work that I have had to put everything else aside.

So Aunt Martha's legacy vanished in an afternoon. The legatee had no regrets—unless he had hoped his play might find a backer to give it a wider hearing. It had been money well spent even if the run for it had been, alas, too brief to work *Uncle Silas* out of his system. The performance had threaded together filaments that would be woven into the pattern of my uncle's life and, to some extent, of my own. The authors had enough good sense not to be misled by polite applause or to be discouraged by *The Era*'s salutary strictures.

Laurence was soon at work on two more plays; both were one-act pieces in a grim vein.

The first, *Godefroi and Yolande,* was inspired by R. L. Stevenson's recent defence of Father Damien and of his conduct of the leper settlement at Molokai. The plot was set against a medieval background. The first forbidding stage direction was 'Enter a chorus of lepers'.

Irving was on tour in the United States when he received a copy of the play from Laurence.

My dear Father,
I hear of your great doings in America. You will see by the play I am sending you that I have not been idle. I dare to think that if I could get an opportunity of playing the part of Godefroi I might do much good for myself. Will you put up the play at the Lyceum when you return to England? I want to see my play acted of course. I turn at once to you, my dear Father.

Your affectionate son,
L.

You have your triumphs to chronicle, I have none.

Irving probably read the play with distaste for its theme, and passed it on to Ellen Terry. She found the piece an inspiration, and felt that

---

I return 'Uncle Silas' which I have read with much interest.
Although the play was not I think well adapted—I mean it is not suitable for the stage—I think that you and Laurence have done your work very well indeed. I shall certainly look forward with pleasure to any other venture by the author of the...[indecipherable].
With all good wishes.

Sincerely yours,
H. Irving

13th October 1892.

by instinct the author had done everything right. She persuaded
Irving to take an option on it, and made him promise to put it on
for her when opportunity arose; the sincerity of her appeal could be
judged by her willingness to appear in the part of Yolande as a leper.
The play served the immediate purpose of awakening in her a curiosity
about Irving's strange son; henceforward she would be his champion,
and would rally to his support the stranger, George Bernard Shaw,
who would soon be sniping at the Lyceum from his critic's chair at the
Saturday Review.

Laurence's second play was a turgid slice of Russian life in the
Gorki manner with an uninviting title—*Time, Hunger and the Law*.

Meanwhile he had been gaining experience as an actor. When the
ailing Toole finally gave up his theatre and disbanded his company
in the spring of that year, Laurence was engaged to lead the touring
company of *A Bunch of Violets*, an adaptation by Sidney Grundy
of a play by Octave Feuillet which Tree had been playing with some
success at the Haymarket Theatre. His part, Sir Philip Marchant, was
based on the character of Jabez Balfour, a hypocritical swindler recently
convicted of extensive frauds. The tour opened at Worcester. His
performance was well received—admirable, wrote a critic, if occasionally marred by affectations, and excellent in scenes that called for
mental and nervous tension—'gifted with an ideal tragedian's face
and with a voice that in subdued passages bears a striking resemblance
to his father's'.

Before he left London a charity matinée had been arranged at the
Haymarket Theatre which included *Time, Hunger and the Law* in
the bill. The author played the lead and was supported by Harry,
Tom Heslewood and a more experienced young actor, Cyril Maude,
who at the time was rehearsing for *The Second Mrs Tanqueray* at
the St James's. Charles Wyndham was taking part in the programme.
No doubt he had heard of Laurence's presumption in *David Garrick*
and had witnessed Harry's failure with Hare. He watched the brothers'
performance with some curiosity. 'I dare say you're very clever young
men,' he told them afterwards, 'but you've got to learn your business
as your father and I did.'

Laurence was trying to do so. Harry was learning his business as
a lawyer. He had been called to the Bar, but was not yet convinced
that advocacy was his métier. At the suggestion of his Oxford friend,
Theo Mathew, he had gone on circuit as marshal to Theo's father,
Sir Charles, a judge after his own heart, terse in his judgments, voluble,

entertaining as a raconteur and, to Harry, agreeably radical. Over dinner they must have traced their common ancestry to an earlier Charles Mathew whose brother, Father Theobald, had stirred the consciences of inebriate Irishmen while John Cornelius O'Callaghan inflamed their republicanism. But for all this, and though the processes of the law fascinated him, Harry hesitated to commit himself. No doubt his immediate need to earn a living had something to do with it. He had by now developed tastes and cultivated friendships that would, unless he gave them up, prove costly in the lean years before the briefs came in. Would it not be folly to risk his long-term prospects at the law, for which he may have acquired an aptitude, when quick returns might be had from hereditary gifts that he believed to be unusual and marketable? Not long after he was called he had been his father's guest at the Arundel Club when Irving had reminded the company that his son, as a member of the Bar, had the right to pay his respects to his sovereign, but if he became an actor would cease to possess that right—an official ban that was the remnant of ancient prejudices. Perhaps as an actor he might be among the members of the profession to put an end to such ridiculous discriminations.

Fate, this time in the form of Joe Comyns Carr, again intervened. Carr, who was now in management at the Comedy Theatre, offered Harry the part of the dramatist in a play *Dick Sheridan*, that he was producing in February 1894. Though he was already working on a play about King Arthur that Irving had commissioned, it was unlikely that he consulted him before doing so. It would not be the only time that his well-intentioned intervention proved inimical to Irving's interests. For my grandfather still had reason to believe that one of his sons was resolved on a less hazardous profession than his own.

Harry, heedless of Wyndham's warning, succumbed to temptation. Once again his manner, that was totally out of key with the character he was portraying, and a lack of technical resource that might have disguised this, proved disastrous. Nor was he less of a fish out of water as a lover in *Frou-frou*, a piece of melodramatic *pâtisserie* with which Carr hoped to redeem earlier losses. In the face of failure Harry, unlike Laurence, was prone not to despair but to a stubborn determination to have his way. It seems that while the portals of the Bar were invitingly open to him, the stage door had been slammed in his face. Such a challenge had to be met.

It was in this mood that, when Carr's son Philip asked him down to Oxford to see his production of *Pygmalion and Galatea*, the idea of returning to the scenes of his illusory success as an actor seemed attractive. As he watched the play and tried to dismiss its nagging association with his own problems he may have been only dimly aware of the naïve charm of the pretty, rather plump, girl playing Galatea. Did his mind wander to the posters outside the theatre advertising next week's attraction—The Ben Greet Shakespeare and Old English Comedy Company? Did they remind him of Wyndham's advice, that he now knew to be sound, and suggest a way of following it immediately?

For whatever reason, things began to move quickly. Harry remembered how a kindly, rather fussy, actor had helped his mother when as children he and Laurence were being coached to act for a charity performance in Kensington. Ben Greet certainly remembered him, and his eye for a promising recruit had marked young Irving's successes at Oxford. Within a week or so Harry had enlisted as a member of Greet's company. Greet, unlike Benson, was wise enough to realise that such a mettlesome horse needed plenty of rein. It seemed to Harry a very short time before he was back in Oxford playing Beauclerc in *Diplomacy* and parts of equivalent weight in the rest of the repertoire. It was pleasant to hear the congratulations and criticisms of old friends like Hutton and Morris. And it looked as though his colleagues would be congenial; they seemed to be well-mannered and to welcome the authority which, in spite of his inexperience, he could bring to their performances.

A short break before rehearsals began for the summer season gave him time to tidy up his room in the Temple, and at Gilston Road to bid farewell to his bewildered mother. The company reassembled at the Metropole Theatre, Camberwell. The first rehearsals were of *The Winter's Tale*. As Leontes he was on the stage throughout the first act and the first scene of the second act. He was glad of a break to study his notes during the prison scene.

> As well as one so great and so forlorn
> May hold together...

Surely he had heard the voice of Emilia before. He looked up and saw that the lines were being spoken by a newcomer to the company. If he had been introduced to her he had not caught her name. But her pretty face was as vaguely familiar as her voice. Yes—of course —she was the Galatea of Phil Carr's production. He recognised her air of amused and innocent self-assurance—a kind of confident humility—certainly as little like a mummer in a touring company as he felt himself to be.

...Now you be blest for it.
I'll to the Queen: please you come something closer

Greet made her rehearse the awkward lines again, regrouping her and Paulina for their revelation of the royal obstetrics to the gaoler.

Harry closed his book and came forward to begin scene three. It was a pity, he thought, that the poet in such a long play had provided no scenes between Leontes and Emilia.

PART III

THE STAIRS TO MARRIAGE

'No sooner met, but they lookt; no sooner
lookt, but they loved; no sooner loved,
but they sighed; no sooner sighed, but
they asked one another the reason...
and in these degrees have they made a
pair of stairs to marriage.'

As You Like It

I

ON ANY SUNDAY in the summer of 1894 many special trains threaded their way over the complex railway system of Great Britain; their progress, routed, as it were, across the grain of the normal flow of traffic, was spasmodic as they halted politely to give way to other self-important trains intent upon their timetables. They were made up of a few passenger coaches and one or two 'flats' or elongated goods wagons. Each contained a small nomadic tribe, self-centred and self-sufficient, prone to internal discords but defiantly united in its posture to the world outside or to what it called its 'public'. Such were the theatrical touring companies that at the end of each week were shuttled to and fro between one provincial engagement and the next—moving like snails, trailing behind them their make-believe habitations of scenery. Often two such caravans would meet during a brief halt at some junction. Heads would pop out of windows as each assessed the quality of the other. The No. 1 Company of some current London success would eye with condescension the travel-worn retinue of some time-worn melodrama; melodrama, in turn, proud in its legitimacy, would scan disapprovingly a train bursting at the seams with its gay noisy cargo of an illegitimate musical. Shakespearean troupes quizzed all these with a kindly, if patronising detachment, like an Anglican mission falling in with a Non-conformist choir outing. Ordinary travellers waiting on country platforms would be thrilled or shocked when an antiquated loco-motive pulled in with its burden of carriages and passengers that had seen better days, catching a tantalising glimpse through windows opaque with internal fug of MISS CARLOTTA DAVENANT'S EAST LYNNE COMPANY or of some SPECIALLY SELECTED LONDON ARTISTES that on closer inspection resolved themselves into tousled females with a few dishevelled children yelling their tired heads off, while several dapper young men and dignified veterans with long hair and tinted noses set in pale parchment faces—long familiar as 'heavy tragedians' in the pages of *Punch*—swaggered up and down the platform. The presence or absence of children was an indication of a company's professional status, and many managers discouraged camp-followers that might lower the tone of their troupe.

These nomadic mummers were content to make their careers in the provinces. Most of them were too modest or lacked the self-confidence to compete for social or professional success in the capital. They ventured through the stage doors of London only for rehearsals before the touring season began. Their corporate life made them self-reliant and kind-hearted; they were highly skilled in the exacting work of the repertory player. They would not have claimed to be great artists, but they had no false modesty about their status as 'artistes'. If a newcomer showed pretensions to intellectuality, he or she would be suspect. 'Talent' was the thing; and if you had talent there was no need to be 'brainy'.

So the special trains with their cargoes of talent puffed their way through the long Sundays. Segregated in their carriages by sexes (no corridors admitted a modification of this convention), the players passed their time with games of nap or whist, singing well-remembered songs, springing practical jokes on each other and confiding to each other under oaths of secrecy the scandal and gossip that was the daily office in such enclosed orders. And many a theatrical romance began by a juvenile helping an ingénue with her luggage, and many theatrical lovers plighted their troth sitting on a dress basket at Crewe junction.

Two or three journeys of this kind had initiated Dolly Baird into the life of players on the road. For the most part she found it intensely amusing and exciting. Naturally gregarious and easy-going, she was soon on good terms with the rest of the company. The leading lady, Ada Ferrar, had served her apprenticeship with Benson and to the Bensonians would soon return. Dolly found her haughty and unpredictable, but a capable actress. At first they shared lodgings, but after a week or two they parted; perhaps Dolly's extrovert ebullience was not conducive to the study of five leading roles. The other ladies of the cast were, as Dolly reported to Emmie, '...an extraordinary mixture...Hermia played by a black-looking woman, bad form and very fast, paints awfully. A jolly little Puck. Of gutter origin I should say from her speech who is quite a match for Mr Greet. When she misses a cue she bounds on to the stage crying: "Hullo!" Jessie Ferrar, who makes a sweet Titania, and five lady supers most of them wives of the company. How can they all agree? It is interesting to look into the future.' On one point, however, all were in agreement, namely the captivating austerity of their *jeune premier*, H. B. Irving.

At first Dolly found him a bit stuck-up—not surprisingly when all the ladies of the cast (to say nothing of the charwomen at the theatres they visited) doted on him, vying with each other to arrange the folds of his costumes and the set of his wigs, so that by now he came to them like a child to his mother, holding out his arms to be powdered as he waited in the wings for his cue. All these attentions he accepted with a certain disdain, and his brusque manner, Dolly reluctantly admitted to herself, added to his distinction and even to his charm. The rest of the men were not particularly distinguished or attractive. Some of them were competent actors but few stayed long enough to become identified with the company.

Over this assortment of talents and temperaments Mr Ben Greet presided with stern benevolence. The son of a captain of a training ship, he had an instinct for command. Indeed, with his ruddy complexion and stocky build he would have been less remarkable on deck than on the boards. His homespun manner and gruff voice were not the attributes of an heroic or tragic actor, but he made the most of them in broad comedy. There was a weather-beaten look about him that suited his fancy for open-air performances. He was less of a scholar but more of a man of the theatre than Benson, to whom he conceded nothing as an ardent champion of Shakespeare. He expected his company to work as hard and as earnestly as he did himself. He knew that most of them were birds of passage learning their craft; in return for what he could teach them he insisted that their behaviour in and out of the theatre must be a credit to their profession. In his view the demands of his repertoire should engage all their mental and physical energies; he regarded the hours spent by Bensonians on playing-fields as good rehearsal time wasted. If the company made fun of him among themselves, they respected his authority. There was no denying his skill in stagecraft or his single-minded devotion to the theatre. These qualities and the first-rate training he offered endeared him to all but the dullest and most wilful young player. In his company the novitiates could count on learning the traditional technique at the hands of an experienced actor of the old school; whereas Bensonians had to fend for themselves, picking up what they could from older members of the company like George Weir, and watching the intuitive acting of their empirical leader. On the whole, while Greet's aims were more modest, he was more concerned than his fellow-missionary for the quality of his company's performances.

The rehearsals at Camberwell had been a bit awesome. Mr Greet
had sat in front of the unlit footlights, prompt-book in hand, illumined
by the light of a seven-branched candelabra that made the cavernous
auditorium behind him an infinity of darkness; beside him had stood
his secretary like an acolyte, repeating his instructions with a clerical
intonation that had given the rehearsal an air of religious observance
—as indeed Greet regarded it. But once on the road, rehearsals were
less formal, though far more strenuous and haphazard when only a
week and sometimes as little as a day was allowed to bring a new
piece into the repertoire. This in a short time included *The Winter's
Tale, The School for Scandal, A Midsummer Night's Dream, Masks
and Faces* and *Money*, in which Dolly was to play respectively Emilia,
Maria, Hippolyta, Kitty Clive and Smart. So what with eight performances a week and attention to Mr Greet's notes after each of them,
rehearsing all day and dress-making during any lull in acting or study,
it seemed to Dolly that she had barely settled in one theatrical lodging
before she was hunting for the next.

Finding good lodgings was the chief preoccupation of players on
the road. As the salaries of the junior members of Ben Greet's company
did not exceed 30*s* a week, not more than 15*s* could be spared for
board and lodging. Consequently the weekly search often ended in a
dreary room in a dingy house in a dingier street, that was let to 'professionals' all the year round. Some of these were depressingly dilapidated, with furniture shedding its stuffing, chimneys that smoked,
and landladies who consoled themselves for having to live in them
perpetually with palliative gin. There were of course exceptions—
well-kept rooms with kindly landladies proud of their reputation in
the 'profession', genuinely fond of their bizarre clientèle and happy
to provide late suppers and even tea in bed for late risers. Their
addresses were handed on like valuable legacies from player to player.
The evidences of their popularity were the signed photographs in
the parlour and the entries in the Visitors' Books that assured newcomers that THE MARGATE HIGH KICKER, THE THREE SLASHERS, or
THE ROWDY-DOWDY SWELLS had found the lodgings a Home from
Home, or that Mrs —'s grub was excellent. Dolly soon learned to
view the Home from Home with caution, for it often meant that the
landlady and her children (if she had any) would, on the slightest
excuse, settle down in the lodger's room for a good gossip. She also
found that most landladies had come down in the world, or had
been cheated of an inheritance, or in better days had driven in their

own carriage and pair. So the addresses of clean lodgings and considerate landladies were as important to strolling players as the whereabouts of safe anchorages in uncharted seas were to the early navigators.

Dolly spared her mother none of the harrowing circumstances of her new life:

Theatre Royal, Stockton-on-Tees

My dear Mother,

I have got the cheque cashed and am going to sew the money in my stays when I go to bed and will use it in driblets. My salary is one guinea a week and it has begun. Do you know Miss Newton had been 8 months in the company without one but then she has no agreement and I have in my box.

This is a horrid place, squalid and pokey. Everyone is on strike, theatre very grubby but nice dressing-rooms. I actually had a bath today, the second since I started, it was so nice—they generally give you a tumbler full of water in a pint basin and one cotton towel. But they made it up in fleas. I caught 6 this morning in my bed.

We are rehearsing the School for Scandal every day as it is produced next Wednesday. I have been busy today doing my other Maria hat, it is very large, grey velvet with a white ostrich feather, and looks very pretty.

This is relaxing after Scarborough so I am taking Steel Pills which I got for 1s for 144, wasn't it cheap? I don't get a bit sleepy now staying up till 12 every night and am quite ready to get up at 7.45 when we have our tea.

Everyone has bad colds. Irving's is dreadful.

Love to Mary and Daisy
Your loving
Dorothea Baird.

The following week she wrote from Blackpool:

Prince of Wales Theatre,

6 p.m. Sunday.

We have just arrived after rather a long journey from 7.15 this morning up at 5.30. There is a bath here and it's clean. The last place was filthy and we were eaten up with fleas.

I have got my Maria frock nearly finished, it's rather pretty. I think you would like it. I did not make it myself but got a little

*dressmaker at Stockton. It is blue-grey cashmere or delaine flowered
in darker and ligther grey, white lace underskirt and drapery lined
with white fichu and sleeve cuffs dark grey velvet hat and white
feather. It cost (making hat etc. everything) £1 7s 6d so I don't
think it was very much.*

*Mr Hearn has gone back to Oxford today, we are all sorry as he
was jolly and acted awfully well. We have got a new man in his
place called Mr Nutter; he is tall and thin, quite the reverse of
Mr Hearn.*

*I don't think we have secured the best theatre here. It's such a pity
as the dresses are beautiful. Miss Ferrar has got a new one for
'School' in white satin and silver.*

*Now I want a commission done if you can, on receipt of this.
Will you send me a 23" Duchess of Fife stays from Elliston.*[1]

My grandmother was hardly to blame for being slower than her
slim peremptory daughter to understand the nuances of theatrical
costume:

Dearest Mother,

*Awfully sorry I could not acknowledge the peaches etc. before
but I have been so busy—not a minute to spare. The peaches were
very good but why did you send black stays? They were so heavy
and I always wear white, black would show through all my dresses.
However I sent them back to Ellistons to change for white...School
for Scandal came off last night. My dresses looked so nice. Tell
Daisy Irving was splendid as Charles Surface and our Joseph was
I am sure better than Bourchier.*

At Southport Dolly became the focus of Greet's growing vexation
with the ladies of his troupe; this came to a head when she and Ada
Ferrar, over the matter of a sewing bee, showed signs of insubordina-
tion. A night or two later, when they were playing *Masks and Faces,*
Dolly finished early; not feeling very well she accepted Mr Nutter's
offer to see her home. She was nearly dressed when she heard a knock
on her dressing-room door. 'Is that you, Mr Nutter?' she called.

In reply came the angry rumble of Mr Greet's quarter-deck voice.
He rebuked her rather incoherently for a mistake she had made in the
first act; when she protested that in fact the mistake was Irving's,

[1] Drapers in Oxford.

Florence Irving.

arry and Laurence Irving, *circa* 1878.

Harry and Laurence Irving at Marlborough, *circa* 1885.

he went off grumbling down the passage. The following day a letter was delivered to Dolly at her lodgings.

Dear Miss Baird,

I must really ask you not to encourage in any way what might end in being 'attentions' from a gentleman of the company. I see certain signs of it already and I must now beg of you to put a decided stop to it. It has happened four or five times before in this company always commencing in the same way and allowed to continue. Flowers, walks, seeing home at night, presents and then inattention to business and inconveniencing and bothering everyone in the company.

I simply won't have it and am determined to take decisive measures directly I see it appearing again. Your remark to me last night in your dressing-room was quite enough for me to go on. Whether I'm mistaken or not I at any rate give the warning.

If people choose to be interfered with 'off the stage', as far as it suits their own ends, I don't care twopence. I don't intend to allow the horrible experiences of four or five other ladies of the Company to be repeated so please have regard to what I say. You are a strong-minded young woman and you must quietly and inoffensively put a stop to it, however mild it may be or you will be very sorry for it afterwards. If I am wrong in my suspicions I only say once more, that this note can serve once more as a warning. I am quite prepared to take all the responsibility.

> *Yours truly,*
> *Ben Greet.*
> *Nov. 13th.*

Flabbergasted but relishing the intrusion of a little genuine drama into their world of feigned affections, Dolly confided in Emmy.

> *Opera House, Southport*
> *Nov. 14th*

I am writing to you a very exciting letter and enclosing a copy of another but don't show it to Mother as she would not understand it probably…How dare he write like that. Nobody has ever given me flowers or presents and I told him so, and I gave it him well in a letter which I left on his dressing-table. I knew I might get my dismissal for it, but apparently I'm too useful for that and besides I'm cheap, for he came to me during School for Scandal last night and began rather rudely, but I cowed him and at last he made out

G

that he was only doing it for my own good as the young man was constantly falling in love...

Mr Nutter is interesting in his conversation and does not flirt, and as you know I don't and if you ask Miss Ferrar or anybody they would tell you the same thing. As far as I can gather he was only in love once and the lady behaved very badly. She accepted many presents from him and was engaged to the stage manager all the time and he said he would blow out his brains. But really I only talk to him about books etc., and most ordinary conversation and nobody else goes walks and it's dull and bad for me to stop in the house all day. However I dare say it will pass off like his (Greet's) swearing at Miss Ferrar.

After this week I am living by myself because Miss Ferrar wants to work up her part. I shall find it so lonely especially at Edinburgh and Glasgow...I don't like the idea of being quite alone in a big city like that. I have had very good notices for Kitty Clive and Maria this week, so that ought to cheer me up.

With best love to you and Teddie (don't show him the letter if you think he'll be angry about it). I've squared Greet all right on my own account.

> *Ever your loving,*
> *D.B.*

The account, however, was not finally closed, before Maria, distracted by Benjamins Backbite and Greet, flummoxed Joseph Surface by declaring:

Oh he [Sir Benjamin] *has* done *nothing; but 'tis for what he has said; his conversation is a perpetual libel on all his...*

and then she dried up—a lapse which left her 'shivering with fright all the evening after'.

The Cooks were amused and reassured by Dolly's spirited assertion of outraged innocence. Greet, having indulged his *amour propre*, noted that Miss Baird now had a brace of escorts. As she told her mother, 'Mr Nutter has to see me home as I won't go by myself at 12 at night—the way is dark and ghostly. However now Mr Topham has arrived and three are better than two in some ways.'

Greet was astute in his concern for the good name of the company. There was a new audience to be exploited in the respectable middle classes if their belief that players were rogues and vagabonds could be overcome. Social acceptability could, therefore, be a commercial asset. Dolly, had she realised this, would have been less puzzled when she read 'such a funny notice in the Ipswich paper'.

Mr Greet's Company ought to be very popular here. Miss Dorothea Baird, a lady in the Company, is a friend of the vicar of Holy Trinity and Mr Greet has some friends in the Barracks.

Harry, no doubt, had been vastly entertained by Miss Baird's defiance and Greet's discomfiture, and by her fall under duress from her accustomed word-perfect grace. Shortly after this he enlisted her as a willing accomplice in a plan to relieve the tedium of the long empty Sunday evenings.

Irving and I [Dolly reported to Emmie] *have established a Dramatic Court of Justice which meets on Sundays, it's very exciting and I think beneficial, everyone belongs.*

He is a splendid judge and we get up cases and try them. Irving simply revels in it and buys reams of blue paper, red tape, and quill pens. We did four cases last Sunday and it lasted from 7–12 with intervals for refreshments.

I can hardly believe that we have only one month more, time seems to have flown with such rapidity.

The tour ended at Glasgow in the middle of December. Greet, reconciled to his *enfant terrible*, had offered Dolly an engagement for next year's season. Ada Ferrar was returning to the manlier world of the Bensonians. A popular actress, Beatrice Lamb, was to take her place, to be starred with Harry Irving. Dolly accepted on condition that she could join Philip Carr and her Oxford friends for a performance of *Pygmalion and Galatea* in Cheltenham just before Christmas.

Carr arranged for rehearsals in London. Dolly stayed at Tavistock Square, where she was plied with questions by Emmy, who, now a journalist in her own right, planned an article on the 'profession' that she could scan through her sister's keen observance. Yet, for all this, and the fun of *Pygmalion* reunions and of getting up her old part, Dolly found herself missing the strenuous and intensely intimate life of the Old English Comedy Company. Sunday came round and seemed tame without travel and mock trials. She had promised Daisy a photograph of Irving. Surely there could be no harm in asking him to sign it—after all, it was not for herself—and in writing to him to convey a little of her nostalgia?

When she returned from Cheltenham, a letter was waiting for her at Tavistock Square:

> *10, Gilston Road,*
> *The Boltons,*
> *South Kensington, S.W.1.*
>
> *Dear Miss Baird,*
>   *Will you tell your sister that I sign the photograph with the greatest possible pleasure and am honoured to do so.*
>   *I am sorry you are having a 'horrid' time. But in this deplorable climate little more can be expected by thinking people. Therefore as belonging to that class you must be content!*
>   *With all good wishes,*
>   *Very sincerely yours,*
>   *H. B. Irving.*

Somehow this made her very content and anyway they would all be meeting again at Camberwell early in the New Year.

II

IN 1879 CHARLES EDWARD FLOWER, the Warwickshire brewer, had built a theatre in Stratford-upon-Avon as a practical and long overdue memorial to its native dramatist. Initially 'the profession' responded feebly to Flower's generous enthusiasm; for the first few years Shakespeare's birthday was celebrated with unworthy performances by such touring companies as could be diverted to the Birthplace from their well-worn provincial trails. Six years later Flower, with some courage, after seeing the Bensonians in a ludicrously ramshackle production of *Macbeth* in Leamington Spa, invited them to do the birthday honours. This had long been Benson's ambition, and with gusto he inducted himself as the high priest of the temple of bardolatry; he remained the incumbent for forty-six years, and officiated for the last time as Shylock at the opening of the new theatre in 1932. But in 1895 the governors, favouring a change, invited Ben Greet to bring his Shakespearean and Old English Comedy players for the Festival. So when the members of the company assembled at the Metropole Theatre, Camberwell, for rehearsals they found their leader heavy with the gravity of his commission.

They were promising material for such an occasion—certainly a stronger team than he had had last year. Beatrice Lamb had taken the place of Ada Ferrar as leading lady. She came with a London success to her credit having starred in *Niobe All Smiles,* a farce that had run for months at the old Strand Theatre. Only last autumn she had appeared in *The Derby Winner* at Drury Lane, wearing a black dress covered with sequins that had shown off her superb figure to perfection. She would make a robust Rosalind and a statuesque Hermione. Dolly took to her at once, for she was a keen cyclist, and also looked forward to exercising her singing voice to the accompaniment of Dolly's guitar. Louie Freear, the irrepressible Puck, was still with them. A newcomer, Winifred Fraser, did not yet know she had helped to make theatrical history by being in the original cast of *Arms And The Man* at the Avenue Theatre—Shaw's first play to have a popular hearing. As for the men, Harry Irving would be sharing the leads with Frank Rodney, a young actor who throughout his all too brief career would, on the stage, vest his naturally modest bearing and commonplace appearance with a rare nobility, and match it with a voice that became a Bensonian legend. William Farren was on his way to creating Sir Patrick Cullen in *The Doctor's Dilemma*; Dawson Milward, a Colonel's son, would find a theatrical niche for himself as the reticent English gentleman—strong and as silent as dramatists could afford to let him be. And later they were joined by a pale, earnest youth of seventeen engaged for supernumerary odd jobs and understudying, Granville Barker.

So it was with a sense of high purpose, and conscious of their ability to fulfil it, that Greet and his players began their circuitous advance on Stratford-upon-Avon, working themselves up with endless rehearsals to a festival repertory that would include *The Winter's Tale*, *As You Like It*, *Much Ado About Nothing*, *Masks and Faces*, and *She Stoops to Conquer*. Harry, now gaining confidence in work he found as congenial as the company, was therefore the more distressed as news reached him of the misfortunes that were besetting Laurence as a result of his impetuous folly.

Towards the end of the tour of *A Bunch of Violets* Laurence began to chafe with restless frustration; his bounding self-confidence had battened on a modest success that, indeed, he had every reason to be proud of. A letter to his mother, shortly after she had seen the play in the provinces, revealed his perilous optimism:

> *...So glad to know that you drew such favourable comparisons between us and the Haymakers.*[1] *With no slight pride I read your judgment out to some of the company who flatter themselves as being keen and critical.*
>
> *Now as ever, in the hour of undertakings, I turn to you. List! List!*
>
> *I want to become my own manager with an honest competent adviser. There is no doubt that Y –* [his present manager] *is making a nice profit out of me...and does not want to pay me according to my drawing power. In myself and in the name I possess I am a valuable property. Why should I not exploit myself?*
>
> *And this is the result of my observations and conversations. £500 is the sum required to start a company to ensure one against all*

[1] The original cast at the Haymarket Theatre.

*eventualities, that is to say £200 preliminary expenses before one
puts one's foot in a train—the remaining £300 in reserve. I have
thoroughly thrashed out the matter. Our expenses on tour would
average £60 a week, inclusive fares, printing and everything. The
takings would average £200 of which we could take 60%...I have
thought of asking the Ancient (H.I.) to lend me £400 and find one
hundred myself. If he refuses unpleasantly no harm done. I should,
of course, refund him the money. All say now that I ought to be
playing long parts.*

When Laurence told Harry of his calculations and plans he had a letter
back in which Harry wrote '...I have written to the Chancellor of the
Exchequer for £500 to start a company with'. Laurence, assuming
that by the 'Chancellor of the Exchequer' Harry meant their father,
was dismayed, believing that his brother, Jacob-like, had forestalled
him. Harry, of course, had not taken his brother seriously. When
Laurence realised that his alarming remark was 'mere hilarity', he made
an urgent appeal to his father.

Though my grandfather may have been impressed by Laurence's
grasp of theatrical business, it is hard to believe that, when he agreed to
help him, he had been warned of the artistic blunder that his son was
about to commit. For Laurence, with his father's backing, flushed with
the flattery of friends and still in thrall to an earlier prepossession, had
decided to stake his debut as an actor-manager on another production
of *Uncle Silas*, with himself in the title-role. Collecting together a
company as inexperienced as himself, in March he raised his standard
at Folkestone and committed himself to an extensive tour. Folkestone
was kindly and uncritical; the small audiences were attributed to the
size of the town and the season. Thereafter he reeled from one provincial
theatre to another, taking harsh criticism on the chin and rarely more
than £15 for each performance at the box office. Ever buoyant, his
failure in 'No. 2' towns only fed the hopes he centred on the larger
cities that lay ahead—'...where I am known and my previous efforts
appreciated'. Undaunted, he felt he must finish the tour at all costs.
'It would never do to surrender it to the tongues of calumniators,'
—though these were less of a threat than the foreseeable exhaustion of
his resources. A desperate appeal to his mother to suggest where a
further £150 could be found drew a blank. The Antique, aware that
his son was suffering as he had done at the hands of critics, sent him
kindly messages of encouragement. Some of the cast abandoned the

sinking ship; the indomitable captain signed on replacements and doggedly drilled them into shape. But his hopes of Manchester proved illusory; Birmingham and a Bank Holiday failed to recoup his losses:

> *In the depths! de profundis!* [he wrote in despair to his mother].
> *Business has steadily declined. They will not have Silas at any price.*
> *I have written to the Ancient asking his advice. If he proffers no*
> *pecuniary assistance, the notice goes up on Saturday night and*
> *Mr Laurence Irving's tour concluded...Tout est perdu sauf*
> *l'honneur. I have been lately so schooled to disappointment that I hope*
> *for very little. If I can get over this rack and shoal of time I still*
> *believe everything may be retrieved.*

Mercifully nobody subscribed to his further discomfiture. To add to his depression news reached him at Manchester of the conviction and imprisonment of Oscar Wilde.

> *Yes* [he wrote to his mother], *Wilde is in the dust. Retribution has*
> *certainly overtaken him. I wonder how Mrs Palmer feels. What*
> *puzzles me is his ever having faced the thing out. I think old Queens-*
> *bury's a brick.'*

Laurence's uncharacteristic opinion of the Marquis indicated the bitterness of another disillusion. Harry did not share it, but was as shocked as his brother. Neither had an inkling of the ugly toils into which their kindly and flamboyant friend had fallen. They were more affected by Wilde's dishonour than by the honour that the Queen, on the day of his conviction, had bestowed upon their father. The knighthood that Irving's fellow-players and his public welcomed as a tribute to his profession left his sons unmoved—they had lived with the idea too long, and its realisation reminded them of their bitter reactions at Marlborough when it had first been mooted. My grandmother tacitly accepted her entry into Debrett. The days had passed when she could derive much pleasure from deriding her husband's achievement, or from persuading herself that his distinction was undeserved.

Harry, as he neared Stratford, received from Laurence a postscript on his disastrous venture. The old nicknames were outworn. Somehow since his 'accident' Laurence had grown out of his altogether; to him Harry was now 'Lemagne', their father the 'Antique'; their mother was no longer the 'Malcho' of their earlier mock endearment:

...Oh, but Lemagne, Lemagne! Could you but know the cares that
brood on the once open and joyous brow. I am more certain than ever
I was that our true policy is combination. Therein I believe lies our
strength. The subscribed capital is fast vanishing leaving perhaps a
chequered light of glory behind it. One hopes so. I do not think the
money has been spent in vain. No phantasy to relieve the gathering
gloom. Goodbye, dear Lemagne ... Oh the comfort of the engagement
permanent, a good salary and no cares!
                          Thine ever,
                          Young Laurence.

Harry would have welcomed the idea of their playing together but, in
the light of this fiasco, not under their own management. Perhaps this
setback might leave Laurence in a mood to accept even an impermanent
engagement with Greet—that is, if Greet would offer him one. Something must be done to prevent him brooding on his failure; there rose
unbidden the uneasy memory of his earlier despondency. But, for the
moment, Harry's immediate concern was to do justice to Leontes,
Jaques and Don Pedro in their creator's birthplace.

The festivities at the Memorial Theatre began on Monday, April 22nd.
The bills stated simply that the 'dramatic performances' would be under
the direction of Mr Ben Greet; the Bard needed no bush in his home
town. The company played itself in on the eve of the Birthday with
She Stoops to Conquer and a new one-act piece, *Judith Shakespeare,* that
was based on an apocryphal incident in the life of the poet's daughter;
and in it a handsome well-built young actor, Bertram Wallis, played the
first leading part of a career that would make him the undisputed *beau
idéal* of musical comedy for twenty-five years. The birthday functions
wound up with a performance of *The Winter's Tale.* It was the first
time the play had been seen at Stratford, and in presenting it Greet had
stolen a march on the Bensonians. The play was well received. Dolly
enjoyed her brief appearance as Emilia. After the usual notes the
players dispersed to their lodgings. There would be a run through of
the next play, *As You Like It,* in the morning.

Early the next day the news spread that Beatrice Lamb had been
taken ill—so ill that certainly she would be unable to play that night.
Greet was frantic. At first it looked as though the performance would
have to be cancelled. Here was an hazard he had not taken into account.
In the pressure of rehearsals he had given little thought so early in the

tour to understudies; it had not occurred to him that so apparently robust an actress could fall by the way. His temper was not improved when during the morning his youngest and least experienced actress, Miss Baird, volunteered to play Rosalind. He rebuked her for her presumption. But on second thoughts he reflected that when she claimed to know the lines she was probably speaking the truth—moreover as Phebe she must have gained a fairly clear idea of the rehearsed action. And he was reminded that once, when Miss Ferrar was unwell and her understudy did not know her words, Miss Baird had played Helena at an hour's notice without rehearsal. He knew, too, that this strong-minded young woman would not, if she could help it, let him down. Very well then, let her do her best as Rosalind. Indeed there was no alternative but shameful closure.

Dolly, as she tried on Beatrice Lamb's wardrobe, was a bit dazed by her sudden promotion but less apprehensive than Greet and the rest of the company. She had felt a momentary chill of irrevocable commitment when she saw the blue leaflet announcing the change of cast:

ROSALIND   MISS DOROTHEA BAIRD
PHEBE   MISS EVELYN NEILLDA
OWING TO INDISPOSITION MISS LAMB IS UNABLE
TO APPEAR TONIGHT

but this was dispelled by a glow of justifiable confidence. She had providentially studied the part with Rosina Filippi. She wished that Mrs Dowson and the Christmas Dramatic Wanderers could be there to share the fearful joys of her unexpected opportunity and to see her leading a professional company in Shakespeare's town. The few remaining hours before the curtain would rise were spent rehearsing the moves; there was little time for more. As she made herself up her bright eyes did not leave their reflection in the mirror as she nodded thanks to each of the company when they looked in to wish her luck.

'I pray thee, Rosalind, sweet my coz, be merry.'

At the beginning of her first scene with Celia she was in her heart as merry as could be, though she was conscious that her voice and gestures were constricted by nervous tension. But this soon wore off as she began to feel the warm sympathy of the audience, sensible of her ordeal. Of the two, Celia had less cause to be merry, for Winifred Fraser, an experienced actress, who would play Beatrice in *Much Ado* the following night, should have stepped into Beatrice Lamb's thigh boots had she been ready to do so. Soon Dolly was taking the part in her stride. Now and again a glimpse of Irving watching her from the wings, wrapt 'in a most humorous sadness', that he had no need to affect as Jaques, was strangely heartening. In their first scenes together there was a note of daring mockery in her challenge—'They say you are a melancholy fellow'; and of gay assurance as she retorted 'I had rather have a fool to make me merry than experience to make me sad; and to travel for it too!' At that moment she would not have bartered for a princess's ransom the endless rehearsals, the heat of limelights, the clammy chill of dressing-rooms, the tedious travelling, the slatternly landladies, Mr Greet's fussiness and the fleas that were the ingredients of her present intoxicating happiness.

As she came forward to speak the epilogue she could feel surging towards her across the footlights the delight of any English crowd that loves to see an outsider romp home to a win. She would gladly have kissed as many as had beards that pleased her and complexions that liked her; and the applause that greeted her final curtsy left her in no doubt that all those good faces that were now pink blobs seen mistily through her brimming lids did indeed bid her fare well.

The few critics present wrote in kindly praise of her; the sense of emergency and the breathless waiting for lapses that never came precluded judgment. A year later, when she had played the part many times, she ran the gauntlet of Shaw's amused scrutiny. His verdict was clairvoyant in its attribution of present weaknesses to past influences. As Ann Baynton, her nurse, had remarked of earlier teasings, what he wrote may have been rude but it was probably neither more nor less than the truth:

Rosalind is to the actress what Hamlet is to the actor—a part in which, reasonable presentability being granted, failure is hardly possible...Miss Baird plays it intelligently and nicely; and this, to such a very pretty Ganymede, is enough to secure success...All that can be said at present is that Miss Baird's Rosalind is bright and pleasant, with sufficient natural charm to secure indulgence for all its shortcomings. Of these the most serious is Miss Baird's delivery of the lines. Everybody by this time knows how a modern high-school-mistress talks—how she repudiates the precision, the stateliness, the awe-inspiring oracularity of the old-fashioned schoolmistress who knew nothing, and cloaks her mathematics with a pretty little voice, a pretty little manner, and all sorts of selfconscious câlineries and unassumingnesses. 'Poor little me! what do I know about conic sections?' is the effect she aims at. Miss Baird's Rosalind has clearly been to the high-school and modelled herself upon her pet mistress, if not actually taught there herself. But that dainty, pleading, narrow-lipped little torrent of gabble will not do for Shakespeare. It is so unintelligible across the footlights that even I who knows As You Like It almost as well as I know Beethoven's Pastoral Symphony, could not always catch what she was saying. This being so, it may safely be said that Camberwell did not catch more than a very small conic section of it. For even an expert cannot make sense of Elizabethan blank verse...when it is delivered at the rate of 200 words a minute and upwards. Besides, its lyrical flow, if such a tiny ladylike patter can be credited with so broad a quality, is not that of Shakespeare's verse. The effect is like a canary trying to sing Handel.

Happily on that first night there was a young man in the audience at the Memorial Theatre less impervious to charm than the disenchanted critic of the Saturday Review. Nigel Playfair had played with Dolly in the O.U.D.S. production of *The Tempest* and later in *Pygmalion and Galatea*. Even then her appearance and her voice had together given him a theatrical thrill he would remember all his life. To him her Rosalind seemed to fulfil her promise as a professional. This impression lingered with him long enough for him to be instrumental in keeping her star in an ascendancy as unpredictable as its lightning course had been during that week in Stratford. Meanwhile she had little time to worry her pretty head about criticisms good or bad. It was now known that Miss Lamb could not continue the tour. After the Saturday matinée Harry Irving was sent to London to find another leading lady. Oddly enough, he returned empty-handed and appeared to favour the suggestion that her place should be taken, for the time being at any rate, by Miss Baird. Greet may have demurred, on the reasonable grounds that Miss Baird's name would mean nothing on the bills; on the other hand there was no doubt about her ability and charm, and economically the idea had much to recommend it.

A week later Dolly wrote to her mother:

I have just got your letter and can answer it before I go to rehearse Hermione this morning. You can't think how glad I am I have got it, but I hope you will see it yourself in June at Oxford. You will if I am a success in it but don't spread this about as it's not officially announced. I simply love the part, and Irving says it's not so difficult as Rosalind but I believe it's harder for me, as it's an older part. The statue scene is I think the most trying as the standing is for much longer than Galatea.

You must buy this week's Stage, there is a splendid notice for Rosalind in it, the best one I've had. I enclose a cutting from the Sunday Chron: the most widely distributed paper in England. The interview is rather bosh I think.

I am to see Latham on Wednesday but I shall not sign an engagement. I'd much rather stay with Greet for the autumn. I know it would be a good company, as he's going to star Harry Irving but he will tell me this week. It's a blessed arrangement that I play both Hermione and Rosalind as they are different as the poles and he cannot say I am a one part person—that is if I do H. satisfactorily.

It was as flattering to receive an offer from another manager as it was pleasurable to refuse it. For as yet she could hardly believe her good fortune. Less than a year ago she was a nervous novitiate; now, if not much less nervous, she was leading a company, in fact if not officially, with the estimable Irving, who seemed as concerned for her success as his reticence would allow him to convey. To wish for more would be to tempt providence. But had she known it, providence was already contriving further temptations for her that she would find irresistible.

III

URING THE PREVIOUS YEAR a story had been serialised in *Harper's Magazine* that had delighted its American readers and had attracted 100,000 new ones. The tale was called *Trilby*. It was the second novel written by the Anglo-French artist, George du Maurier, who for thirty years had been gently satirising Victorian modes and manners in his drawings for *Punch*. The plot, set in the *quartier latin* of Paris, was original, and the characters in every sense unconventional. The heroine, Trilby O'Ferrall, a Franco-Irish artist's model, falls into the hands of an unscrupulous German musician with hypnotic powers. Under his influence, though she is tone deaf, she is able to use her physically perfect vocal organs to such effect that she soon wins fame as an exponent of *bel canto*. Her evil genius succumbs to a heart attack. No longer able to sing, and stranded in a world far removed from the humble origin, she languishes and dies. Her Bohemian friends, an Englishman, a Welshman and a Scotsman who share a studio in the Place St Anatole des Arts, provide the comedy and pathos of a romantic novel that was perfectly attuned to the prevailing taste. She sits to them as a model, but never in the 'altogether' (as they coyly spoke of the nude), as she did for the French sculptor next door, to the embarrassment of the Englishman, Little Billee, who had fallen in love with her.

In due course *Trilby* was published in England and America as a book; its sales were phenomenal. du Maurier's illustrations added very much to its popularity, and soon Trilby hats, Trilby dresses and Trilby hair-styles were the vogue. Even as far away as Arcachon, Toulouse Lautrec named his little yacht after her. And, as Trilby smoked cigarettes, thousands of women who in deference to convention had denied themselves that pleasure now fashionably followed her example.

It was not long before the book was adapted for the stage by an American dramatist, Paul Potter. The play was an immediate success, and after a short run in New York toured the large American cities.

It was being played in Philadelphia when the English actor, Herbert Beerbohm Tree, arrived in town with his company, and at another theatre gave proof of his astonishing versatility in a repertoire that ranged from Falstaff and Hamlet to Sir Philip Marchant in *A Bunch of Violets*.

Unable to go himself, he sent his half-brother, Max Beerbohm, to see *Trilby* and to report on its possibilities. Max, when he left Oxford, had a vague intention of reading for the Bar; after, though not necessarily as a result of, meeting Harry Irving in George Bancroft's rooms, he had decided that he was not 'for the Forum'. Consequently he had been at liberty to accompany Herbert to America as his private secretary. It was a mutually agreeable arrangement. Herbert was much too entertained by his brother's whimsical conversation to allow him to waste his time on secretarial duties that Max found tedious and unsuited to his literary style. This visit to *Trilby* was his first and last mission of the kind. Over supper he declared that the play was great nonsense, and with variations on this theme convinced Herbert that it was not for him. Tree thought no more about it until he returned to New York, where he found that *Trilby* was being played at the Garden Theatre. On the eve of his embarkation for England he went almost as a duty to see it. At the end of the second act he bought the English rights.

The contradictory reactions of these two otherwise wholly sympathetic brothers was a perfect example of the theatrical paradox that mummers and men of letters had never resolved. Max, the fastidious literary artist, found the banal situations, and creaking stage contrivances of *Trilby* ridiculous—as they were. Tree recognised Svengali as a bizarre character that might have been written for him and fitted his eccentric genius like a glove—as it did. He, like Irving, was not at all concerned for the literary merit of any play that would give him plenty of scope as an actor. Indeed, after *Trilby* had won Tree a fortune and he was beginning to tire of its success, he spoke of it affectionately as 'hogwash'. He had placated Shaw by playing Ibsen. His honour, as an exponent of the new drama, was satisfied—but not his appetite as an actor. He could make a meal of Svengali, and with any luck would redeem the losses of his American tour. For all his deceptive nonchalance, Tree had the stubborn courage of his theatrical convictions. He was returning to England more or less empty-handed, with plans already in train for building his own theatre on a site opposite his leasehold, the Haymarket. His conception of it was grandiose. Success was imperative and *Trilby* was instinct with it.

As soon as he got home he discussed the play with du Maurier, who agreed to those alterations and additions that a dramatist would be wise to accept from an experienced actor with a well-developed audience-consciousness. Tree undertook to produce *Trilby* at the Haymarket Theatre after Sardou's *Fedora*, to which he was already committed. There was only one contingency. Everything depended on the proper casting of the part of Trilby, and as the weeks went by the difficulty of this became more and more apparent.

Towards the end of June the fashionable physician, Dr William Playfair, and his wife gave a dinner party; their son, Nigel, happened to be home at the time. Among the guests were Mr and Mrs George du Maurier. Naturally the conversation turned to the success of his new novel and so to Tree's hopes of producing the play if, as was beginning to seem doubtful, a girl could be found to play Trilby. Nigel pricked up his ears. With some daring, for his status as a theatrical was still amateur, he told du Maurier that he had seen a young actress playing Rosalind at Stratford who had all the qualities the part called for and one that few ingénues of experience retained—a sort of innocent candour that shone through her limitations as an actress. Her name was Dorothea Baird. Later, du Maurier, seeing from a photograph that she closely resembled his ideal, reported the conversation to Tree who, having located the Ben Greet company in a seaside town, set off to see *As You Like It*. He returned convinced that but for her evident inexperience their search was at an end. He and du Maurier agreed that together they should seek an interview with Miss Baird and if, in the course of it, du Maurier still felt that in appearance and personality she matched his heroine, he was to signal his approval by pulling at the lapels of his coat.

Dolly was at Tavistock Square recovering from a chill. When they broke in upon her they found her, as they recalled, 'lying all her lovely length upon a sofa surrounded by books' and engaged in studying the part of Desdemona. As she rose to greet them Tree's earlier impression was confirmed—'...form and features alike suggested the ministering angel of *les trois angliches* at the Place St Anatole des Arts. The singularly level brows were not thick and dark, but finely pencilled as if drawn with a camel-hair brush in a tone that exactly matched her beautiful golden brown hair, which hung down below her waist and clung in delicious little curls round her broad low brow'. As his brother Max wrote later, it had seemed an impossible task to find an actress 'who should embody literally from head to foot *la grande Trilby*. Great height, a perfect head, a perfect foot, joyous youth and health, brown

hair, blue eyes, the figure of a Venus de Milo and at last and above
everything else an actress. How could such a combination ever exist,
much less be ready to hand? Yet it was found and exact in every detail
in Dorothea Baird who would seem to have fallen from heaven in
answer to the prayers of author and manager.'

During those moments of appraisal Dolly and du Maurier were too
preoccupied to remember that they had met before when this 'roarin'
gal', as he came to call her, was the eight-year-old daughter of his
friendly neighbour in Hampstead, John Baird. For the novelist was
already tugging vigorously at the lapels of his coat. Tree discussed the
possibility of her playing Trilby in rather vague terms. After they left,
Dolly, though her head was spinning with the prospect they had
envisaged, was so conscious of Tree's misgivings about her as an
actress that she resumed her study of Desdemona.

Two days later Tree called again. The script of *Trilby* had arrived
from America. He asked her to come to the Haymarket Theatre after
the evening performance of *Fedora* to read the part to him. She seemed
scarcely to have begun the ordeal of construing the part unseen to an
audience of one from an empty and dimly lit stage when, interrupting
her, he asked her up to his office to sign a contract. She agreed, subject
to Mr Greet's approval. Tree's reservations were expressed in a clause
that her appearance in London must depend on her success in the
provinces.

Next day Daisy received a laconic telegram:

GREET RELEASES TRILBY TREE HAYMARKET

A day or two later du Maurier wrote to his friend Sir John Millais, on
whom he had modelled the character of Trilby's friend, the Laird:

> The Trilby and Little Billee are to be played by two beautiful but
> quite unknown little people whom I myself discovered. Tree took an
> immediate fancy to such a lovely Trilby. You would love her—5 ft.
> 9 ins.—and made like a slender Venus; the little Billee...sat for my
> illustrations of him in the book—the first portrait, that is, the front
> face. They neither of them have much experience of the stage, but Tree
> believes in them both, and he and I have been doing our little best to
> coach them.

Parting from Mr Greet and her companions of the last strenuous
months was a sorrow no less sweet for her friend Irving's undisguised

disapproval of her departure. It was, after all, a poor reward for his aiding and abetting her substitution for Beatrice Lamb. She was touched by his umbrage; as a propitiary offering she gave him a pocket edition of *Much Ado About Nothing,* inscribing it with a quotation from Browning—'The aim if reached or not makes great the life'. But her last thought was for a friend in the company, who, she feared, might lose her job in the re-shuffle she had provoked.

> *Of course,* [she told her mother] *M– isn't to take my place, but I sent a cheque to Greet and begged him to take her on for small and walking on parts for the tour and he complied.*
>
> *I have sold and lent my dresses to Miss Olive who is playing my parts. I like to feel anyway if I can't be acting there myself my clothes will be.*
>
> *Irving told me yesterday he couldn't bear the idea of my going away and he said he was afraid he'd been cross, but he was so upset. He's quite nice now and very glad of my chance.*

Harry was, in a measure, consoled for her absence by the arrival of Laurence, who had been engaged by Greet to play Iago to his brother's Othello. The new Desdemona would be Miss Lillah McCarthy, a girl with little more experience than her predecessor, though she, like Harry, had studied elocution with Herman Vezin.

After a brief holiday with Emmie at Southwold, Dolly returned to London in August to start rehearsing. From what she had heard and from the little she had seen of Tree she realised that though his company was going to be very different from the prim and penurious one she had left, it would never be dull. For Tree and his wife, as theatrical partners, lived on an emotional level that was charged with electricity generated by their opposing natures. Tree, for all his frailties, was sincere in his quest for the beautiful and good, pursuing happiness with the bumbling optimism of a retriever chasing a butterfly; his wife was as practical and hard-headed as he was visionary and unworldly—once he had protested that she did not understand the difference between happiness and pleasure. Both had a ready wit—his fanciful and kindly, hers brilliant and, when she wished to wound, incisive. By this time they were more or less necessary to each other, and so they remained, in spite of intermittent estrangements, until he, more or less by accident, left her a well-to-do widow.

Dolly soon discovered that she and Mrs Tree had reached the theatre by similar routes. Maud Holt came from a home that set great store by education, and in due course she took an honours degree in classics at Queen's College, London. She would have been among the first undergraduates at Girton College, Cambridge, had she not, like Dolly, been drawn into the vortex of amateur theatricals. When she met Tree she was bent on the stage, and their marriage gave her the key to the stage door. They had played together for ten years, but by now her limitations as an actress were becoming apparent to her husband, if not to herself. She did not and never would develop the style and personality of a leading lady. As time went on Tree's choice of a new one for successive productions was the signal for tears and recriminations and elaborate if unconvincing explanations. Happily Dolly's engagement was as welcome to Maud as to her husband, for the long search had eliminated all her professional rivals from the contest. Consequently the Trees as a family (including their ten-year-old daughter Viola) received the god-sent Trilby with open arms. And whatever gossip-born misgivings Teddie and Emmie may have had about Dolly's new employers were dissipated by a supper or two in the bright homely atmosphere of the Tree's house in Sloane Street.

Tree planned to start his autumn tour with a repertoire that included *Hamlet*. No actor, since the Lyceum production of 1878, had dared to challenge Irving's supremacy in the part. By playing it Tree declared his rivalry and betrayed his inadequacy as a usurper. He loved the part, which he interpreted in terms of his own abstracted idealism; but he lacked the physical temper that is necessary to Hamlet's consistency as a character. His failure in London must have been hard to bear, but he made a brave show of accepting the ridicule of his critics with amused resignation. He knew that provincial audiences welcomed *Hamlet* in any guise; by taking his production on tour he could recoup a measure of his losses and his self-esteem while rehearsing *Trilby* for its first performance in Manchester in September. Dolly began rehearsing the Player Queen. The holiday had done her good but anticipatory nervousness had taken its toll:

Emmie is going to take me to Mary's lady doctor [she told her mother] *to find out if I am quite sound before going on tour. I do want a tonic and hope the doctor will order one as I lived on Bengers four days last week; now I get indigestion if I eat meat, but I'd rather have that than feel hungry.*

We start on Saturday at 2.30. Little Billee is very beautiful and extremely pathetic dreading rehearsals. Annie Hughes is playing

Madame Vinard, the concierge, and Miss F. Ivor (the Rosalind of the All Ladies As You Like It show last year) is Mrs Bagot. The men are very superior, except H.B.I., to Greet's. The women are, with the exception of Annie Hughes and Mrs Tree, not so superior as far as bringing up goes. They are somewhat actressy.

The superior men included Lionel Brough, who would play the 'Laird' and make up to resemble the author's friend Millais, du Maurier's younger son, Gerald, who had all his father's gallic charm, and Raymond Roze, the musical director, who had been engaged primarily to accompany Svengali's mimed virtuosity as a pianist on another instrument behind the scenes.

Dolly's chief regret on leaving London was that she would miss seeing the two young Irvings in *Othello* at Folkestone, and, as it turned out, meeting their father for the first time.

Papa transpired last night [Harry wrote to his mother from Folkestone]. *He is stopping at the Pavilion and is amiably inclined, though with rehearsals I don't see much of him. He comes to Diplomacy tonight...He talks of coming to Masks on Sat; but whether he will or no I cannot say. He ought to have had enough of my acting by then eh?...*

My grandfather must have been impressed by the vigour of his sons' performances. During the week Iago dispatched Roderigo, played by Granville Barker, with such excessive zeal that he stabbed him effectively in the side. His victim did not 'bleed to death', but was out of the hard-pressed cast for a night or two. This onslaught may have inclined Barker in later life to more temperate perfomances of Shakespeare. Yet out of this bloody essay Laurence forged the most memorable Iago of his time. Perhaps the sight of the wounded, wan young Barker may have kindled in the breast of Lillah McCarthy an affection that led to the partnership Shaw, as an ambitious dramatist, would make his instrument.

A week or two later Laurence, having a night off, escorted his father to Richmond, where Harry was playing Claude Melnotte.

I accompanied the Antique to Richmond [he reported to his mother]. *We drove down together and he and I sat through the performance side by side. How charming! The Antique, as ever, rather sniffed at Harry's performance. I did not tell Lemagne for you know he is tender to criticism. We then all drove back to Grafton Street and*

supped together. The Antique then said—and afterwards performed
his say—he would give me £50. Hence the free and easy independence
of my correspondence. I am going to pay the bills myself each week
so as I may be no drain upon your already seriously taxed resources...
later I accompanied the Antique down to Southampton and received
great attention from him on the way. I thought Terry looked very ill—
worse than I had seen her for some time.

My grandfather left for the United States knowing that his sons were
at least solvent, however perplexed he may have been about their
prospects. To him the improvisations of Benson and Greet seemed like
elaborate charades, though he appreciated that they provided the only
training comparable to his own in the now defunct stock companies.
Harry and Laurence were going their own way, but whither he could
not tell. His road had been winding and rough, but those tough enough
to survive the journey found themselves in a commanding position;
now the road was a short cut, but at the end of it the field was crowded
with actors of ability competing for the prize of management. Nothing
he had seen led him to hope that when he returned their situation would
be much improved. Laurence, as he waved them goodbye, must have
wished Ellen Terry well. For she carried with her the script of *Godefroi*
and Yolande and the secret of her promise to him that she would
persuade his father to put it on before the end of the tour.

Tree, by the time his company reached Sheffield, was beginning to
regret his enthusiasm for du Maurier's 'beautiful discoveries'. Mr Evans
had, no doubt, been an admirable model for the artist's posthumous
tribute to his friend Frederick Walker, the illustrator whose work had
influenced his own style, and who had been, in part, the inspiration for
little Billee; but his quiescent rigidity, so accommodating in the studio,
became an unyielding woodenness on the stage that, with a nervousness
aggravated by a growing sense of his inadequacy, was driving Tree to
despair. Miss Baird, charming and willing as she was, had a primness
of speech that at first seemed to be incurable. After a week or two Tree,
during a long and frustrating rehearsal with her, was heard to groan:
'Give me actresses from the gutter!' Dolly, as she strove to acquire a
convincing vulgarity, reflected ruefully that Greet had worked as hard
and patiently to polish young actresses in his company who were
naturally deficient in ladylike refinement.

In fairness to her, the part of Trilby called for phonetic acrobatics that would have daunted an experienced character actress. The author's directions were clear. She spoke 'in English, with an accent half Scotch and certain French intonations and, in a voice so rich and deep and full as almost to suggest an incipient *tenore robusto*'. Now and again he had added a dash of cockney to her cosmopolitan vocabulary with such expressions as 'Maïe aïe!' And such was the popularity of his novel that the public would detect any deviation from their heroine's engaging traits.

The Scotch accent was soon abandoned in favour of an Irish one; English playgoers had not yet been conditioned to Scotticisms, whereas Irish brogue and blarney had long been popular in melodrama and farce. After all, Trilby's name was O'Ferrall. So without more ado Dolly was handed over to the Broughs to be coached in basic Irish. Svengali, his creator had written, 'before he could teach Trilby anything he had to unteach her all she knew; her breathing, the production of her voice, its emission—everything was wrong. She worked indefatigably to please him and soon succeeded in forgetting all the pretty sympathetic tricks of voice and phrasing Mother Nature had taught her.' Substituting for Mother Nature the South Hampstead High School, the passage presaged the self-identification of Tree and Dolly in the parts they were playing that became more marked as the weeks went by, and in the end paid off handsomely. So by day Dolly strove to coarsen her sixth-form fibre and by night relapsed into the genteel inflexions that traditionally were acceptable in the Player Queen.

For all this Dolly was enjoying herself immensely. 'I'm not one bit afraid of Mr Tree,' she told her mother 'and he is charming. Everyone is so charming to me. I can't imagine why.' She had, of course, become the company's mascot, a lucky charmer upon whom all their hopes were pinned. The strain of endless rehearsal was relieved by the Trees' lavish hospitality at their hotel. Life in lodgings and in the theatre was eased by her dresser, Annie, who was at once duenna and lady's maid, who coped with the weekly packing and unpacking. Even the search for lodgings had become a light-hearted affair in the company of Gerald Du Maurier and Raymond Roze. Dolly and Gerald would wait in halls reeking of boiled cabbage while Roze climbed after the landladies to inspect the upper rooms. Soon his mellifluous tenor voice would come ricocheting down the narrow stairs with a plaintive 'Fil-thy, fil-thy!' —a 'gone-away!' that sent them tally-hoing off on the scent of another mummer's home from home.

The company reached Manchester on September 1st; *Hamlet* would be played throughout the week until the Saturday night, when *Trilby* would have its first performance. Dolly found herself gaining confidence as the rehearsals became more intense. Tree, having given up hope of making anything of Little Billee, concentrated his attention during the few days left to him on perfecting his now malleable Trilby. 'Avoid being genteel!' he told Dolly again and again; as he said afterwards: 'I preached and preached till "genteel" must have stunk in her nostrils.' Yet at the dress rehearsal Dolly showed that she still had reserves of spirit and guile to counter any attempt to impose upon her inexperience or good nature.

The climax of her performance would be when Trilby, now La Svengali (whose voice, according to her creator, had enraptured Berlioz and Theophile Gautier and drawn vast audiences to the concert halls of Europe), appeared with her evil genius at Drury Lane—'in a classical dress of cloth of gold, embroidered with garnets and beetles' wings...a gold coronet of stars on her head'. Furthermore, the author's illustrations had led the public to expect such an effect. Dolly, therefore, was dismayed to find that the management, not usually inclined to thrift, had provided her for this scene with an unadorned dress that Maud Tree had lately worn in *Fedora*.

'I cried on Wednesday,' she reported to her mother 'because there was no gold on my dress, so Mrs Tree said: "Poor baby, we will send up to Nathan's for some nice gold embroidery and a gold crown", so you see I got my way. And now they are sending it back to have it made grander still.'

Understandably, the Trees may have hesitated to lay out much gold on an outsider who still had to prove herself a popular favourite. But on the Saturday night all their doubts were resolved by the triumphant outcome of Tree's patient direction and Dolly's tireless and patient acceptance of it. The public's great expectations were not disappointed. At her first entrance they recognised 'that ideal Trilby whom to look at was to love, who won every heart before her opening: "*Salut, mes enfants!*" '. On that night the cheers and applause of the Manchester audience were but the overture to the ovations that the cast would be given at many hundreds of performances to come. The critic of the *Manchester Guardian* struck the note to which his colleagues in the weeks to come would attune themselves:

Miss Baird looks the part to perfection...and by some happy gift of
nature or artistry or both she is able to play the part with the un-

*hackneyed freshness and candour which it before all requires. It was a
beautiful performance with rare poetical qualities and even the most
hardened old playgoers could not watch it without a thrill of
sympathy and pleasure.*

C. E. Montague, as yet one of the young reporters on the *Manchester
Guardian*, was as moved as any in that audience that called again and
again for Tree to lead to the footlights the unknown enchantress who
had so perfectly embodied the Trilby of its imagination. Years later he
would recall wistfully his innocent pleasure in that 'fresh warm bath of
delicate sadness', though maturity forced him to admit that there was
'something peculiarly fugitive about the triumph of these orgies of
uninspired melancholy about youth and youthful comradeship and the
pace at which these things consign to ashes'. But to Tree the ashes of
Trilby would be those from which would rise the phoenix of his
beautiful theatre in the Haymarket, lavishly appointed and un-
encumbered with debts. And for Dolly there was nothing fugitive
about her success, which at first she could scarcely comprehend.

> *I was not very nervous last night and am quite well* [she reassured her
> mother]. *I have got such a lot of telegrams and things, also there are
> two notices in the Manchester Sunday papers…Tree gave a supper
> party last night—Emmie and Teddie were there. Mr du Maurier
> sent me a telegram. Mr Potter was there also—he has been inter-
> viewed and says I am much better than the American Trilby. But
> Mr Tree will have all the limelight turned on him, which isn't fair,
> is it? But he's very nice, and he told Teddie after the performance
> last night that I was very good.*
>
> *Madame Vinard calls me 'Ma Belle', Mr Brough 'My lassie'
> Mr Roze, 'La Grande Trilby'—and it's one continual squeezing of
> hands.*
>
> *Please give my love to Daisy and say that H.B. sent me a
> telegram last night.*

Leeds confirmed Manchester's verdict. Dolly relaxed to the extent of
sending for her bicycle and leading other enthusiasts in the company
on sorties into the country, enduring politely Maud Tree's tendency
to hysterical imbalance. From Glasgow she confessed to Emmie:

> *I feel miserably incompetent to keep pace with the stream of letters
> I receive and now you say answer the telegrams. Do you know
> I have had 30 and at least 50 telegrams since I came here. What*

*am I to do? I wrote 12 this morning but it takes money and time to
any extent.*

*The play is going like fun and I am much vulgarer now. I'm not
nervous and I love the first act especially. There was £350 in the
house last night, wasn't it good? They simply yelled at Mr Tree
and me when he led me in front the 2nd time after the 3rd act, it was
so nice. At present I'm miserable about the 4th act. I can't do it right
and it seems to spoil the play.*

*I've been a long bicycle ride up to the golf links today. Mr Tree
says he's afraid I shall get too blooming and muscular for the death
scene…and he blues me all over my face with grease-paint before I
go on the stage.*

*I've got tired of saving for a bit so am having a launch at the sales
—there are some good ones going on here.*

She had, of course, sent news of her success to the Greet company,
and it was natural that she should communicate this through her
friend Irving. It was as natural that he should report his discharge of
this pleasant duty.

Dear Miss Baird,

*How sweet of you to send me a line and tell me of your fortunes.
They are most prosperous, are they not? I hear nothing but good
of 'Trilby'. I am sure all are heartily glad to read of your success,
and no one more so than your humble servant. Of course they are
kind to you in the company; they would be churls if they were not.*

*My draperies hang but loosely upon me now that your guiding hand
has been withdrawn. M— is earnest and very kind but her fingers
are not so deft as those of the late gentle lady…It will be very pleasant
to see you again at Liverpool. So ho! You bicycle! I read about your
bicycling in some newspaper. What Greet will say to so bold and
daring a proceeding I dare not think.*

*I still have my book of 'Much Ado' with the inspiring quotation on
the cover! 'The aim—' But no! More of this when we meet.*

Always, my dear Miss Baird,

Most sincerely yrs,
H. B. Irving.

Dolly may not have detected in this letter the writer's awareness
of the sudden change in his professional relationship to her. Only
a few weeks ago Harry as a leading juvenile wearing, whether he

liked it or not, the aura of his father's effulgence, had accepted the homage of Dolly and her fellow devotees almost as his due. The part he had played in substituting Miss Baird for Miss Lamb had been magnanimous, and as satisfying as the dispensation of benevolent patronage can be for the dispenser. Now overnight, the night of September 7th to be exact, their relative positions as players had been reversed. Dolly, he realised, was on her way to shine in the constellation of London stars, while he, having earlier failed to make much impression on the capital, was in the eyes of their theatrical world no more than the leading man in an earnest but rickety provincial touring company.

Dolly was, no doubt, too modest to appreciate at once the implications of her change of fortune. She had no false modesty about her work, nor did she disguise her extrovert delight in doing whatever she undertook as well as she could—and even bragging about it. But she was unconscious of the effects of her charm, and to turn it to account, except upon the stage, never entered her head. Consequently she was genuinely and humbly surprised when people were charming to her. Her unaffected innocence and ingenuous enthusiasm might have made her dangerously vulnerable in the highly emotional world of the theatre for which she was heading, had it not been shielded by the compensatory armour of downright astuteness and a lively sense of the ridiculous that kept her pretty head deceptively below the cloud level. Thus, though she did not disguise from herself (or from Daisy) her admiration for her moody Jaques, it is possible that, dazzled by the adulation that awaited her, his absence and her unawareness of the impression she had made upon him might have prevented or certainly delayed the ripening of their acquaintance.

But already their paths were charted by occult influences. A fortnight later the orbits of their respective companies intersected at Liverpool. Their conjunction gave mathematical proof of the relative magnitude of these theatrical bodies for, while *Trilby* drew £300 a night into the box office of the Theatre Royal, Liverpudlian playgoers had no more than £100 left over to spend on the zealous Greet's eight performances at the Shakespeare Theatre. This meant nothing to Harry and Dolly, nor did it deter him from taking the first chance he got of seeing for himself the marvel of her transformation. He was not disappointed, and his companion, Laurence, marked down Svengali as his quarry when the time came for Tree to cast his No. 1 touring company.

Grand Hotel, Liverpool,
Oct. 3rd.

Dear Miss Baird,

All the adjectives to describe your performance have been long since exhausted by bursting critics. I am only going to tell you that, knowing them as I do, I reciprocate all they have said. This is a rash pledge but no matter! Sincerely I was charmed and touched by 'Trilby'.

I told you I disliked ladies dying on the stage, but I think your last act the best of all. You have overcome my prejudice in this respect.

No more—save all felicitations! 'The aim if reached' will be!

Am I coming to you tomorrow? Then we will discuss these things further.

Always yrs,
H. B. Irving.

They met, though Dolly was not able to see her friend in *Othello*. The hours they spent together were all too brief before she sailed at the end of the week for Dublin. Harry was consoled by photographs of Trilby that would make the dreary days in future lodgings tolerable. Before he left Liverpool he made sure that Trilby O'Ferrall had a thought for him before she became the darlin' of her doting compatriots.

Grand Hotel, Liverpool.

My dear Miss Baird,

One line! If you are drowned (which heaven forfend!) this letter will be an asset. If not let it come as a congratulation on your safe arrival... You will be sorry to hear that you have quite spoilt me while you were in Liverpool, with the result that I am today peevish and captious. Laurence also cheers me and I look to the Clown to make this day pass. To Llandudno I look with horror!

Do not altogether forget me in the grim solitude of my hotel, and cheer me by occasional messages. Laurence is now about to take me out.

Ever yrs,
H. B. Irving.

As it turned out Llandudno was enlivened by the presence of George Grossmith and George Alexander. Though Harry and Laurence knew the old Savoyard as a friend of their father, they were delighted on their own account to meet again the author, with his brother Weedon, of *The Diary of a Nobody* that had been published earlier in the year. Both were early connoisseurs of that tender satire upon the middle class, and they were apt to judge new acquaintances by their reaction to the Pooters.

Dolly had a rough passage across the Irish Sea. Like most of the seasick company, she disembarked at Kingstown tired and careless of her appearance. 'Och, look at horr!' said an ungallant Irish bystander. 'I don't think much of horr!' She did not think much of herself until soon after reaching Dublin she dined with Tree, who prescribed a magnum of champagne for her and his dishevelled family.

> *I am glad you arrived whole and safe* [wrote Harry from Llandudno]. *The deplorable utterance of the onlooker is only another support to my theory that all artists, on landing from sea voyages, should either be closely veiled (if they are well enough to walk) or if not should be carried from the boat in closed litters à la Romaine...*
> *I passed a really delightful Sunday with G.G. He is a most kindly little man and an excellent companion, most indefatigable in amusing the young and old alike. Laurence and I lunched with him and another supped with him in the evening when Alexander appeared and we had a long discussion, the conclusion to which was that of all professions that of an actor-manager is the most ill-paid, precarious and unappreciated; and yet G.G. and Alexander are making fortunes! Such is life! I don't know why...This Llandudno is a strange place. Not too cheerful. The stage of the Hall is 4 ft by 2. We play Romeo and Much Ado thereon. That's the sort of thing to give you breadth of style.*
> *Greet and I dress in a passage about as broad as this sheet of paper. Naturally I cannot avoid the wall in this contracted space, and then the white or pink (I forget which) comes off on my clothes. I have to go on the stage to wash, and the greater part of my wardrobe is stored in an adjoining confectioners! All this is very romantic and is, I believe, called experience. So is penal servitude. However a most intelligent and enthusiastic audience at Two Roses last night did much to make us forget that they were sitting under our feet.*
> *By the way I have gone some distance towards solving a mystery connected with that elegant comedy of James Albery's. I will tell*

you. Whenever we have played it this tour someone has sent me a
flower which I have gratefully worn in the second act. I thought for a
long time that M— was the authoress of this attention, and gave it
to me to make up for the deprivation of the amiable Miss Ferrar's
accustomed gift. But last night I elicited from M— the fact that it
was somebody outside the company who sent it to me.

   Now who can that be? 'Can't guess—can you?' as Digby Grant
says. Whoever it may be—and I have my suspicions, I can only say
that I am sure I am quite unworthy to have been so sweetly remem-
bered.

When Tree returned to England he knew that two changes in the
cast would be necessary. Annie Hughes, though she was a competent actress and had come straight to him from the Lyceum, could
not, as Madame Vinard, convey the tough good nature and broad
humour that the character called for. To Dolly's joy, Tree appealed
to her friend Rosina Filippi to leave her brewer and her babies in
Oxford and to take up the part when the company reached Birmingham. As the concierge of the studio in the Place St Anatole des Arts
she gave the scene a bohemian authenticity it had lacked, with a
performance that would be remembered as long as the play itself.
He would have replaced the unhappy Evans, but H. V. Esmond,
the actor he had in mind for Little Billee, was not immediately available. Esmond, having made his name with Alexander as Cayley
Drummond in *The Second Mrs Tanqueray*, was about to play the
lead in London in his own play *Bogey*; though Tree wished him well,
he felt that the sooner *Bogey* evaporated the better, so that its author
could appear in his handsome flesh at the Haymarket.

   By now Dolly had a shrewd idea of the publicity and flummery
that were in store for her, and with it came the realisation that success
in these terms meant very little to her. The truth was she had not the
temperament and egocentricity that a star actress needs to create
around her a make-believe world of calculated self-importance. She
had a gift for friendship, but none for the affectation of friendship.
To be the focus of attention from fashionable folk, who moved from
one nine days' wonder like herself to the next, embarrassed and
alarmed her. She had, also, the psychic disability of intuitively sensing
the virtue or shortcoming of people she met, of seeing through the
masks and disguises that most men and women of fashion wear for
self-protection, so unconsciously antagonising those who saw in her

innocence a reproach to themselves. In time she would become reconciled to this social handicap that nothing but cultivated insincerity
could overcome. Now she had only a few days left to adjust herself
to the ordeal that lay ahead. She was no fool, and her natural modesty
did not prevent her coolly assessing her chances of success, and
concluding from the assurances of her fellow players and the applause
of her audiences that these were likely to be favourable.

She confided these misgivings to her friend Irving. Oddly enough
he and she had spontaneously discovered that neither had met anyone
before with whom it seemed so natural and easy to exchange confidences. So their letters crossed each other in the post with greater
frequency and were eagerly received from stage doorkeepers in their
distant theatres. Dolly found Harry's reassurances waiting for her in
Glasgow.

>...*I was glad to get your letter this morning. Do you know that your
letters are very welcome to me? So don't be sparing of them, and tell
me all about yourself and your doings...One has so few friends whom
one cares to know at all well! Their sincerity will hardly bear close
scrutiny as a rule.*
>
>*You are quite right about the lionizing. There is much humbug
about it, but still you must put up with a certain amount of it.
And, when people get to know you for yourself, you will no doubt make
some very good friends. And as you rate the whole thing at its proper
value and are neither vain nor silly, you can use it just for what it is
worth...Don't be depressed or feel inadequate! It is a good thing
not to have an* overweening *idea of one's own transcendent abilities;
but don't go too far the other way. You can't go back now. You've
got to do Trilby as well as you can in London, and I for one don't
think you need have any fear of the result. Of course you don't feel
yourself to be all you could wish. But what sane actor or actress ever
did? Haven't I been preaching? I apologise but it is Sunday and I
have only just left Wales!...I supped with the Greets one night. They
were pleased to be rather sly on certain subjects! Indeed Greet
surpassed himself and has become peculiarly mirthful of late...Miss
Greet did* not *send me the flowers. I will say no more until I personally
acknowledge the kind thought of the sender.*

If the donor of Digby Grant's buttonhole had to be divined, a letter
from Dolly had warned him that an Irish blackthorn walking-stick
would be waiting for him at Southport; on the strength of this, a little

box to hold Trilby's tobacco, for the cigarettes she now rolled as to the manner born, was soon on its way to her in Glasgow.

> *The stick is delightful! How sweet of you to think of me and send me such a pleasant companion! At any rate I shall never be alone now when I go out with my Irish friend...I am half Irish, you know, on my mother's side, and her patriotic spirit would be greatly rejoiced if she saw me leaning on Irish support. So that altogether your thought was most appropriate, and if anything can bring me luck I am sure that will.*

The tour of *Trilby* ended in Birmingham barely a week before its opening at the Haymarket Theatre. Harry was playing in Nottingham. It must have occurred to both of them that this consistuted a crisis in their acquaintance. It would be a long time before they would be in striking distance of each other again. Greet's caravan was heading north; if Tree's hopes were fulfilled, *Trilby* would not be leaving London for a long time. Harry knew that the success he hoped sincerely Dolly would enjoy might easily envelop her and make her forgetful of earlier and absent friends; instinctively he felt that if they could meet once more before this separation their friendship would be immune to these dangers.

His reception at the Theatre Royal Manchester had made him bold —'a crammed house and very attentive'. He had good notices. Only the *Guardian* ignored his Leontes and strained his loyalty by declaring Greet's Autolycus as the most interesting performance. 'Of all the big towns where my father's name is so beloved and venerated (!) Manchester is the only one which has made any show of transferring those feelings to his son.'

As soon as he reached Nottingham he made up his mind to see Dolly before they went their separate ways. He wrote to her, with a casualness that cannot have deceived her, suggesting a rendezvous, and marked the urgency of his proposal by dropping for the first time the formality of addressing her as Miss Baird.

Albert Hotel,
Nottingham.

My dear Friend,
...I meditate coming to see you at Birmingham because it seems to me that we are to be parted for an insufferably long time; but it is difficult. It takes 2½ hours to get to you and the same to get back.

Well that doesn't leave much time, and then with Romeo and Leontes at night it's not quite fair to tire oneself on the railway!

I suppose you go to town Sunday or I might have come over then and gone to Stafford from Birmingham on Monday which is an easy journey. Anyhow I suppose you are with the Mundays, so I shouldn't see much of you; and I'm not coming to Birmingham to see anybody else. So there! You see my pathetic situation...I must study Hamlet! I hope you observe how disordered it is making my brain.

Dolly was only too glad to fall in with his suggestion. It could be easily arranged if she stayed behind in Birmingham on Sunday morning, and followed the company to London in the evening. That the plan induced a feeling of pleasurable guilt impelled her to write to Emmie telling her what she proposed to do. She knew that Teddie was a stickler about overstepping conventional conduct and, after all the kindness and patience he had shown her during these last tumultuous months, she had no wish to distress him, remembering how, after a heavy week's work, he had so often planned treats for her and Emmie on Saturday evening, crowning their dinner with a pint of champagne before taking them to the dress circle to see the latest play. Time was short, but she would like to have his blessing on her escapade if she could.

Emmie answered by return:

6 Tavistock Square, W.C.
Friday afternoon.

My dearest Dolly,

I've just got your letter and I don't know what to say. Don't think me a meddling thing—but doesn't it look just a little odd yr staying behind the company just to see H.B.? They'll surely think something's up and it wd be much better not to let them think anything. Of course I know there's nothing incorrect in it—but it seems a pity to make oneself at all cheap...He will think much more of you if you don't—that's quite certain. And a theatrical company is, even more than anything else, a nest of gossip...Teddie feels this strongly (else I wd not have written for as I say I don't want to interfere) and you know he likes young Irving very much...He seems to be quite whiffy about it—I have been thinking all day whether I wd write and now he seems to think I ought.

I dare say you'll hate me for writing this advice and of course you are not in the least bound to take it—If you don't come 'till later we won't allude to it in any way but as you asked my advice I give it—

that's all…Your photographs line the shop windows and I feel it an
honour to have such a celebrated sister!

Yr very loving,
Emmie.

Emmie's reply was a bit of a facer; the more so because her protest
was so reasonable, though the prospect of Teddie's icy silence was
more chilling than of any 'allusions', however severe. But by the
same post came a letter from Harry. He could solve the logistic
problems of the rendezvous by leaving Nottingham after the performance on Saturday night by a milk train that would deliver him
in Birmingham in the early hours of the morning. Thus, after he'd
had a bit of a rest at the Midland Hotel, they could spend the day
together until she left for London in the evening. She knew now that
she was committed to this meeting, and was glad that Harry's persistence made it impossible for her to change her mind. Her acquiescence may have been a little too eager, but by now she knew him
well enough to dismiss the idea that he would think less of her for
snatching an opportunity to share with him the hopes and anxieties
of her success, for which he bore some responsibility. She would have
been ungrateful to refuse him—besides, now that Emmie's reaction made
their meeting seem more of an escapade, it would be enormous fun, and
Daisy (to say nothing of Annie) would be disappointed if she did.

Perhaps it was the emotional strain of coming to this decision that
brought on a heavy cold in her head—an inopportune affliction which
romantic novelists seldom allow their heroines to suffer. She may not
have felt or looked her best, and Harry may have been concerned for
her when he saw her off from the railway station into the bitterly
cold night. But by then they were content. For in those few hours
they had learned that they were indispensable to each other. Though
they had made no confession of this, both of them knew that the
weeks ahead would be endurable in the promise of that stolen Sunday
afternoon in Birmingham.

On the evening of October 27th the Haymarket was thronged with
carriages, broughams, hansoms and growlers discharging their elegant
cargoes at the portico of its elegant theatre. Beams of light from the
crowded foyer shone through the colonnades, illuminating here and
there the scaffolding of Tree's new building on the opposite side of
the road. The manager of the theatre, Mr Watson, hovered near the

entrance, glancing nervously now and again at his watch; he was
waiting for the liveried brougham to arrive from Marlborough House
and to conduct the Prince and Princess of Wales and the Duchess
of Fife to the Royal Box. He had never before received such distinguished company for a first night. Already the Lord Chief Justice,
Mr Asquith, Sir Charles Mathew, Canon Wilberforce and Mr
Labouchère were in their seats. He had seen Sir Edward Clarke and
Mr Charles Gill pass through the foyer and had wondered if they,
as the prosecuting and defending counsels in the recent trial of poor
Wilde, were thinking of that first night, only two years ago, at the
Haymarket of *A Woman of No Importance*, and of the gay, flamboyant
impudence that was soon to be crushed out of the prisoner in Reading
gaol. The Bancrofts, Pinero and George Grossmith were there to see
if *Trilby* would be for Tree, as it had been for du Maurier, the end of
financial anxiety.

Dolly sat before the mirror in her dressing-room nervously combing
the set of her fringe. Annie hovered behind her, now and again
patting and adjusting the thick folds of her mistress's hair that by
now she was skilled in rolling up and tucking into the collar of the
poilu's uniform to look, as it convincingly did, like a page-boy cut.
The edges of the mirror were foliaged with cards and telegrams. On
the table, among her powder and greasepaints, lay two letters. One
was a pencilled note from Teddie:

> *D.D. In case I don't see you this afternoon, good luck! I was
> delighted yesterday and thought you had strengthened your part
> immensely since Manchester. All the press people I talked to were
> enthusiastic—So don't be afraid of the critics. Don't overdo your
> make-up—yesterday eyebrows were too dark.*
>
> *E.T.C.*

Dolly put down her comb, moistened her finger and ran it along her
eyebrows; then, staring critically at her image in the glass, she dabbed
her cheeks lightly with a powder puff. The other letter caught her
eye and for a moment her expression relaxed into the ghost of a
smile—for beside it lay a cheque.

Haymarket Theatre.
Trilby night!

My dear Miss Baird,
    Your success tonight is assured with the altogether—I mean

everybody. I hope it will be an evening of happy memories in a happy future. For me your accession to our company has been productive only of pleasant things—and I feel very proud of my faith in you.

Believe me,

Yours sincerely,

Herbt. Beerbohm Tree.

P.S. I am sending you herewith a little cheque as 'conscience money' for your hard work in the provinces—and a few lilies for Trilby.

H.B.T.

Dear Mr Tree. It was really very sweet of him—especially as she had given him such a lot of worry and hard work. It wasn't perhaps entirely her fault that the last act wouldn't come right. He was still not satisfied with it—even after making a lot of upsetting alterations at yesterday's dress rehearsal. Perhaps it would never come right —but the public so far seemed to like it, for the applause at the end of it was always terrific.

In the distance she could hear the call-boy shouting: 'Overture and beginners, please!' She felt slightly sick as she heard him coming up the stairs and along the passage. He knocked sharply on her door and, with a note of friendly encouragement in his voice, called again, 'Overture and beginners, Miss Baird, please!' She stood up and looked herself up and down in the mirror. She arranged the stiff folds of her tunic and, putting her thumbs into her heavy leather belt, settled it firmly on her hips. Annie handed her the tobacco box and cigarette papers and, wishing her luck, opened the dressing-room door for her. As Dolly went down the stairs she remembered the last lines of another letter that was tucked away safely in her handbag.

Now mind, on pain of death, that you do well on Wednesday evening. I am sure you will. No one hopes for your success more sincerely— shall I say affectionately than

Yr ever devoted and very faithful

H.B.I.

And then, as she passed through the door to the stage, she became possessed by Trilby O'Ferrall and all fear left her.

IV

THOUGH TREE, as Dolly had remarked, had done all that his suborning of Potter, his flair for disguise, his relish of bizarre characterisation and the concentration of limelight on himself could do to make the evening his own, it turned out, of course, to be George du Maurier's triumph. The first-night audience had come to see justice done to a tale that had charmed them all, not least George Bernard Shaw, who declared that what 'Thackeray, with his enslaved mind and clumsy hand, tried to do in vain, is here brought happily off by the pleasantest of freethinkers and the most charming of artists'. It was as though this starched and jewelled epitome of a long-established social order, conscious that it would not long survive the ageing Queen whose name would be the attribute of its times and tastes, was eager to express its gratitude to an artist whose pen had assured it graphic immortality. A glance at the now elderly Prince in the Royal Box, and at the still handsome but evidently ailing author, inspired them to make the most of the occasion. After the second act they called again and again for du Maurier, until he acknowledged their applause with a short speech from the stage—a precedent that Tree cannot have welcomed.

The play itself promoted an atmosphere of carnival. When Holman Clarke, as the American manager Kaw, welcomed Trilby to the *Cirque des Bashibazoucks* with the lines—'You are doing well, Madame. You are booming. Royalty is present. Your stock is up!' there were shouts of delighted laughter as artful glances and applauding hands inclined towards the Royal party. After the third act Dolly was taken by Tree to be presented to the Prince of Wales; she found him, as Harry had predicted, 'very amiable'. At the end of the play the company had an ovation; as Svengali led Trilby to the footlights, with the air of a ringmaster justly proud of his performing seal, du Maurier leant over the rail of the orchestra pit and threw a bouquet at her feet. When at last Dolly was alone with Annie in her dressing-room, as she removed her make-up with cold cream, her mirror reflected a less tense and preoccupied countenance than the one that had stared back at her two hours ago. As she wiped away the last of the grease-paint she rediscovered her natural exhilarated self—ears burning from compliments, cheeks flushed with happiness and eyes alight with pride in her hard-won success. The drive home to Tavistock Square was blissfully quiet, and over supper Teddie's optimistic forecast of critical appreciation sent her to bed tired but utterly content.

Fear not and you cannot fail. Having played the piece so often before you will enjoy it. Why it's nothing to having to play a piece for the first time before that kind of audience. You should be quite at home...

Well—if not quite at home, she had been marvellously sustained by Harry's buoyant predictions, and now was happier above all the evening's felicities in her fulfilment of them.

Dolly's prompt confirmation of this, and Monday morning's papers, were Harry's reward for his exhortations. The critics were generally agreed that Tree had been lucky and wise in his choice of a Trilby, a part which, if it had been played stagily, would have been intolerable. Most of them were astonished that so young a player could act with such distinction and without exaggerated overtones; one or two of them warned the uncritical not to mistake for amateurism the sim-plicity of her performance, that owed as much to her talent as to her charm. Shaw, who had enjoyed the evening, with reservations as to Potter's accommodation of Tree at the expense of du Maurier, found 'Miss Baird's Trilby...a very pretty performance by a very pretty girl', but he was not prepared to hazard an estimate of her future as an actress; of all the cast Rosina Filippi alone moved him by 'a stroke of genuine art'. On the whole Dolly could not have wished for a better press, but she and Harry were as yet unaware that a time fuse was spluttering its way to a critical bombshell in the editorial offices at Peterborough Court.

Just got your letter [wrote Harry from Shrewsbury]. Well done indeed! All seems to have gone as well as possible and you have come out triumphantly. I am so glad! I don't believe anyone can feel happier and prouder than I do at your success! You know that don't you? Now you must enjoy yourself. You have every right to and being in town you can do what you like. You are sure to be made a great deal of and admirers will throng round you. And a very good thing too! Though they may be tiresome at times, they are useful and to be humoured.

I wish I could tell you how delighted I am. But you see I can't! But I know you will do me full justice in your thoughts in which, 'Outcast' as I am, I am bold enough to think I have some habitation. I am not altogether homeless.

Yes the feelings of a première are horrible aren't they? But on the whole, as events have turned out, you were wiser not to bolt into the street. H.R.H. is very kind isn't he? But one does feel an idiot. Why no notice in the D.T.? This is inexplicable I think. Something must have occurred! It is certainly strange...Most affectionate congratulations my dear 'Trilby' (though I expect you're getting rather sick of being called by that name) from

Yours ever and always,

H.B.I.

The reason for the absence of a notice in the *Daily Telegraph* was stranger than they could have imagined. Those among the first-night audience at the Haymarket who could survey the glittering patchwork of stallholders below them may have noticed that two seats remained empty throughout the performance—leaving a small bare patch, as though moths had eaten away the pile on a gaudy carpet. Only Mr Watson and his box-office manager, Mr Leverton, were aware of the identity of the absentees and of the implication of their absence. For a hurried check on the allocations confirmed their fears that the empty seats had been allotted to Mr Clement Scott, the dramatic critic of the *Daily Telegraph*.

Scott had at that time reached the zenith of his self-importance. The power, real or imagined, that he wielded through his columns in the *Daily Telegraph* and in other papers caused a profession vulnerable to criticism to flatter him into believing that he was a quite exceptional person who had claims to exceptional treatment. Consequently it had become a habit of managers to provide on first nights, for him alone among the critics, a box from which coign of vantage he could preside pontifically over the proceedings. That he had recently been the target of a hostile demonstration by playgoers in the pit and gallery did not at all disturb him—indeed the spice of martyrdom added to the relish of his self-importance.

Only a fortnight earlier he had given H. V. Esmond's play *Bogey* an avuncular wigging that had no doubt contributed to its failure and withdrawal after a few nights. The pit and gallery, who had enjoyed a naive variation on the theme of Jekyll and Hyde, resented Scott's rough handling of the young dramatist, and on succeeding first nights had greeted him as he entered his box with ribald cries of 'Bogey!' This had led to altercations in the press as to the fairness or otherwise of Scott's comments and the propriety or otherwise of the pittites' behaviour—attentions that the critic himself found easy to bear. It would be thought that Scott, in hastening Esmond on his way to take up the part of Little Billee, might have earned Tree's gratitude. But that sensitive actor had been too often riled by the critic's disparagements of his performances, and was now itching for revenge. So, when the first-night list was being arranged (admittedly under pressure of an unprecedented demand for seats), like a chess player removing his opponent's piece from the board he translated Scott from a box to the rough and tumble of the stalls.

When the tickets reached the *Daily Telegraph* Scott could scarcely believe that such an insult (for once authentically gratuitous) could be offered to a critic of his distinction and to the widely read newspaper he represented. In his egotistical folly he believed that by cutting the performance he would teach Tree a lesson. When his proprietor, Lawson, whose love of the theatre had made the *Daily Telegraph* pre-eminent in theatrical reporting, opened his paper to read of Trilby's success, he was as astonished as most of its readers to find no mention of that eagerly awaited production.

Scott was immediately called to account and, to his chagrin, was told to buy two seats for the next performance. By that time the only ones available were in the dress circle. Much as this graver deposition must have irked him, he would, had he been a wiser man, have recognised the danger of his position. The irrepressible critic of the *Saturday Review* had been barred from their theatres more than once by aggrieved actor-managers, but their pique had, if anything, inclined Shaw to more genial banter than usual in his subsequent notices of their plays. Not so the inclement Scott.

Mr George du Maurier [his belated notice ran], *sensitive as all artistic temperaments ought to be, must have wept tears of blood when he found the delicacy of his romance ruined to-night by dramatist and artist...We do not want merely a pretty girl for Trilby. We want Trilby, a rare bit of genuine nature...the very keystone of the romance. What do we really get? A very pretty bit of artifice and amateurish-*

ness. It is not the fault of Miss Dorothea Baird. She is a young girl, an inexperienced girl. She doubtless one day will be a clever actress, but she has no idea of what Trilby is or should be. What mistakes even actor-managers make sometimes! What fatal and egregious mistakes! It is assumed by them that any pretty girl with a neat figure and a good foot can play Trilby. Why, Trilby, as put on the stage by dramatists, would tax the strength of our most experienced actresses. She should be natural, not artificial. She should be an artist, not an amateur. She should fill the studio with her presence, be the life and soul and heart of the play. She should lead the attack; never lag behind. But how can all this be expected of a charming young lady who has never been taught to act, and is coolly announced as making her first appearance in a part of exceptional difficulty.

He then turned on Tree, accusing him of engaging so feeble a Trilby in order himself to score off weakness. He forecast correctly that his strictures would be thought 'unkind, ungracious and uncharitable', but he thought that his remarks were less cruel than any that might persuade Miss Dorothea Baird that she could play Trilby and 'by doing so help to ruin a doubtless excellent career'.

Many of his readers must have suspected that Scott was expressing the views of du Maurier, for, after his mild flirtation with my grandmother, he had married the artist's sister, Isabel, who had died a few years earlier. To disabuse the public of any such idea, du Maurier, in a letter to the *Daily Telegraph*, sprang to the defence of Tree and 'his two beautiful little people'.

Will you permit me in justice to Mr P. Potter who dramatised my story and to the Haymarket company generally to state that far from shedding 'tears of blood' on Wednesday night, I was much delighted both with the play and with the performance of it. In justice to Miss Dorothea Baird the critic might have been invited to correct his extraordinary misrepresentation contained in the following line 'is coolly announced as making her first appearance'. When was the 'cool announcement' made? It is a matter of common knowledge that Miss Baird has been on the stage a couple of years and has played an extensive range of parts with Mr Ben Greet.

Scott was not at all abashed by his brother-in-law's disavowal. He had two more shots in his locker; one he fired off anonymously in his column in the *Illustrated London News*; the other, over his signature, burst in the pages of the weekly journal *Today*. Both reiterated his earlier attacks. This brief skirmish in the now openly declared war between the actor-manager and critic did Tree little harm and delighted those who for long had chafed under Scott's presumption of infallibility. Teddie, no doubt, saw to it that Dolly had the measure of him. Perhaps Scott's behaviour was an early symptom of the pathological conceit that in a year or two would drive him to self-destruction as a critic.

But it was a near thing that du Maurier was able to reject Scott's condolences; for, in a few months, he lay dying at his house in Bayswater. He had lived to see his faith in his 'roarin' gal' justified; for the weight of his influence as Trilby's creator made him, above all others, responsible for Dolly's good fortune. She had measured up to his exacting standard, and nobody but Scott had disputed his judgment. During the last week of his life his son, Gerald, brought him news of *Trilby's* triumphant autumn tour, and made him laugh with tales of Tree's whimsical resourcefulness, such as the occasion when Svengali, rising from the piano that magically went on playing, confided to his delighted audience: 'See what Svengali can do!' du Maurier's last words echoed the pathos that had permeated his story-telling:

'Si c'est la mort, ce n'est pas drôle.'

The news of Dolly's success and of Scott's folly were pleasant diversions for Harry during his week at Shrewsbury, most of which was devoted to the study of *Hamlet*, that would be brought into the repertory within a month. His own curiosity and Hamlet's antic disposition led him to the County Lunatic Asylum, where he could observe the tragi-comedy of madness at first hand. There he saw the many and curious gradations between a maniac in a padded room who, the moment the door was opened, flew out upon murder bent and taxed the strength of three attendants to get him back again, and a nameless old gentleman who imagined himself Christ, singing to his visitor as he played upon a tea-table under the impression that it was an harmonium. One of the inmates, a mad doctor, gratified Harry by telling him that he laughed like the devil, and on the strength of this compliment asked for the loan of two shillings.

Yet on most of the strenuous days of study, rehearsal and performance Harry found time to keep open the lines of communication with Tavistock Square.

Raven Hotel,
Shrewsbury.
Nov. 1.

Scott's notice is monstrous and unjust. He has evidently kept his rod in pickle for twenty-four hours to some purpose. You have won the sympathy and approval of the public so can afford to give his remarks their true value. The wisdom of your selection for the part will be abundantly proved in the ensuing months and what you may have lacked in experience, you more than sufficiently make up in charm and feeling. The public want you and will not have anyone else now they have seen you…Of Scott the eternally infamous, I will not utter or write another word, lest I tempt you to over-rate his importance… He speaks well, I see, of dear Laurence in the new piece at the Strand; so he is not quite abandoned to villainy. But I'm afraid the play is no good.

Inevitably these two young players became targets of romantic conjecture in their separate theatrical hot-houses, where conditions were ideal for the cultivation of grape-vine gossip. Neither could have concealed from their companions that they were absent-hearted. The Greets had become increasingly facetious in their coy allusions to Harry's mysterious distraction; at least one of the actors at the Haymarket had been made sharply aware that Dolly's affections were not disengaged. Soon the columnists of Fleet Street, eager for paragraphs about Tree's leading lady, began to speculate on the possibility of a newsworthy betrothal between the current queen of London's hearts and a prince of the Lyceum blood. News to this effect reached Harry in York and it deepened his climatic depression. He was already hyper-sensitive to noises that intruded on his studies, so that relays of barrel organs in the street, ardent performances on the hotel piano, and a nearby instrumentalist practising a cornet, were making his nerves twang like an overstrung harp.

Clarence Hotel,
York.

…Come now I have no right to be depressed (but I write to you just as I feel and think) for according to some of my friends I ought to be the happiest man alive. In the last three days I have had three letters congratulating me on an approaching event which, if it were true, would, I frankly confess, be the happiest thing that could befall me or any man. How it has originated I cannot tell, but the fortunes

of public characters (!) are not their own. I dare say you have guessed what this rumoured event is; and I shouldn't tell you of it, but I know you too well to have any secrets from you, but this I will add that I am sure there are many far worthier of the great happiness, which my too eager friends are so delighted to award me, than one who will always be your very devoted and affectionate friend.

If you have ever thought of me in any other light, I am all the prouder and all the happier; but when you have and yet will have so many around you who can offer you greater happiness and fortune than I could ever hope to do, is it for me to ask you the question which others have already answered, as I could wish it to be answered?

If I am wrong or presumptuous in writing thus to you forgive me! I know you will! But I should not have wished any report of this kind to reach your ears without your knowing that they in no way originate with me and that I should give them no countenance 'till I had the right to do so...

My existence is not particularly exhilarating, rather different to yours isn't it? However I work on, and perhaps something will come of it some day.

and a day later:

Don't imagine for one moment that the cackle of the unemployed makes the least difference to me. As somewhat of a public character myself, and the son of a very public character, I have been accustomed to this sort of thing all my life, so accustomed that I have grown careless of it and I should be very angry if I thought you would let it affect you at all...As to reproaching yourself with our meetings that is absurd and not for one moment to be endured! If we are fond of one another why shouldn't we see as much of one another as we like? And in other matters we will take the liberty of choosing our own time and deciding our future for ourselves...

Indeed I should not have written on the subject at all but that I conceived it to be right that I should do so. I am only sorry that I allowed a depressed habit of mine to give you the idea that I was in any way worried by news which, though impertinent and untrue, was not the most terrible thing in the world that could befall me. Indeed it is seldom that the reports of these good people are so kindly and considerate!

Enough of this. It's an 'ill wind' etc. and these excellent folk may

*congratulate themselves on having enabled us to show to one another
how true and how strong is the bond that unites us...*

  *I forgot to tell you that both Laurence and I had been married
in newspapers before now. Poor Laurence went to concerts with an
amiable young lady of musical leanings; and you can imagine the
horror of that severe youth on reading of his approaching alliance
with his companion of the Albert Hall and other respectable musical
centres! So you see it is rather dangerous to speak to us in the
street!*

Harry's equivocal abnegation may have puzzled Dolly who, by now,
was do deeply in love with him that the denials she made to the
press made her feel a traitor to her true feelings. Yet she may very
well have been alive and sympathetic to Harry's dilemma. This
unwelcome publicity had caught him off balance when he knew that
he was not in a position to pledge himself to marry any woman, least
of all the one whose friendship he valued most and wished least to
hurt.

  For their relative situations, so swiftly reversed, made him deeply
conscious of his own precarious prospects. He had abandoned the
long-term chance of making a reputation and an assured income at
the Bar, and had chosen the insecure life of a player with its immediate
if modest rewards. So far he had had no regrets. He was learning
his craft in a practical if not very congenial school, convinced that
apprenticeship in the provinces was, in the long run, the quickest
road to London. But the year had seen little change in his professional
status. His earnings as Greet's leading man were barely sufficient to
keep him going and to give what help he could to his mother at
Gilston Road. Ruefully he realised how little he had to offer as a
husband. Had Dolly remained in the company, they might have
drifted into the kind of theatrical marriage that was the end of all too
many brave hopes and ambitions, committing its partners to a crip-
pling interdependence that left neither room for manoeuvre to the
advantage of their separate careers. Now, oddly enough, their separation and the frank communication it had inspired made them mutually
aware of shared values and principles that would have made such
tame surrender unthinkable.

  Though Harry was proud of Dolly's success, his own pride was
touched by the change in their fortunes, and it was pride that prompted
him to temporise rather than let wagging tongues drive him to a

premature proposal. The decision cannot have been easy. Her affection and concern for him had breached the curtain-wall of his introversion, and had released him from the prison of his emotional reserve. He had hoped that their present easy-going friendship would continue until he was in a position to ask her to be his wife—if, indeed, at this juncture and in the midst of his other preoccupations he had faced the consequences of their growing intimacy. If he had reflected on her reaction to the *démentis* to which they had subscribed, it may have revealed to him for the first time her self-effacing forbearance that later would be his enduring wonderment. Her level-headed response to public adulation had reassured him. He could not know that she valued her own success only in terms of her promotion in his esteem.

Having disposed of the rumour-mongers, Dolly wrote to him urging that he should not linger in the provinces after he had submitted himself to the ordeal by Hamlet and, as a companion volume to her earlier gift, sent him a copy of the play to be the tablet of his studies for an interpretation that, if it proved him, would be the order of his release.

Other repercussions of her success provided some comic relief to these perplexities. Now, for the first time, she experienced the unashamed cadging for seats that in those days every popular player had to endure. It had long been the practice of actor-managers to give seats, if they were available, to members of their profession—a courtesy particularly beneficial to young players learning their craft. But the surviving correspondence of leading actors and actresses shows that they were expected to provide free seats to a section of society that could best afford to buy them—notably the aristocracy. The box, not as easily sold to the public as stalls, was the usual response to such polite requisitions. The records of the Lyceum indicate that my grandfather was a willing dispenser of such tributes. Indeed, he may have been largely responsible for encouraging his patrician patrons to regard playgoing as a condescending benevolence like visiting the sick. Such bounty was not expected of the management of opera houses. At Covent Garden boxes were rented like annexes to town houses, and used by their tenants to provide their guests with entertainment that had been paid for. As most of the performers in opera were foreigners, there was not the same sense of privilege that, in addition to the free seat, the visit to the dressing-room of a popular star afforded those complimented playgoers. There is no doubt that this traffic played its part in the overdue elevation of the stage in the public esteem and in the social acceptability of the theatricals. For the players were becoming more and more socially conscious, and not a few actor-managers were glad to exchange a box for the pleasure of hobnobbing with the noblemen that occupied them. But the profession as a whole spoke uncompromisingly of those who expected to see them perform for nothing as 'deadheads'.

Dolly's first begging letters of this kind were in delightful contrast. The first was from the head of her mother's family, who had protested against her compromising its good name by going on the stage—Savile Crossley. The second was a kindly intercession on behalf of a most deserving deadhead who, as one of the 'sun-burnt sickle men' in the Draconian *Tempest*, could claim to be a fellow-player.

> School House,
> Bardwell Road,
> Oxford.
> 6.xl.95

Dear Miss Baird,

I must write to tell you how delighted and charmed I was with Trilby! And it seems so strange that two years ago Trilby was helping to teach little boys at Oxford—what a change! I hardly can wish you greater success—I can only say may it never grow less! Do you remember Eric? I have written to tell him all about it. He will envy me! You must send him a ticket for the Christmas holidays.

> *Yours very truly,*
> *C. C. Lynam.*

Seventy odd years later Eric[1] recalled his adulation of the under-matron who, as Trilby, had been so marvellously translated.

In the course of each theatrical century few actors attempt to play Hamlet, and of them only one or two bequeath intellectual conceptions or technical innovations that are reflected in the performances of their successors. The decision of an actor to submit himself to this test appears to be intuitive, and often is taken before his maturity as a player would seem to justify the experiment. In doing so he faces the

---

[1] Sir Eric Macfadyen, J.P. Member of the Federal Council, F.M.S., 1919–20. M.P. (L) for Devizes 1923–24.

moment of professional truth. For, though it has been said rather
foolishly that no actor can wholly fail in the part, partial failure will
preclude the pretender from any claim to sovereignty of the English
stage; success, in so far that it enhances the understanding of Hamlet
by contemporary playgoers, ensures him a niche in the ghostly
pantheon of our theatrical heroes.

The fourth theatrical century (which I reckon from 1860–1960)
saw the rise and now scarcely perceptible decline of Henry Irving.
His Hamlet had been judged to have exerted an enduring influence
on the actor's study and on the playgoer's conception of the play
until the present day. This does not detract from the excellence of the
most distinguished of later interpretations, but it means that historic-
ally they will be pendants to the one that created the climate for their
fruition. Forbes-Robertson, though younger than Irving, was of his
generation. His Hamlet, perhaps, excelled my grandfather's with a
perfection of elocution that made verse seem the natural expression
of his more profound intellectual reading. But the younger man
lacked the electrical discharge that shocks playgoers into creating
legendary actors in the image of their recollection.

Of the next generation of actors, turning away from a long tragic,
tradition and facing the economic disintegration of the system it had
imposed on the English stage, critics and commentators seem to have
conceded pre-eminence as Hamlet to Irving's son, Harry. It was not a
generation distinguished for Sheapearean production, and, as it reached
maturity, war and war-sick audiences cheated it of tragic fulfilment.
But it was a period of acute dramatic criticism that makes this concession a valid excuse for focusing on my father's Hamlet the magnifying
glass of filial pride.

There was a curious coincidence in the chronology of the Hamlet
urge in father and son. Both played it first at the age of twenty-five,
both waited eleven years before submitting their performance to London audiences, and both were forty-seven years old when they played
it for the last time. My grandfather, as a stock actor, had played with
most of the reputable Hamlets of his youth—Phelps, Barry Sullivan,
Fechter and Edwin Booth—the latter inspiring the princely melancholy
and quiet humour that marked his own interpretation. Harry, when he
began to study the part, had no such exemplars. It is doubtful if he saw
his father as Hamlet, for the only time he could have derived much
impression of it was during Irving's last brief revival in May 1885—but
by then the summer term at Marlborough had begun. Had he seen the

Hamlets of Tree and Wilson Barrett, he would have recognised their respective physical and cerebral deficiencies. All he knew of the Hamlet tradition he had to pick up at secondhand from his father's contemporaries.

An actor who strives to harmonise the infinite notation the part affords with the expression of his own temperamental idiosyncrasies will win a hearing; if he imposes a contrived impersonation on the text, audiences will not tolerate his affectation. Harry found nothing strange or paradoxical in the extremes of Hamlet's emotional behaviour, for in them he recognised his own inner conflicts—the craving for affection repressed by an almost savage aversion to sentimentality, an optimistic humanism bedevilled by cynicism nourished by the vicarious study of human weakness, and a violent though volatile temper that warned him to recoil from physical violence.

Harry would discern all these contradictions in Hamlet's disposition, and he would exploit them with a natural style that relied more upon self-identification than upon histrionics for its effect. My grandfather, when, as a young stock actor in Manchester, he played Hamlet for his benefit, had an untutored instinct for the part that he interpreted by harnessing his intuitive genius to a wagon-load of technical devices and traditional business; his son had a more scholarly grasp of the dramatist's intention, but lacked the technique and artistic self-discipline necessary to give the reading of the part controlled expression. The circumstances of their first essays were markedly different. The young stock actor played the part as he conceived it with the conventional support of a well trained company. Harry had to submit to the direction of a provincial actor-manager who, no doubt, felt it his duty to combat the enervating effects of 'braininess' on so young a 'talent'. Friction of this kind between director and actor often puts a nervous edge of the latter's performance. But Greet failed to determine the flashpoint of Harry's combustible temper.

Harry left his depression behind in York. He found Middlesbrough bracing, though, opening with *Much Ado*, he found 'Beatrice is very heavy. But we must trust to luck and an indulgent public.' He welcomed Dolly's news that she now had the support of a new and more experienced Little Billee.

> *Esmond is sure to be a comfort to you. He is a charming man and an artist. Poor little Evans! He has had hard measure dealt him, not from the press for they could not praise him, but from those who*

should have kept him out of the part when they had once removed him. Though, if once an incompetent person is allowed to play a part, it is difficult to get rid of him without much heart-burning and distress.

The Sunday evening mock trials were resumed. Harry would have missed his Portia more but for the arrival in court of a newcomer, Sidney Blow, whose singular personality and inoffensive familiarity with all the ladies made him, as defendant, 'good food for nonsense'. If the sharp east coast air put an edge on his enthusiasm for Hamlet, it also whetted his impatience with Greet's pedestrian direction.

The Grand Hotel, Middlesbrough.
I have been very anxious to write to you, but I thought I would wait till I got your letter.

Well, you will not be surprised perhaps to hear that Greet has been a little too much for me over Hamlet. Ever since we began the rehearsals, instead of leaving me any latitude in the matter of stage management, he has grumbled and argued against any suggestion I have made and if he has ever given way, has only done so in the most ungracious manner possible. Of course such conduct is intolerable and idiotic towards anyone who is entrusted with such a part as Hamlet, as you would see at once. No one, except a born fool, would study such a part without forming some very strong ideas of his own and a conception of his own; and, if any success is to be made in such a part, it must be by the force of a man's own conception of the character. This is the commonplace of acting.

Well after some time of this sort of thing I am happy to say that at rehearsals yesterday the storm broke and the rehearsal was dismissed in confusion. I knew an outbreak must come. Greet has worried me nearly to death ever since this play was rehearsed, and, with the anxiety and excitement of the part, I have been utterly depressed and irritable.

However we must play the piece; and of course I can never make any further suggestions. I shall play the part to the best of my ability, absolutely in the way Greet wishes. But my heart is gone out of the undertaking and it has ceased to be—what such a beautiful part should be—a labour of love.

Naturally I am very disgusted. I had hoped that after being with a man more than a year and having done work that has not been, I hope, without some merit, he would have had more confidence in me, or at least be more considerate and amiable. But I am afraid that poor

B.G. is doomed to finally sicken all who come in contact with him. At any rate I have done with him; and in so doing I am but following your advice...So you see I've been rather worried lately, for you can well understand how worrying that perpetual feeling that everything one suggests or wants will be made a theme for argument and ungraciousness must be after a time. And I have stood a good deal of it for some time. For you know that I'm not an unyielding and irreconcilable person. And I have considered Greet perhaps more than I ought.

Perhaps only my grandmother and Laurence were aware that Harry's anger, when aroused, was indeed a brief madness. Greet may have been the first of his colleagues to experience its instantaneous and terrifying intensity that paralysed those unlucky enough to be in the path of its whirlwind track. Suddenly a man of good humour and equable charm was transformed into an unreasoning basilisk. By the time any stout-hearted onlooker had made up his mind to face the withering fire of the dark eyes glittering in the pale tense mask, the frenzy was over, leaving the air a-quiver with its simmering turbulence. The demon had departed, leaving the man it had possessed humiliated and ashamed, as were those who witnessed this appalling transmogrification.

This latent demon would plague Harry all his life; for, in the nature of things, those whom he loved most were the most exposed to its trap-door visitations. His paroxysms of rage were not as a rule provoked by hardship or misfortune (these he bore with good-humoured resignation), but by such trivial aggravations that in retrospect were seen to be ridiculous. In after years we, who lived in apprehension of these volcanic eruptions, came to laugh about them—but at the time they were no laughing matter. They did most violence to the spirit they afflicted. No doubt this demon emerged from some dark celtic cavern, though there is no evidence to show whether it lurked in the blood of the Brodribbs or of the O'Callaghans.

In fairness to my father it should be remembered that the uninhibited expression of rage by men, particularly by gentlemen, was a characteristic of the Victorians. Choler was regarded as a manly humour, and the bursting of blood vessels as the supreme sacrifice to outraged propriety. Men in authority, such as schoolmasters and senior officers in the services, bellowed and blustered at their subordinates, creating legends of wrath that often enhanced their popularity. Colonels were 'peppery'; headmasters were reported to be in 'towering rages'; masters

of foxhounds were in graver danger from apoplexy than from breaking
their necks in the chase. If fortunes were no longer lost in the card-
rooms of clubs, tempers were; and the losers of them were cherished
as 'characters' that gave a club an enviably eccentric flavour. All this
I remember. At the time, though always fearful of my father's
paroxysms (as he himself called them), I came to regard them with a
certain pride—as superb manifestations of the unpredictable passions
to which my elders seemed so prone. As I grew older I realised that
this popular heat of temper had begun to cool, that some subtle change
had taken place in the chemistry of the British characteristic and social
ethos. The spleen was no longer worn upon the sleeve; biliousness
called for patent medicines rather than aggressive self-assertion.
Irascibility died of ridicule, drowned in the laughter of my generation
at Colonel Blimp and Donald Duck.

Harry's confession to Dolly of his rumpus with Greet was the
first hint she had of the sharp squalls that, in the years to come, they
would have to weather together intermittently in the prevailing
clemency of their dependence on one another.

V

HARRY MUST HAVE BEEN STRUCK by the coincidence of the peregrinations of the Greet company and the climax of its peripatetic rehearsals of *Hamlet* determining his first performance in the part at the Theatre Royal, Sunderland. For it was there (then the New Royal Lyceum), nearly forty years ago, that his father had made his first inauspicious appearance as an actor, and had been advised by a local critic to take the first steamer back to London—the critic hoping, perhaps, that this leisurely transport and the sea air would dispel the young man's artistic pretensions. When my grandfather heard in New York that Harry was to be tested in Sunderland, he must have chuckled, as he composed a benedictory cable, at the thought that the town was not infallible in its theatrical judgment. Neither Harry nor Dolly had any idea that their fathers had collaborated so long ago in filling the double bill of its then proprietor, Mr Davis.

The storm that had disrupted the rehearsals at Middlesbrough evidently cleared the air; Greet, with his usual common sense, bowed to it; he realised that however wild and wilful Harry's interpretation, it would not at least be dull. Harry was mollified by the arrival of Mrs Charles Sim, the gifted amateur who had played with him in *Strafford* and *King John* at Oxford and had been engaged by Greet to play Queen Gertrude. However tense the rehearsals and sharp his own anxieties, Harry found plenty of domestic comedy and gossip to report to Dolly—particularly of the protégée she had left behind to minister to his player comforts.

Mrs Sim comes on Monday. I shall be glad to see her. She is always bright and sanguine and has a good effect on B.G...M— is ill! She has been seedy for a few days and last night she had an approach to hysterics! I found her lying on the sofa after the play, shivering and sobbing, refusing to be moved and bursting into tears if anyone approached. However the sober Topham ultimately conveyed her home...where she now lies. I don't really think there is much the matter. She doesn't eat enough, only bread and butter and sweetmeats, so I have learnt; she's probably caught a chill and for a person living on a diet of that kind you can imagine how undesirable that could be...Poor M—! She really ought to eat a little meat...

I don't know what you've been doing to Laurence. But he writes to me so delightfully about his meetings with you on Sunday and Monday! And, as you probably know, he is not a youth who likes everybody he meets all in a minute and calls people 'charming' because it's a pretty or popular thing to do. But you and he would be sure to get on, because you are both so original and so unaffected by the society in which you live. Your accounts of the Savoy and other social functions are most entertaining to me! I wonder if the people who sit next you are at all conscious of how thoroughly you appraise their value.

The week at Sunderland opened with *The Winter's Tale; Hamlet* was billed for the Thursday night.

> *Queen's Hotel, Sunderland.*
> *Monday.*

Your letter is splendid! How good of you, rushed as you are, to write at such length...You have really much less time than I, for you know how much time one has on one's hands in these uneventful places...Fancy your reading Hamlet on Saturday! How happy I am to be so much in your thoughts. I feel that in the midst of all this curious and inconstant world there is one to whom I can look for consolation, by whom I can hope to be understood and who will forgive one's failings. Don't think this egotistical, but some of us need sympathy more than others and therefore we cannot help being very grateful when we find it. It may be a weakness but it is a very pleasant one when the sympathy comes from one we love.

That is very pretty business of Tree's with the flowers. But I put the flowers in on the speech 'I loved Ophelia; forty thousand brothers', picking up some flowers lying near the grave. I am rather averse to bringing Hamlet back at the end of the scene. It is not in Shakespeare and people are so fond in a part like Hamlet of filling it out with improvements on the bard, though I've no doubt it was very effective as Tree did it.

I wish you could be here, for you would know what I mean in the part and that is half the battle in Hamlet. Whether I shall be able to express it to an audience is another matter. B.G. thinks I'm going to make him very mad; but it can hardly be said that Hamlet was a very reasonable man, and as he was deliberately acting as a madman for the mystification of his uncle and his court, the part should bare some trace of eccentricity. A naturally excitable and unstable mind, simulating insanity, would, I should think, and was meant by Shakespeare to appear very mad to those about him. Nobody reading the play can doubt this.

Yes—my father was born here dramatically speaking. He made his first appearance on any stage at the old T.R. now burnt down, in a small part in Richelieu in, I think, 1857. The fortunes of the family may be said to have risen out of this rather maligned town. It is not so bad as people led me to think. My father does not like the thought of it, but I should think it's much improved since his time …The lowering of the south cone implied that the Greet depression had passed. It did not last long. I did not speak to him after his fatuous conduct at the rehearsal and maintained a dumb front to him the rest of the day. Then I wrote to you in the morning and when I went to rehearsal, found our friend quite amenable and accommodating. His amiability has continued undiminished since then. Indeed whenever he begins to get gloomy again I must get up another scene! They seem to do him a lot of good.

and later:

> *Queen's Hotel, Sunderland.*
> *Week-end.*

I dare say this letter won't reach you till the second post. I've been very harassed today. A four hours rehearsal of Hamlet in the morning and then Mrs Sim came and had dinner with me and left me in time to get a nap and now it is 6 o'clock!

Well we opened to a very good house indeed with Romeo and the play went well for here; but they are terribly unenthusiastic, notoriously so; very attentive but quite undemonstrative. Last night they waxed somewhat more excited over the Winter's Tale but still well within the bounds of reason.

One paper here was extremely patronising to me over Romeo and held out polite hopes that I might with earnestness play the part some day. But I am accustomed to this sort of thing. The fact that I am my father's son (which after all is no fault of mine) is a red rag to the critical bull, and the creature frequently tosses me, whilst bestowing unreserved eulogies on Greet, Miss McCarthy and Westerton!

*However he's made some sort of retraction tonight over Leontes which
is very kind of him. Well the time draws nigh for Hamlet and to tell
the truth I'm not very nervous. I dare say I shall be as the actual
moment approaches but so far I feel a certain confidence, which may
be misplaced, or may arise from the fact that I feel the part suits me.
Let us hope the latter will turn out to be the true course.*

*I had a letter from Laurence this morning. He tells me he is
going to you on Sunday evening. I envy him. O Dorothea! Dorothea!
I am so sick of this tour and shall be glad to get back to town. Sunday
the 15th is a consummation devoutly to be wished and thank goodness
an inevitable one! As early as I can I shall be in London!*

*No I can do nothing with Jeffreys on tour. You know I have a
room in the Temple where all the materials for that great work are
stored. I sometimes wish I could afford to give up this acting and
go away quietly into the country with my books and papers and
finish the work which is very dear to me but these are dreams, the
product of an idle fancy.*

Such fancies, whether of the heart or of the head, were forgotten in
the surge of his performance and of the audience's response to it.

Queen's Hotel, Sunderland.
Friday.

*Well, my dear Dorothea, it is all over and I feel a worm this
morning; quite washed out after all the excitement; life seems to have
lost all purpose, etc. etc! You know the state of mind.*

*Well, if I may believe those who were in front, I got on far better
than I could have hoped or anticipated. And one moment in the evening
the audience testified to their satisfaction by an enthusiasm which was
certainly overwhelming to me, and very surprising to all concerned,
even to old E— who has played in the place many times and with
many different Hamlets. This was after the Play Scene.*

*With us a front cloth comes down directly after the scene; and the
king and court are seen hurrying across, followed by Hamlet, who
begins his scene with the recorders and Rosencrantz and Guildenstern
straight away. You'll see that by this arrangement the audience
cannot get a call for the Play Scene but no sooner did I appear with
Horatio following the king than they came down in a tumult of
applause, and for some minutes I could not go on with the scene. It
certainly was very gratifying, for they are an exceptionally cold
audience here; it is difficult as a rule to get even a call for an act out of*

them. But they did come down last night with a vengeance, and I think one may take it as a sign that they were pleased.

So I suppose I ought to be satisfied, when one considers one is only five and twenty, playing it for the first time on a week's rehearsal, and you know how different Greet's rehearsals are to London rehearsals. Of course it's a great and infinite part and one is only now beginning to realise it, but I think it suits me better than most parts and I shall hope to make something of it some day. And I ought to consider myself very very lucky to have had an opportunity of starting on it so early in my career.

I expect the impertinent gentleman in the 'Herald' who speaks of… Greet's 'Damas'[1] as the best ever seen in Sunderland, and passes Claude [Melnotte] over as a 'studied' performance with qualifications, will be very patronising about Hamlet, but, if it is any satisfaction to him, I have made up my mind very firmly not to read his precious and discriminating 'criticism' (God save the mark!)

Now no more of Hamlet. 'It wearies me, you say it wearies you'. Well you haven't said so, you're much too considerate to say anything so abrupt, but let me imagine it does, for, as I have told you, I feel so mouldy this morning that only the interest which you are sweet enough to take in my poor doings could have induced me to allude to the subject at all.

I am now returning to a rehearsal of Othello and will finish this on my return…

I have been to rehearsal and take up my pen again. Would you believe it, the Herald has written a notice of Hamlet which is certainly extraordinary, I send it to you at once. I certainly expected quite different at their hands, but you see even the dubious one has yielded at last. I'm sure you'll be glad to read it…

Adieu best of friends,
Ever thine,
Henry.

(What does that signature mean! I don't know!)

It meant, of course, that in Hamlet he had found himself—not only in Hazlitt's sense—'It is *we* who are Hamlet'—but in his success, however modest, in the part that had proved his potential as an actor and thereby had justified his stubborn determination to become one. It was this that for the first time inspired him to declare the deeper devo-

---

[1] In *The Lady of Lyons.*

tion that this signature, in spite of his equivocal parenthesis, implied.
Unhappily his declaration coincided with another outbreak of gossip
in the press.

> *Yes, it's too bad of these papers! Of course I see nothing of them,
> being practically in exile, so that I am as little affected by them as if I
> were in Armenia or Timbuctoo. But the annoyance it must give you
> causes me pain. Would it be any use for me to write to them and give
> them the lie? If it appeared in any paper of consequence I will do so
> with pleasure. Or ask Mr Cook to write in my name. He would no
> doubt compose a more discreet epistle than I should. I am altogether
> at your service.*
>
> *The whole thing is most impertinent and highly officious and it
> would be a pleasure to disappoint the curiosity of the rascals. I really
> think you will find that it will exhaust itself very shortly and, as soon
> as I get to town, I shall deal very firmly with anyone who brings their
> chatter to me.*

His reactions must have been more than ever perplexing to Dolly. Her
letters to him had always been cheerful and amusing, sympathising with
his worries and anxieties and making little of her own; now she confessed she was 'sick and tired to death'. This caused Harry a pang of
guilt—'Is it by some superhuman effort that you summon up your
good spirits for my selfish edification?' It had not occurred to him that
the remedy for her heaviness of heart was in his hands. Teddie and
Emmie were becoming exasperated, for their sense of propriety and
their concern for Dolly's reputation were beginning to make them
wonder if young Irving's intentions were entirely honourable. But the
days of Harry's indecision were numbered. In less than a month the
tour and the season of their separation would be ended.

A fortnight later he played Hamlet again in Edinburgh, in another
playhouse that had many paternal associations. For, in an earlier
theatre on the same site, my grandfather, after his false start in Sunderland, had served a three-year apprenticeship, and in the course of it
played, as 'walking gentleman', more than three hundred parts. In
those days the theatre, the Queen's, was under the management of
R. H. Wyndham and his wife, Rose Saker. When in 1883 Wyndham
pulled it down and built a new one, Irving, as a token of his affection
for his old manager, contributed £1,000 towards its cost, a gift that
Wyndham acknowledged by naming it The Royal Lyceum and
inviting the donor to open it with a performance of *Louis XI*. Wyndham

and his partner, J. B. Howard, prospered. Thus, paradoxically, my grandfather unwittingly helped to promote a theatrical octopus, the firm of Howard and Wyndham, that by gradually getting commercial control of the theatre robbed the actor of the authority and managerial responsibility that had been so laboriously won for him.

After his performance in Edinburgh Harry wrote:

> *Hamlet really went immensely on Saturday night. Three calls at the end of the play and people waving handkerchiefs and showing other signs of unwonted joy. Gilbert of the 'Scotsman' said it was the best Hamlet seen in Edinburgh for years, but he dared not say so in his paper, as such comparisons give offence. In any case it was the crowning event in my career so far (whatever that career may be) for I really felt from the beginning of the play to the end that the audience was with me and that at any rate in that part I have the power to hold their attention. It was all through a more enthusiastic night than Sunderland and of course a more cultivated and experienced audience.*
>
> *But 'something too much of this'. You see how exuberant my vanity becomes with a little success. If you are not sick of the subject by now, go and see Mrs Sim, she will tell you more. And then I will thoroughly sicken you of the subject by sending you the papers. What more can I do to show my gratitude.*
>
> *B.G. is very angry with Wyndham. He had arranged to play Othello and Romeo at Glasgow and the latter cut them out of his bill at the last moment without saying a word to him. It was ungentle-manly conduct at the best, and was all done to save fresh scenery coming into the theatre and interfering with his pantomime prepara-tions. W. seems to be a rude boor. Though his father and mine were old friends and he was in the theatre every night he never came near me. Quite unlike poor old Howard, a rough but good fellow—dead now as many good fellows have been before they could be spared.*
>
> *B.G. is thick in 'Dream'. Miss Bruce is passionately desirous to play Hippolyta but will, I have little doubt, be returned to Philostrate and washing the fairies. She complains pitifully to me of her 'drudgery', and certainly bathing promiscuous professional infants should come under that head. Poor dear! Smike's sorrows pale before hers! It is terrible when the dreams of Juliet and Lady Macbeth find their realisation in 'Mrs Triplet' and the tending of unclean children.'*

Edinburgh, owing very largely to the excellent theatrical fare that the

Wyndhams had provided over many years, had a discriminating theatre-going public and a newspaper with a long tradition of enlightened dramatic criticism. We can, therefore, even at this great distance, get a glimpse of the intention that lay behind Harry's interpretation of Hamlet and the manner of his performance. *The Scotsman*, reporting on his performance on the Saturday night, did not detect any sign of fatigue, though he had played Benedick ('characterised throughout with dash and verve') in the afternoon; at the end of the first act Harry, when he was recalled twice, knew that he had his audience with him, a stimulant that endows any actor with superhuman powers of endurance.

> *His Hamlet* [wrote the critic] *was an excellent piece of work— thoughtful, scholarly and well sustained from the rise to the fall of the curtain. It was not perfect, but it was more than promising, for in every act there was great achievement in it. He attempted no fantastical new readings; on the other hand, there was no blind following of tradition. Mr Irving had brought to the reading of the part his own cultivated intellect and imagination. His Hamlet was a living and vital personality, which from the first commended itself to the intelligent sympathy of the audience...The keynote of the impersonation was struck in the mental excitement and unsettlement of thought which results from the message of the ghostly visitor...He is the philosophising, excuse-seeking, mentally unhinged Hamlet, working under the domination of what to him is a monomania which colours his thought and action, and which leads him to sacrifice even his love for Ophelia, lest that passion should interfere with his purpose of revenge. This was the Hamlet which Mr Irving consistently worked out with admirable dramatic and elocutionary effect...The ear of the house he reached by his well studied and pleasing elocution; the intelligence of the spectators by the general appropriateness and convincing character of the impersonation, and by his well attuned accord between voice and action.'*

The last week in Hanley was something of an anticlimax. Greet wanted to end his tour with a flourish of *Hamlet*, but the parsimonious manager of the theatre would not change his bill. So Harry took farewell of the company he had led for more than a year as Claude Melnotte in *The Lady of Lyons*. Greet had made a few vague proposals for the future. Among them a performance of *Hamlet* at Camberwell in the spring, an idea attractive to Harry in that '...one could get some critics down without the folly and presumption of giving a performance in London itself which would be...an egregious blunder'. But Greet did not commit himself to any of his suggestions. Harry, on the other hand, knew that pleasant as the prospect of a few weeks leisure might seem at the moment, his affairs, artistic and financial, had reached a juncture that would allow him no rest.

He had accepted an invitation from his Oxford friend, Willie Goschen, to spend Christmas with him at his parents' house, Seacox House, near Hawkhurst. Mr George Goschen had just begun his second term of office as First Lord of the Admiralty. Twenty years earlier he had done much to restore the public's waning confidence in those responsible for Britannia's unopposed ruling of the waves; now, as on every hand forces were gathering openly and secretly to dispute her sovereignty, he was energetically overhauling and expanding the Navy, and with his considerable powers of persuasion had induced Parliament and the public to pay for it. Happily these distant clouds could not be seen from Hawkhurst in the twilight of that Christmas Eve, and Harry was more annoyed to find that his luggage had gone astray at the railway station. He was, however, able to borrow a dress suit from Willie and thus, *sans gêne*, could enjoy the convivialities provided by his kindly hosts.

> *Seacox House,*
> *Hawkhurst.*
> *Christmas Eve.*
>
> *They have just had a Christmas tree for the children or rather one child, and I am writing in the interval before dinner. They have presented me with a very charming and rather important looking writing case. It will go towards making me a person of some consequence on tour, if I walk about with it under my arm. Of course I shall do that when I feel in want of additional dignity. It will look so easy and natural.*
>
> *Tell Mr Cook there's a profusion of portraits in the dining room, one in the billiard room, a print of David and Goliath in my bedroom, and there, as far as I can see, the family pictures end.*
>
> *I hope the little gift reached you safely and that you will like it. I felt very inclined to post myself instead but it wouldn't have been so useful...Your letter was the only Christmas greeting I received, except a hairdresser's bill, but it made up for the absence of any others.*
>
> *I saw Laurence before I came away. He seems well and prosperous. He is to be at home all next week as they have a week out.*

His brother's improving prospects, and his presence at Gilston Road over Christmas, eased Harry's conscience and promoted a seasonal peace of mind. Laurence, after his brief spell with the Ben Greet company, had made an even briefer appearance at the Strand Theatre in a 'whimsical comedy and melodrama', *The Lord Mayor*. The play evidently fell between two dramatic stools, and the author-actor-manager, Harry Paulton, failed to find in it a profitable successor to his *Niobe All Smiles*. It ran only three nights, but long enough to come near doing the cause of English literature grave disservice. For among the cast was another of Harry's Oxford friends, Harold Child, a gentle scholar who had drifted on to the stage and by now was nearly convinced that he had no future as an actor. Clement Scott, seeking something to praise in this lamentable production, wrote of Child that he was 'a bright, intelligent and clever novice who showed great promise'. For a time this Leading Juvenile Gentleman's confidence was restored, though, happily, it had evaporated a year or two later when Bruce Richmond was looking for an assistant to help him edit the new *Times Literary Supplement*. For this part Child was perfectly cast and in it he enjoyed a lifelong run. Laurence, on the other hand, if only at rehearsal, had made the play serve as an experiment in dramatic hypnotism. For his appearance as a fraudulent theosophist 'of unearthly pallor and tragic demeanour' may have led to his engagement for Svengali in the *Trilby* No. 1 touring company. He opened at Torquay, where playgoers were, according to the *South Devon Advertiser*, 'unprepared for such genius'.

> *From his entrance until the weird awful death, he held the house spellbound. The lithe, nervous, commanding personality, the suggested demoniacal influence, the weird chucklings, the queer abrupt changes, were all vividly real. But the best of the superb performance was the suggestion of loss of vital power. With every effort of his will there was a supreme exertion of nervous force and the reaction has shown his wonderful power...the storm of applause which greeted him after the third act was a tribute to one of the cleverest performances we have seen.*

Even if Torquay did not lie in the track of stars of the first magnitude, its acclamation was heartening music for ears so long unaccustomed to the sound of applause.

> *All has gone well* [wrote Laurence to his mother]; *as well as the most sanguine of Laurence's well-wishers could have hoped. Great*

houses! Great notices! Great enthusiasm! And it was good news hearing what a success Lemagne had made simultaneously with Hamlet. Harry and Laurence are certainly bursting about a bit. Anyhow Laurence's star seems to be in the ascendant...I've not had much leisure these last days. The nerves of excitement and fatigue are just beginning to subside.

Happy and relieved as my grandmother was to read of Laurence's response to a breath of encouragement, she must have marked her elder son's proud show of indifference to praise or disparagement, in contrast to the younger's hunger for a crumb of critical comfort, and his deep despondency when critics failed to discern in his performance the height and purity of his ideals. Yet, of the two, Laurence was the more pliant and Harry the more rigid when expediency called for a readjustment of prejudices and principles.

So through that Christmas day Harry at Hawkhurst and Dolly at Tavistock Square thought of little but their approaching reunion. On paper their relationship had changed very much since they last saw each other; the significance of their next meeting was apparent to them both. As the evening drew in, Harry went for a solitary walk—'the woods and groves and the old church and other features of the landscape were at their saddest and best in the winter darkness'. Perhaps when he returned to tea at the welcoming fireside in the galleried hall, he knew that the prospect before him was tolerable on only one condition.

VI

THAT CHRISTMASTIDE Teddie had more than Dolly's dilatory suitor on his mind. He had just taken his last farewell of Mr Gladstone, who, now in retirement at the age of eighty-two, had dominated his life as a Liberal journalist. Thirteen years earlier he had written in one of his first leaders for the *Oxford Chronicle*: 'It used to be the boast of French kings to be able to say "the State, it is I, and I am the State"; so it is with Mr Gladstone. He is the Liberal Party and the Liberal Party is Mr Gladstone.' Now the torch that for so long had welded the Liberal party together had lost its heat; soon imperial issues and personal ambitions would engender dissensions that would prove to be a fatal weakness in the face of the Tories' ruthless unity. That last night at Hawarden Castle marked for Teddie the end of the simple loyalties and clear-cut principles that Gladstone had inspired. The G.O.M. had seemed vigorous enough. Through dinner (politics barred), while playing backgammon, and during a prolonged leave-taking of his guest ('I don't appear in the mornings now') he talked unceasingly on a wide range of subjects. Before they parted Teddie asked him what he thought of Joseph Chamberlain's colonial policy. Gladstone, smiling contemptuously, answered: 'Most mischievous!' and with that prophetic utterance went to bed.

In the early summer Teddie had done his best, after Gladstone's resignation, once again to rally the party and to recommend the policies of its leader, Lord Rosebery, to his readers. He and the new Prime Minister had much in common. They had met for the first time at Oxford. Teddie, as President of the Palmerston Club, had entertained him at dinner. Later Rosebery found him a 'gifted and delightful friend' whose opinions he sought increasingly as the years went by. Once, when Teddie had failed to keep an appointment, in gentle rebuke he said: 'You didn't come...it was like missing the morning sun.' Teddie's friendship for Rosebery did not make it easier for him when, shortly before that Christmas, Morley had appealed to him to mediate in the quarrel between Rosebery and Sir William Harcourt that threatened to split the Liberal party, now in some disarray after losing the election. Harcourt had never disguised his dislike of journalists and his ill-temper contrasted unfavourably with the sunny disposition of the Primroses. Teddie failed in his mission; had he succeeded he might have prevented the endemic factional disputes that have plagued the Liberal party ever since.

On top of all this he was, over Christmas, deciding on a step that would be the turning-point of his career. He had edited the *Westminster Gazette* for three years. He had made it a paper of influence out of all proportion to its circulation. The leaders of the Liberal party found it 'difficult to exaggerate as to its helpfulness'. But in those three years its proprietor, George Newnes, had spent £35,000 on it, and now claimed that it was still losing £250 a week; in return, he probably owed his recent baronetcy to its prestige and literary quality. Teddie could bear the paper's economic stress. But when Newnes complained to him that he found the paper was very uninteresting he was justly irritated as, no doubt, Newnes had been by his strong views on editorial independence. The time had come, perhaps, for them to part company. He had been offered, at Morley's suggestion, the editorship of the *Daily News*. Its offices were a few yards from his present one, and it was pledged to support the Liberal party, so that the move could be made conveniently and without prejudice to his political principles. A contributory factor in deciding to reorientate his life to the routine of a morning rather than an evening paper was his determination to take up the task of editing an edition of the entire work of his hero, Ruskin. He had already discussed the project with Alexander Wedderburn, Ruskin's literary executor, and had invited him to be his partner in this colossal undertaking which, with his own *Life of Ruskin,* would be his preoccupation for the next fifteen years. The editing of an evening paper occupied those morning hours that his collaborator could most conveniently put at his disposal; a morning paper would leave his morning free for work at home. His agreement with Newnes was for a three-year term; as that would end in January, a change seemed timely and desirable.

So, when Dolly told him that Harry would be coming to see them after Christmas, he was in a frame of mind to bring at least one of his problems to an issue. It was high time the young man declared his intentions and that Dolly, evidently wilting under the strain of suspense, should know what they were. And one way or another an end must be put to speculation in the press. Teddie was prepared to deal firmly with him, and the fact that Harry was on his way from a Tory stronghold did not incline him to leniency.

If Harry, during his solitary walk on Seacox Heath, had decided to let his heart govern his head, he would have been amused had he known the reception that was awaiting him at Tavistock Square.

In the event Teddie soon discovered that Harry had in fact come to ask Dolly to be his wife, and that his hesitancy had been the natural caution of a young suitor with very little in the way of worldly goods to offer his bride. This, too, had been his first opportunity for many months to make a proposal that could not be adequately expressed by post. When he and Dolly were at last alone together, if there was any sighing, they had no need to ask each other the reason, and all that remained was for them to ascend hand in hand the last flight of the stairs to marriage. There followed diplomatic exchanges between Tavistock Square and Gilston Road and the despatch of a cable to America asking the Antique's blessing on their betrothal. A few days later Dolly announced their engagement in the Green Room of the Haymarket Theatre, thus launching a thousand paragraphs already set up in type in a hundred newspaper offices. Apart from royal marriages and births, the gossip writers had not for a long time had such a delectable dish to put before the public. It was eagerly lapped up. Shop windows blossomed with 'cabinets' and postcards of the happy pair. If my grandmother had other matrimonial ambitions for Harry, she held her peace. After all, there must be something in a girl who had captivated both her boys.

They planned to be married in May but, hearing that the Antique would not be home from America until June, they thought it better to wait until July. *Trilby* would run until February. Meanwhile Harry needed work. An offer of a part in a play *The Fool of the Family* seemed immediately attractive. It meant that he would not have to tear himself away from Dolly and trudge the provinces. The respite was short. The play ran three nights and his second appearance in London was scarcely noticed. He was, therefore, in no position to resist overtures from Ben Greet.

In the first week of the New Year a play had been produced at the Lyric Theatre that, such is the incalculable sorcery of the theatre, had tickled the palate of the Victorian public with its appetising hash of religiosity and pagan sensuality. Though the critics scoffed at *The Sign of the Cross*, it happened to suit the mood of playgoers at that moment and they flocked to see it, ignoring the notices, most of

I

which made game of the author and leading actor, Wilson Barrett.

Wilson Barrett, now rising fifty, had no rival in the field of melo-drama. His episcopal good looks, his powerful physique and a resonant voice issuing from a manly bosom revealed by the habitual *décolleté* of his costume, inspired the admiration of his devotees and the derision of his fellow players. 'Here comes Barrett—bubs and all!' grunted my grandfather, as the darling of the gods approached the supper table at the Garrick Club. Content with supremacy in his chosen field, Barrett melodramatised it up and down the world, making and losing enormous sums of money. He was, perhaps, the most popular actor of his time. He was, moreover, a kindly man, generous to his own ruin and genuinely committed to the simple moralities he affected on the stage. In writing *The Sign of the Cross*, he had contrived for himself a vehicle that, without hurting Victorian susceptibilities, dramatised Christianity and allowed him as an actor to give full rein to his religious convictions and heroic powers. Shaw saw that the whole drama lay 'in the spectacle of a hardy Roman prefect, a robust soldier and able general, gradually falling under the spell of a pale Christian girl, white and worn with spiritual ecstasy'. Barrett was the first, perhaps, to discover the box-office value of an entertainment that administered the purge of quasi-religious experience in the appetising jam of voluptuous orgies and titillating tortures—a recipe that since has often filled the depleted coffers of Hollywood. If Nero played only second fiddle while Rome was illuminated by burning martyrs, it was because Marcus Superbus, the Prefect, played by Barrett, joined them in penitential rapture at the fall of the curtain. Such a play could hardly fail when sumptuously mounted and acted for all it was worth by a competent and well drilled cast. Though there was nothing epicene in Barrett's virile exhibitionism, it was apt to defeat its own ends. 'The one conspicuous and laughable oversight', wrote Shaw, 'is in Mr Barrett's own make-up. Instead of wearing the proper cropped Roman wig, he wears his own hair in his old familiar feminine fashion, with the result that when he first steps on the stage...instead of applauding him, I stared with a shocked conviction that I had a lady before me in the costume of a Roman warrior. The effect is amusing; but it spoils an otherwise manly picture.' *The Sign of the Cross* not only enabled playgoing clergy to extol unashamedly from their pulpits the evangelical mission of the theatre, but planted in the gestating mind of a critic and dramatist-to-be an idea of the fun to be had with such a theme when it came to writing *Androcles and the Lion.*

Laurence Irving, *circa* 1892.

Harry Irving at New College, *circa* 1894.

H. B. and Dorothea Irving in J. M. Barrie's *The Wedding Guest*.

Ben Greet's brother, William, had acquired the provincial touring rights of Barrett's piece. Ben, having disbanded his own company until the spring, was glad to fill in the time as Nero. After a week or two William became dissatisfied with his Marcus Superbus and his 'worn Christian', Mercia, and, no doubt at Ben's suggestion, invited Harry and Lillah McCarthy to take over those parts. Harry, with new responsibilities staring him in the face, and chastened by his second failure to make a mark on London, reluctantly accepted the offer on condition that when Ben reassembled his own company *Hamlet* would be included in the repertory.

Harry joined *The Sign of the Cross* company at Oxford, where his memory was sufficiently green to ensure him a warm welcome on and off the stage. He was rapturously received at Rawlinson Road by Daisy, who had long been privy to Dolly's infatuation for him. As a prospective son-in-law, the handsome but intimidating young play-actor can only have added to their mother's growing conviction that the world she lived in was less comprehensible than the firmament she raked with an astronomical telescope through an attic window, or the kingdom of heaven that was so confidently mapped for her at the church of St Philip and St James. Harry paid a dutiful visit to Mary and Arthur Smith, whose philosophy was not much troubled by the intrusion of the arts, least of all by the one in which Dolly had attracted more attention than might be good for her. He was amused by Mary's caustic comments on the weaknesses of others, and attributed her disinterest in his and Dolly's profession to the fact that, as she boasted, having never been without a baby in her arms since her marriage, her mind was wholly concentrated on maternity. He complimented her on her recently delivered sixth daughter, though to Dolly he confessed that he found the infant 'very red and of a weird appearance. No doubt when that first blush of modesty in a new and inquisitive world has worn off it will have acquired the necessary assurance and uniform colour that such confidence bestows.'

While at Oxford, he managed to persuade Dolly's family that the wedding should be in London. The Cooks were agreeable to this and to the reception being at their house. For the majority of their friends and for the public, whose curiosity was being stimulated by the press, this would be much more convenient. Among other old friends whom he revisited at Oxford was William Hutton of St John's College, who gladly agreed to conduct the service that would be held in St Pancras Church.

After this pleasant and opportune week at Oxford, the tour realised his pessimistic expectations. With the exception of Lillah McCarthy, the company were strangers to him. For all their faults and follies the Old English Comedians engendered a domestic warmth. Now no mock trials or other spontaneous jollifications enlivened the tedious Sunday evenings; the daily rehearsals that so often had seemed burdensome were sadly missed. The company appeared to be made up of married couples who thought it improper to speak to anyone but their spouses. 'They are', he complained to Dolly 'all intrinsically dull, so if they did revel it would be tedious.' He found a kindred spirit in a young actor, Scott, who to his surprise turned out to be the son of Dolly's persistent critic. His mother and father had parted when he was a child, and since then the latter had ignored him. He was a bright intelligent youth, with his quota of du Maurier charm. They made common cause of their broken homes. Harry, from all he heard, was thankful that the Antique, whatever his shortcomings, was not like Clement Scott, a sentimentalist—'...invariably the most heartless and unfeeling of creatures in all those relationships in life that demand real and true qualities and not the falsetto make-believe of so-called emotions'.

The small provincial towns were all too familiar; the only compensation for their slated, chimneyed uniformity was the enthusiasm of their unsophisticated audiences. His Marcus Superbus was everywhere well received. Wilson Barrett liked him in the part so well that he asked him to play it in America. With Dolly to play Mercia this, after their wedding, might have been an attractive proposition—but nothing came of it and, perhaps, the Antique had been wise in warning him against it. The hotel rooms were bleaker than ever and his separation from Dolly a keener vexation. The few hours snatched on occasional Sundays at Tavistock Square and Gilston Road were hardly worth the torture of recurring farewells, compared to which the sufferings of Marcus Superbus seemed a light affliction. Now and again, in the mahogany recesses of a sitting-room, he found a dissonant piano that, as he ploughed his way with reckless brio through a favourite opera score, made his own company less intolerable. With Camberwell in the offing, *Hamlet* was constantly on his mind, but he was sick of study and longed for rehearsals. So, when early in April the Shakespeare and Old English Comedy Company reassembled at Southampton, his old friends appeared to the martyr as ineffably lovable as a revelation of the heavenly host.

Dolly joined them at the Metropole Theatre, Camberwell, for

Greet's Shakespeare Festival to play Rosalind. Harry was to play
Hamlet, Romeo and Jaques. *As You Like It* had gained strength from a
new Orlando—Mr Bernard Gould, the sobriquet of Bernard Partridge,
the brilliant draughtsman who had already begun the graphic record
that alone would convey to posterity the splendour of the Lyceum
productions. Among the metropolitan critics condescending on
Camberwell were William Archer and Bernard Shaw. The latter, after
asserting his reluctant Bardolatry, found 'Mr H. B. Irving . . . in the full
flood of that Shakespearian enthusiasm which exalts the Bard so far
above common sense that any prosaic suiting of the action to the word
and the word to the action seems to be a degradation of his genius to
what Nicholas Rowe called "a mere light of reason".'

Unfortunately Shaw arrived late for an afternoon of Shakespearean
snippets, to see among others the closet scene from *Hamlet,* into which
Harry may have concentrated all the energy he normally expended on
the whole play.

> *He was resolved to make an effect by seizing the Queen and throwing*
> *her down on the floor; and the moment he selected was in the middle*
> *of the following passage:*
>
> At your age
>
>   The heyday in the blood is tame; it's humble,
>   And waits upon the judgment; and what judgment
>   Would step from this to this?
>
> *The Queen was floored after the phrase 'and waits upon the judgment',*
> *shewing that at Mr Irving's age the heyday in the blood does not wait*
> *upon the judgment, but has its fling (literally) regardless of reason . . .*
> *Nevertheless, the performance, nonsensical as it was, was not*
> *ridiculous. Mr Irving is not altogether unsuccessful in his attempts*
> *to be tragic and to make effects; and if he could only bring his tragedy*
> *and his effects into some intelligent relation to the drama in hand, he*
> *would find himself highly complimented in the Saturday Review.*

It was on this occasion that Dolly drew Shaw's waggish fire at her
Rosalind. Though she and Harry may have smarted under his penetrating badinage, they were sensible enough not to underestimate the value
of the merciless but salutary dramatic criticisms that would enliven
that paper for the next decade. Archer conceded that Harry had
'unmistakable gifts' and that he gave 'a gallant and picturesque performance as Romeo, though his voice lacked tenderness, intensity or
passion'. 'If only', he added, 'Mr Irving would find time and opportunity

I*

to cultivate his very real talent instead of Marcus Superbussing about the world.'

Harry was not downcast by the strictures of these two fastidious but eminently sane critics. He knew as well as Archer that he was wasting his time in the shadow of Wilson Barrett, and that he had exhausted the benefits to be derived from rudimentary productions of Shakespeare. It was, therefore, with immense relief that, while he was at Camberwell, he had an offer from George Alexander to join him at the St James's Theatre in a season of romantic plays at £20 a week. This meant that he could leave Greet shortly before the wedding and could take up this engagement after the honeymoon.

After the 'Festival' that Dolly's presence had alone made festive, the resumption of the tour at Birmingham was an anticlimax, and the prospects of the weeks ahead a melancholy one.

> *Grand Hotel, Birmingham.*
>
> *My own dear love,*
>
> *Here I am without great spirits, great voice or great anything at all …It is a damp and depressing evening and I wish the week was well over. I thought bitterly of the last time I was in Birmingham Station when I alighted from the train. Then you were with me and I bade you God speed with Trilby! And you looked so sweet and loving in your fur cap! Oh! Why am I here at all? To the lions with it all! I nearly came to see you on my way to Euston, but I didn't feel I could stand parting from you again! Write to me as often as you like, and don't be diffident and think I don't love every line you write, for I do to all eternity as I love you. O, Dolly, it's no good. I am wretched without you! Pray for me!*
>
> *Yours loving desolate*
> *Harry.*

For an actor loss of heart is the *sequela* of loss of voice. Archer had detected the first symptoms of what a doctor diagnosed later as 'clergyman's throat'—an ailment that Harry attributed to an excess of playing his sanctimonious part. By the end of the week, after playing Romeo and Hamlet in one day, he became speechless. He reached Wakefield only to take to his bed and give himself up to a regimen of hot baths, eucalyptus and ammoniated quinine. Rejoining the company at Sheffield, he had the good fortune to fall in with a friend of his father who was staying in the neighbourhood and proved to be the ideal companion for a depressed convalescent.

I had a pleasant surprise [he reported to Dolly] *which promises to beguile in some fashion the ennui of this woeful town. Whilst I was having my dinner who should walk in but old Henry Kemble (do you know him, the actor, member of the Garrick, an amusing creature). He is stopping at Buxton for his health and came over here to see a friend, and reading my name looked me up, for which I am eternally grateful to him.*

I am going over to lunch with him at Buxton tomorrow and so breath again for a few hours, for squalor and reeking dust and all manner of vile town pests infect the air of this miserable waste of dirt and ugliness...at all times drunken men seem to reel about and every face looks sodden and beastly.

Henry Kemble, though short and portly, had a powerful presence on and off the stage. He came of a family that had dominated the English theatre for 150 years. Mrs Siddons was his great-aunt; Fanny Kemble was his aunt, who had adopted him and provided for his education. At last a long line of heavy tragedians had produced an incomparable comedian, timely born to interpret the more subtle style of comedy that was on the way. Already his pungent observations were treasured and circulated by raconteurs—his imitable delivery of them adding to their rotund humour. His utterances were heralded by a fretful bass tremolo that rumbled in the recesses of his double chins, and on these waves of sound he launched drolleries that long survived him. It was he who, after seeing the Jubilee procession, described Queen Victoria as 'a ruby set in jet', and when one of her inspectors of taxes grew importunate, he warned him sharply that he must 'tell the Berkshire widow that she cannot look on me as a perpetual source of income'.

Dolly was paying the price that society exacts from popular players by enlisting their charms to advertise its works of charity—though, for the most part, they are willing victims, responding to an audience of any kind like flowers to sunlight. Trilby was still the rage and her appearance behind a stall at a bazaar could be guaranteed to stimulate sales. At first she found this amusing, but soon there were too many such functions, entailing too much standing about all day before her performance at night. One of them, a theatrical bazaar, produced an embarrassing peace-offering in the shape of a large wedding cake that Clement Scott bought and with a flourish presented to her. Having denied her one of his usually sugared notices, this was at least a token of his approval of her as the daughter-in-law of an actor who in his eyes could do no wrong. Reconciliations were in the air, for at about the same time Scott and Tree, like Tweedledum and Tweedledee, decided to resolve their quarrel. When the news of this reached W. L. Courtney, he commemorated it with a ballad that ended:

> Press! Let thy trumpeters announce
> An echoing strain through all the lands!
> Great men their enmities renounce
> And Tree and Scott have shaken hands!

When Harry reached Bolton at the end of May he found there a pleasantly macabre surprise awaiting him. During that week the public was reading in the newspapers of the last hours of Mrs Dyer, who was awaiting well-deserved execution in Newgate Gaol. She had been a baby-farmer or foster-mother and had been convicted of murdering a number of her little charges while continuing to pocket the money she received for their keep. Harry and Dolly, who by now shared his interest in crime, had followed closely a case which was particularly repellent to one whose conscience was already stirring with concern for the wretched lives and premature deaths of under-privileged children.

I see [wrote Harry] *the trial of your dear friend Mrs D. begins today. What a pity you are not here and being here are not a man, for then you might go and be shaved by the Hangman who is a barber in this town. In any case he might cut your hair. I went to the shop this morning but it didn't look inviting from the shaving point of view and as he doesn't like people calling on him in his official capacity, I didn't go in, but I shall hope to get a glimpse of him. Billington is his name. He will have a good lot of 'jobs' as he calls them at Newgate in a week or two if all goes well.*

Harry, however, stalked the modest executioner at first in vain.

Bolton.
I haven't seen the Hangman yet. He hasn't been to the play, though he is very religiously minded, preaches on Sunday and turns people out of his shop if they use bad language. He fitted himself for his present high office by experimenting on cats and dogs. He always goes to the theatre when he comes back from a 'job' and once when there was a play with some hanging in it he was there every night.

In the event he had to leave Bolton without having had a glimpse of his quarry; worse still, he had heard that Dolly would not be at Tavistock Square to greet him when his tour ended. But the week at Blackburn had its consolations.

Blackburn.

The wanderer, the exile returns after four weeks of lonely despair only to find that you are going off at the earliest opportunity to Oxford to take part in this pastoral masquerading. Practice! How can there be any practice in a thing of which the physical conditions make acting *impossible and encourage all the worst faults that can be acquired by a necessarily forced and inexpressive style. I despised the thing before, now I abhor it. But go and play on the grass! Only don't call it practice or acting because it is neither. And if you're going to leave me, leave me for something better than Mr Ben Greet's Woodland Folly! I hope it will rain very much and be quite horrid.*

Having mildly *expressed my anger I shall take a new nib (this one is worn with the vehemence of my indignation) and resume the story of my life during the last 48 hours which will be found not to be without its tragic moments.*

On Monday night I had the McCarthys to supper. All the shops being shut the poor things had been living on eggs all day, so I took them in after the play and gave them meat and drink. They seemed to enjoy themselves.

Yesterday I went to Bolton, a journey fraught with adventure. I lunched with Mr Ellison heartily and drank a good deal of some very fine and old Port (the importance of this detail appears later on). After lunch, instead of sitting quietly, I hurried him off to see Billington the Hangman. He was at home, we saw him and mirabile dictu! (remnant of Latin) we had our hairs cut by him. And well cut too. He had a sure and careful hand. He is rather a forbidding looking man and seems to relish putting criminals out of the way. He speaks of it with a gloating kind of satisfaction as though he were doing a very good thing in ridding the earth of such vermin. A man told me his great pleasure as a boy was killing vermin of the rat type. His father was in an asylum. The man really seems to have been born with a kind of passion for execution which beginning in rats and mice has ended in vermin of his own image. Quite an interesting character, original, and I've had my hair cut by him so I have not lived in vain.

Well, Billington interviewed, I departed for Blackburn and then the trouble came. Whether it was the lunch or the port or the hurryings about but in the train I felt quite miserable. You have seen me en route for the Channel Islands. Well I felt like that, ready to die at any moment. I would have welcomed Billington as a happy deliverance. More dead than alive I got home as I thought at 5.30 and flung myself on my bed. But my watch was an hour slow and the next thing I remember was someone coming over from the theatre and telling me it was a quarter past 7! By something little short of genius I was on the stage at my time and got through the performance. But it was a tragic day and the deception of my watch was a cruel piece of treachery on the part of that companion...

Well, my father has wired me that he goes to London today, so you will see him. Have no fear. You cannot fail to make him very proud and pleased with his daughter! And I am sure he will think a great deal more of me when he has seen what a treasure I have found in his absence. You are my greeting to him on his return and I am awfully glad he has gone to London that he may receive it at once and rejoice, as I know he will, accordingly...

I shall expect a full *very full* true *and particular account of the scene between*

Sir Henry Irving
and
Miss Dorothea Baird

I love you except when I think of the Pastoral Plays and then Othello is tame by my side. The first week of my return too! More coming and going and meeting and parting. If I didn't love you so much and despise P.P.s so heartily I should be calmer.

Dearest farewell,
Harry.

When in due course Billington exterminated Mrs Dyer, Harry noted that she 'did not hold out to the last. You see it doesn't require much courage to squeeze a little baby's neck but it does to let Billington squeeze your own'.

The despatch of Mrs Dyer coincided with the arrival of my grandfather from America. From Liverpool he went directly to London, returning again two days later to start a short provincial tour before his coming season at the Lyceum. The public on both sides of the Atlantic had been kept fully informed of his triumphant progress through the United States and of the banquets, receptions and academic honours that had been strewn before him like laurels on his line of march. He had attracted enormous sums of money into American box-offices, and his share of them amounted to £75,000. But the expenses of transporting and maintaining his large company, and the vast accessories of scenery and properties, had whittled this down to a profit of a mere £7,000—a trifle when it came to replenishing the depleted coffers of the Lyceum, and a poor reward for the expenditure of so much of his time and energy. Though he was not given to self-delusion, his sanguine temperament (so much a part of his genius) may have masked the sense of foreboding that these figures should have inspired. The affectionate farewells of his American admirers and the adulatory paragraphs heralding his return gave no hint that he was entering his climacteric year—not, perhaps, as an artist but as the proud autocrat governing the prime theatre of the world. If he had any inkling of this he kept it to himself; the public, his friends and his family continued to regard him as an indestructible institution. Harry's only concern, therefore, was that his father should share his love and admiration of Dolly and that she, free of ingrained prejudices, might win his affection and so help them all, including Laurence, to a more sympathetic understanding of each other. He was glad, in a way, that he could not meet the boat:

> I didn't go to meet him at Liverpool because I couldn't get an accurate account of the boat and because such meetings when he is mobbed by the fulsome and the curious are always unsatisfactory to both of us. I shouldn't have got a word in and as I don't think I have Mr Craig's craving for advertisement I stayed away. But I have written to him and told him I shall try and stop with him in Manchester the week we are at Preston...
>
> I am wondering and thinking of you. Has the great meeting, to which that of Wellington and Blucher is but a wayside greeting, yet taken place? or are you still in the throes of fearful anticipation? If the former has occurred, I have no doubt it has been quite as satisfactory as that of the two historical personages I have mentioned. If not, then you must have no more misgiving than they had. For they had already won their battle before they met, and as you have not had to depend on the issue of any battle at all, why should you be less confident?

Two others awaited Irving's return with equal impatience. Laurence was eager for news of the production and reception of his play *Godefroi and Yolande*, which Ellen Terry, true to her promise, had persuaded his father to put on for a few performances in Chicago, she herself playing Yolande the leper. She was able to tell the author that those who saw it, in spite of its unpleasant theme, recognised the genius of the little piece and 'received it splendidly'. The Antique, though he found it distasteful and put it on only to indulge his impulsive partner, went out of his way when talking to reporters at Liverpool to praise his son's talent and to forecast a bright future for him in the theatre. 'Did you see', Harry asked Dolly, 'the interview with him in the D.T.? Half of it was devoted to Laurence, which is nice for him and will raise him in the public estimation, for on such things does that estimation depend. I am sure nobody has deserved it more for he had worked hard and amidst much that was discouraging.'

Very different was the reaction of another frustrated dramatist to whom Ellen Terry sent the laudatory notices of Laurence's play in the *Chicago Tribune*.

9th March, 1896

Ellen Terry: What do you mean by this? Have you no respect for my years, my talent, my reputation, my feelings, that you play these games on me? Here is a newspaper—a miserable American newspaper—containing a monstrous statement that you insist on playing the part of a—a—no: I cannot write it, speak it, think it. Far be all such horrors from you for ever and ever and ever!

'And he went out from his presence—a leper white as snow.'

How could you have the heart to threaten me with such a thing? Do you want me to go out from your presence also white as snow, blanched by a tormented, wounded heart? Wretch! perverse, aluminium-hearted wretch! I do not know any other way of expressing the lightness, the hardness, the radiance of that centre of your being.

Ugh? It is not an idea, but a pain too deep for surgery.

Let me shake it off. To business!

Shaw's business was to get Irving, with her help, to produce his own play *The Man of Destiny*. This other piece that Ellen Terry had carried in her knapsack drew only a polite and non-committal response from my grandfather—though in reporting this to the author she translated it into her own hyperbolic idiom as 'H.I. quite loves it and will do it finely!' This was the signal for Shaw to begin the skirmishes before the fortress of the Lyceum (using her as a partisan vedette) that would be the comic sub-plot to the drama of Irving's year of adversity.

Meeting a young woman like Dolly was a new and, as it turned out, delightful experience for the Antique. Though she could not have concealed her very proper awe and respect for him, she showed no trace of sycophancy nor of any self-conscious effort to please him. She was so transparently unaffected, so lacking in cautious reserve, so frank in her expressions that he found it hard to believe that she was an actress; for she bore no resemblance at all to the egocentric professionals of his company, who too often imagined that their flattery and shallow reverence impressed him. Yet here she was, the talk of London; and it had taken her as many months as the years it had taken him (and Ellen Terry, for that matter) to win its homage. Yet as she chattered away to him of Harry and their plans for the future, he saw that she and another young actress, Lena Ashwell, who had played Elaine to his King Arthur, had much in common. Perhaps they were the prototypes of the better educated and more percipient actresses that the exemplary theatre he had striven to create would need in the future. And, when he and Johnnie Toole compared notes about Dolly and found themselves in complete agreement as to her charm and intelligence, he saw his intractable and moody son, who had wooed and won such a bride, in a different and less austere light.

Dolly's report to Harry of her visit to his father reached him as he was starting out for Liverpool for a reunion with him that he hoped would usher in a change in the climate of their relationship—the chill of mutual suspicion giving way to the warmer promise of a home where the Antique could be sure of a welcome and an easement of his loneliness.

York.
June 1st.

I can't tell you how glad your letter made me. I told you the meeting would not be awful and it has turned out triumphantly. You have come away with a father's blessing which I have since heard was no empty form.

Well I journeyed to Liverpool and reached there about 4. Who should I meet but E.T., Marion and Craig all in a carriage going to meet my father. I followed them and greeted the Ancient about 4.15 on the platform of Lime Street Station. He rallied me on my beautiful straw hat and was altogether in a most gracious humour. No sooner had we got into the corridor of the hotel than he confided to me his opinion of you, told me I was very lucky indeed and con-

gratulated me most heartily. I offered no serious objection to any of his remarks on this head.

E.T. was effusive on the same subject and said she is going to give you a miniature of my father which she values as one of her most treasured and sacred possessions. I can only say that it is much better in your hands than hers. She was very cordial and well meaning, but she is a nonsensical creature. They all had dinner with us after which my father and I withdrew and talked into the morning. I told him all the news, he asked when we were to be married and seemed to quite approve of July, and Bloomsbury as a place of abode...I have never known him so really friendly before, I mean in the sense of treating one more intimately and as a son. He spoke very nicely of Laurence too and altogether between you you seem to have cheered him. He looks very well and unchanged...

When is the wedding to be? When will Tree let you go free? I don't think E.T. will give much trouble. When she sees you you must expect to be flopped on and gushed over, but I don't think she'll expect to be asked to the wedding and will be quite content with giving us her blessing...I hope my father will contrive to be present for many reasons, though I think he means to go away for his holiday pretty soon after he returns from the tour.

Harry's hopes that the Ellen Terry situation would resolve itself were confounded, not by her, but by those who could see no further than the end of their noses, that for years had been scenting the air for any gossip that would serve to colour their caricature of Irving as a libertine. Needless to say, the clouds that threatened the bright prospect of the wedding blew up from South Kensington. The O'Callaghans (with the exception of D.O'C, who was snoozing through the evening of his life in the lobby of the United Services Club under a tasselled smoking cap) were working themselves up into a frenzy of conjecture as to whether Irving would be at the wedding, and if so, whether Ellen Terry would be there too. My grandmother had already swallowed her pride and appealed to her husband to attend their son's marriage. By this time she had made her righteous indignation known to Teddie and Emmie, who in turn communicated it to Dolly. When Harry heard of his mother's ridiculous qualms, he had the last word on a subject that had been a burden to him all his life.

I am sorry [he confessed to Dolly] *all this E.T. business is cropping up again in South Kensington. How wretched it is! I had*

*hoped they would have spared you all unpleasantness. Whatever the
whole business means my father is now at an age when the matter
may surely be set at rest, and the family linen not washed to every
newcomer. Heaven knows it is distressing enough to Laurence and
myself to be planted in the midst of all this scandal and we have
done our best to steer some sort of course between it. And why all this
excitement? I don't anticipate any trouble from E.T. She is not so
blind or foolish as yet.*

*You will have to meet her as I met her and be rather bored by her,
but she will not want to come to the wedding or to our house or do
anything that might be inconvenient. It is too improper on their part
to attempt to dictate to you at all in the matter. If they don't know
you well enough by now (and by their protestations one would think
they did) to know that in such a matter as this you are your own
guide of what is right and you can have no better guide than your
nature, then they must acquire that knowledge.*

*It is a difficult position but a little forbearance and wisdom might
have spread one the necessity of ever troubling you with the subject
and have enabled one to quietly take the line we have always con-
templated and so avoid all difficulties. That line we shall of course
take, but it will be wiser of others to leave us to ourselves. They can
get no good by interfering. But I must confess I had hoped that
perhaps the time had come when this luckless affair might be passed
over and surely there could be no better time than when a sweet young
girl like yourself has brought so much happiness and so many bright
and kindling hopes and sympathies into the family to forget whatever
might mar the promise of her coming.*

Dolly, having had her pastoral fling, returned to London and to the
now urgent task of finding a flat. Emmie, no less appalled than Harry
by the prospect of the wedding and by the logistics of accommodation
at the church and the reception that had to be revised almost daily,
had an influenzal *crise de nerfs*, leaving Teddie to deflect Dolly from
rash decisions, and to help her make up her mind when a small but
pleasant flat was found in Southampton Row. For Dolly's comfort
it was within hail of Tavistock Square, and for Harry's convenience
only a few yards from the Reading Room of the British Museum;
its front windows caught the afternoon sun that, after it had set,
would be put out of countenance by the newly installed electric light.
The Antique, suddenly alive to the pleasures of paternal responsibility,

had been assiduous with enquiries and suggestions; but, as became the impresario of the Lyceum, his ideas of mounting their marriage were out of all proportion to their resources—his area of search being limited to Mayfair and Belgravia. When, however, he heard that Dolly had decided on Russell Mansions, he showed his approval by sending her a cheque for £500 so that, as Harry said, she could go shopping 'with haughty mien and head erect having at her back well lined coffers'. He had yet to learn that, erect or not, her head was screwed on the right way when it came to business and to the planning of a home, and that an inability to even affect a haughty mien was an asset when it came to picking up bargains in the Cumberland Market and in second-hand furniture shops. Her letters to him were now illustrated profusely with sketch plans of their new home, drawn with inherited skill. He was most concerned with the bestowal of his books— '... It must all be left to you except when I interfere with worrying criticisms and become teasingly captious for the sake of my being captious. I know you love me so much when I am in these moods.' She did—and their well matched sense of the ridiculous helped her to distinguish between competence and bossiness, and him to understand that habits indulged by a doting mother were better not imposed upon an adoring wife.

Harry's pilgrimage with Ben Greet, that had led him to this supreme happiness and had weathered him from a gifted amateur into a skilled and disciplined professional player, ended characteristically. In York, while the Old English Comedians played the staff of the Lunatic Asylum at cricket ('not covering themselves with that glory that might be expected from such good Christians') Marcus Superbus spent the afternoon among the inmates. During his last performance at Preston the gas men rose to the spirit of the occasion.

We have never had such an enthusiastic audience as it was last night. The piece went like wildfire. This was some compensation for playing in a very poky theatre and the most extraordinary limelight effects I have ever encountered. During the revel scene Miss McCarthy and I were purple coloured, the last scene varied between pitch darkness and a kind of tremulous twilight that was most distressing. But it didn't matter, the audience enthused all the more.

The next day he wrote the coda to the romantic duet that he and Dolly had played together through the long months of their segregated wooing.

No more, the last page, the last words are being written. We shall never be separated again until we have been 'joined together' and then we shall endure parting better for we shall belong to each other and shan't mind lending ourselves occasionally to the necessities of a profession to which we owe our greatest happiness. We can afford to be grateful and generous then!

On Sunday I shall take you in arms which have been so long robbed of their precious burden, and no cruel train will drag away on Monday.

Your longing and expectant
Harry.

It was now settled that July 20th should be the date of the wedding. The Antique had at last made it clear that he would not attend it. No doubt his infallible audience-sense warned him that this was not a very suitable occasion for staging a reconciliation with Flo and that, from his recollection of her, the scene might very easily get out of hand. Harry and Dolly, appreciating the hazards, accepted his decision perhaps with unspoken relief. Laurence was less tolerant, and in the old vein wrote indignantly to his mother:

The Antique has only put himself once more in the wrong. Ah, how unsatisfactory and insufficient he is! He has as yet given no shadow of a reason for not coming to the wedding. But I don't think it's worth troubling oneself about such a shifter. I never thought any good would come of your writing to him; he has evidently determined not to be there.

My grandmother's forlorn invitation cannot have been very whole-hearted; for the encounter, whatever may have resulted from it, could not have added to the harmony and tranquillity of her son's marriage. Perhaps unknown to her, Harry and Dolly had asked my grandfather to join them for the second part of their honeymoon at Bamburgh, and to this he had agreed with evident pleasure. Though no Forster of the Bamburgh line would lead Dolly up the aisle on her wedding day, she remembered her Northumbrian ancestry when she ordered her wedding dress from Fenwicks of Newcastle, on condition that it was made on the part of their premises in Northumberland Street that was the stone house built there by her grandfather John Baird, the surgeon.

The morning of July 20th was bright with the promise of a fine day. It was as well, for by 9 o'clock crowds were surging into Tavistock Square and into Upper Woburn Place, the short approach from the Square to St Pancras Church. Emmie and Teddie had their hands full helping Dolly, preparing for the reception, and keeping at bay the crowd that thronged their front door.

The arrangements for the service were in the hands of the vicar of St Pancras, Luke Paget, a dear man radiating dreamy compassion but scarcely able to organise himself, let alone such an affair as this wedding promised to be. His wife, Elma, having a well developed sense of fun, had early appreciated the situation and decided that, *faute de mieux*, she must put her hand on the affair. Early that morning she tried to alert the police to keep order, but they refused to believe that, as she said, 'a star turn of the playhouse could draw a royal crowd as if queens were parading'. They were hardly to blame, for this was the first time the public showed its infatuation by mobbing a popular player; in years to come such demonstrations would be commonplace and often discreetly organised by publicity agents; this was the first that ever burst spontaneously upon the astonished targets of its acclaim. What Elma Paget knew of Harry and Laurence made her wonder if they had remembered to get the special licence, without which her husband could not officiate. At about 9.30 a.m. she fought her way through the crowds to Tavistock Square, where she found the Cooks happily and vaguely in despair. She suggested to Teddie that he should put a notice on the door to keep out the uninvited, and to warn people that no more tickets were available for the service. Absentmindedly he wrote the notice on the back of one of the coveted tickets and pinned it on the door; in a flash it was gone, and another uninvited ticket holder was on his way to add to the congestion in the church. There were, of course, no telephones. Mrs Paget, having imparted her doubts to Teddie, with his help sent off a message that she hoped might reach the bridegroom and the best man.

Having struggled back to the vicarage, she busied herself in the preparations for the luncheon that she had arranged for Harry and his brother. She was justly proud of the *chef d'oeuvre*—a brace of pheasants from the ice-house on the Norfolk estate of her father, Sir Sam Hoare, the banker who shared with his neighbour, Savile Crossley of Somerleyton, a passion for shooting and the parliamentary representation of the county. When Harry and Laurence turned up they were full of gratitude for the timely message, having indeed forgotten all about the licence; they had been able in the nick of time to get one on their way. At luncheon, Laurence tucked into the delicious and unseasonable birds; Harry, in no mood for this rare experience, paced nervously up and down the hall. When the time came for them all to leave for the church, they had to take a circuitous route by the Euston Road to avoid the crowds besieging the church, and to make their entrance through the vestry at the back of it.

The floor and galleries of the great basilica were crammed to capacity. The friends of the bride and bridegroom were equally matched in numbers. Behind Dolly's mother and sisters and the latter's large families were ranged rows of Bairds, Brintons and Crossleys. Anne Baynton, having wheeled Daisy into a commanding position between the front pew and the lectern, sat near her charge, nervously clasping and unclasping her big, capable, ceremonially white-gloved hands. Across the aisle Flo was supported by Gran and the Morgans, the only surviving O'Callaghans; D.O'C had not been encouraged to leave his club; the Donovans were not invited to leave Ludgate Hill. Under the shimmering gasoliers, that shone like great moons from the dark canopy of the church, celebrities of the world of affairs and letters eyed with curiosity the company of distinguished theatricals who, with practiced composure, gave the impeccable performance that the occasion and the setting called for. All rose to the opening bars of 'The Voice that Breathed o'er Eden'.

Down the aisle came Dolly on Teddie's arm, the court train of her white satin dress borne by six of Mary's daughters and Vera Morgan. She carried a bouquet that was the gift of the Antique and was his proxy. Ben Greet, by right of being the only true begetter of this union read the lesson with the husky clarity of a ship's captain conducting a service at sea. Laurence, by some miracle of organisation, produced the ring at the right moment. The responses of the bride and bridegroom were firm and clear. The stairs to marriage were behind them.

William Hutton, who must have been aware of Harry's scepticism, drew from Shakespeare and the Brownings the text of an address perfectly attuned to the sentiments of that heterodox assembly.

How can I put in words for you the wishes that your friends are thinking as I speak—for you who have so much before you, as we hope and believe, of all that may raise and brighten and inspire the lives of others? He who wrote the song for Hymen when he brings Rosalind

*to her father and her lover could speak for us; or he who sank to rest
with Cymbeline at his pillow: not we for ourselves.*

*It was an old custom, George Herbert tells us, to say when light
was brought into the room 'God sends us the light of Heaven'. It is
true of the light of life, for all of us; most of all for the artist, for all
those who see visions, who live among ideals, whose joy it is to present
characters as GOD made them, and man marred...'I lived' said she,
who had written The Cry of the Children, 'I lived with visions for
my company instead of men and women...nor thought to know a
sweeter music than they played to me.' How beautiful a life
it was among the visions: yet how far transcended by that ideal
marriage!*

*It is a new world: the old lies 'wrecked behind' us. 'Hark how
Ariel sung overhead! What splendour in the heavens! What marvels
of beauty about his enchanted head! And, O you wonder! Fair
Flame! by whose light the glories of being are now first seen.'
Yes, Ferdinand and Miranda stand still, as our great master sees,
as pictures for the new life that begins, for us all, with love.*

And he ended:

*So go brightly and boldly forth together...True marriage cannot be
ended. It is the new life into which GOD has brought you, and it is
eternal like the life and the love of GOD.*

*And the future? In the great hand of GOD you stand, and what is
to come will be given you by Him who has given you today. Work,
and He will reward: love, and He will bless. We, as we have prayed
today, can still pray.*

'And with GOD be the rest.'

'For thus it was and is, and shall be ever more...' The echoes of the
great thanksgiving hymn died away. Over Dolly and Harry, kneeling
below the altar, Luke Paget pronounced a benediction that, if the
efficacy of the transmission of divine benevolence can be measured
by the simple godliness of the intermediary, meant that they were
indeed blessed.

An incongruous party assembled in the vestry to sign the register
—the First Lord of the Admiralty, Tree vaguely benevolent, Arthur
Smith cheerfully aggressive, Laurence pale and distant with emotion,
and Teddie very much alive to their incongruity. They regained their
places in the expectantly murmuring congregation. The wedding

march pealed out. Harry led Dolly confidently down the aisle; after them streamed the wedding guests, telling each other that it had been as pretty a wedding as they remembered. They came blinking into the sunshine and heard the cheers receding as the bridal carriage drew away from the church. Other carriages picked up their elegant cargoes and clove their way slowly like icebreakers through the press of sightseers. When the last had delivered its occupants to No. 6 Tavistock Square, as it drove away the crowd closed in, eyes bent expectantly on the balcony outside the drawing-room on the first floor. At last, in response to sustained shouts of 'Trilby! Trilby!' Harry and Dolly came through the open window and waved their thanks for the ovation. They were called again and again until Dolly appeared finally alone with a champage glass in her hand and toasted the host of her admirers with an all-embracing gesture. Not until the carriage had borne the bridal pair away towards Euston Station did their well-wishers, tired but content, begin to melt away.

At Hayburn Wyke Harry and Dolly found peace and contentment after the rapture and confusion of their wedding day. Only now they realised how rarely and for how short a time in all the months, since that day in Birmingham when they became aware of their mutual destiny, they had been able to enjoy the quiet study of each other that would be the foundation of their happiness. They had the place to themselves, and they discovered in each other an unsuspected zest for tramping over the moors and clambering down crumbling chines to rocky coves wedged between the sea and the beetling cliffs. 'We are happy indeed,' wrote Harry to his mother. 'What more can I say or you wish?...For I know that if you are satisfied of this your heart is light.' Dolly endorsed this with an appeal to her to superintend the redecoration of the flat, asking her to see that 'the two long bookcases in the drawing-room are stained a deep walnut...I think white would look a little trivial for the Newgate Calendar'.

Bamburgh, by contrast, was a well-manned family fortress. The Smiths held the southern approaches between the castle and their crowded house, St Aidans; the western outpost, the Victoria Hotel, was occupied by Aunt Jane Baird, cheek by jowl with the Antique. Dolly had taken a cottage near the Wynding Lane, where older inhabitants remembered her as a long-legged schoolgirl wandering up from the sands strumming on her guitar. Now she led Harry off to picnics on the Stag Rocks; while she sketched with an inherited facility for laying on pure luminous washes of watercolour, he browsed and nodded over his books. There they received from Laurence the first act of a full-length play he was writing on Peter the Great of Russia. 'It is worthy of him,' Harry reported to his mother; 'we have shown it to the Antique who is delighted and full of confidence. He is very well.' Mary's boy, Lionel, now at Rugby, was summoned by my grandfather to dine with him at the Victoria Hotel; he found his host kindly, awesome but, as always, aloof. Once more Harry made his short sight an excuse for avoiding organised games. Arthur Smith, a dynamo of intellectual and physical energy, would rope in everyone he could muster to play violent games of hockey with walking sticks and a tennis ball on the hard smooth sands at low water; with lower jaw out-thrust and whiskers steaming in the slipstream of his velocity, he rushed up and down, like a character of Edward Lear, exhorting his team to 'go like billy-o!' and tackling his opponents with a ferocious disregard of age or size. Further up the beach, near the high water mark, Mary sat with her latest babies, smiling inscrutably as, stitching and piping and smocking, she tried to keep pace with the ever-increasing demands for sun bonnets and pinafores.

All too soon their honeymoon was over. They returned to London and to the possession of their flat. Wedding presents in their planned positions were milestones along the road that had led them to Russell Mansions—over the fireplace, three views of Stratford-upon-Avon given them by the Old English Comedians, and in the hall, a handsome grandfather clock that ticked a constant reminder of the tactful absence from the wedding of its donor, Ellen Terry.

Dolly found a letter of greeting from the Antique.

My dear Dorothea,

Welcome, welcome home—and thank you for the picture which I was delighted to get.

Would you be able to come to Cymbeline tomorrow (Saturday) night?

If so, you can have my box and come round during the play and we'd all have supper afterwards in the Beefsteak Room. I know Harry will come—he's always ready for a bite of something to eat.

Affectionately,

H.I.

A bride might well have bridled at her implied failure to nourish a ravenous husband; but Dolly knew by now that of the few indulgences her lonely father-in-law allowed himself, wining and dining his friends was his favourite one.

Harry at once began rehearsals for taking over the part of Rupert of Hentzau in Alexander's production of *The Prisoner of Zenda*. Dolly set about organising the domestic routine peculiar to the lives of players—the late breakfasts, the quiet hours for rest before the performance, and the leisurely relaxing suppers afterwards. She had a natural gift for cooking, and soon learned the suppertime uses of a chafing dish and the temperamental advantages of not keeping the servant up late.

At the Lyceum *Cymbeline* was in the middle of its three-months' run. It was a success in terms of everything but the box office—for it brought in barely enough to pay for its costly production. Again the applause of his devotees deafened Irving to signals warning him of his financial insecurity. With Ellen Terry in her fiftieth year affecting, as Imogen, 'a divineness no elder than a boy' and Irving, nearing sixty, coming as fresh to Iachimo as he had done to Synorix in *The Cup* fifteen years ago, the Lyceum troupe lulled theatre-goers into an acceptance of its apparent agelessness—and, for once, won the qualified praise of the *Saturday Review*. Early in December Dolly began rehearsing with Harry at the St James's for *As You Like It*, which Alexander was bravely putting on with a novel absence of 'cuts'. As Phebe and Oliver they found themselves stepping back to take a look at their own shortcomings as Rosalind and Jaques, measured against the erratic charm of Julia Neilson and the sound competence of Frank Vernon.

By the middle of the month London theatre-goers were keenly anticipating Irving's revival of *Richard III*. It was twenty years since he had restored Shakespeare's text and had given a reading of the part that exorcised for ever the preposterous demon portrayed by his predecessors. With a more mature reading and with a worthier production he felt he could count on it to redress the adverse balance of his theatre's accounts. Harry and Laurence, though appalled to hear of the accident after the first night that crippled him, and virtually closed the Lyceum for several months, were unaware of its grave significance.

Dolly, sharing Harry's determination to be independent of his father, was thankful that being both in work they had been able to make ample provision for the arrival of her baby in the spring. Unfortunately Phebe, the shepherdess, tightly corseted in a costume of indeterminate period could not for long conceal a fecundity that led the audience to suspect Silvius of being more than neighbourly. Regretfully, my mother had to leave the cast, but not before I had suffered pre-natal stage fright that sowed deep in my subconscious the seeds of a recurring nightmare that I must appear in a play having totally forgotten my words.

So she bore me to that Easter morning. Lazily I absorbed the diffused pattern of light and shade that gradually resolved themselves into my mother and the topsy-turvy view of skies and ceilings that for months are the perspective of a baby lying on its back in its cot.

I had a kindly reception from the Press, apart from the *Daily Telegraph*, which announced me first as a girl and, by correcting this the next day, gave the impression that my mother had had twins. *The Court Circular* opined: 'May it some day be said of the son and the grandson, as it was said of Sir Henry Irving, "They were honoured in their generation and were the glory of the times".' *The People* hailed 'the entrée of the latest offshoot of the Irving family as... almost a national event'. The *Morning Post* rashly predicted that 'the boy will probably carry on the acting traditions of the Irving family'. It was in any event unlikely that these sanguine hopes could be fulfilled. For, oddly enough, it occurred to nobody in Fleet Street to wish me luck, and without a generous measure of luck, millions of male babies born in Europe in 1897 would have a slender chance of reaching their majority.

APPENDIX

Towards the end of September 1954, while staying in Rome, I received the following letter from Sir Max Beerbohm:

Villino Chiaro, Rapallo.
20th September, 1954.

My dear Laurence Irving,

You may conceivably remember that at that long-ago dinner of E. V. Lucas's at the Orleans Club I told you that I had once written an account of my first meetings with your Father, and had afterwards told him about it one night at the Garrick, and that he was much amused.

Well, the B.B.C. wishes me to 'record' any unpublished 'things' that I may happen to have, and it has occurred to me that this thing (with one or two others) might be suitable; but I wouldn't dream of using it without consulting you. It might very likely seem to you disrespectful to your Father's memory.

So would you please read it and not for one moment hesitate to say Nay instead of Yea.

The B.B.C. technician will be here on Thursday the 30th of this month. So would you please let me have your answer rather quickly? With all good wishes and great respect,

Yours very sincerely,
Max Beerbohm.

Ladies and Gentlemen,

Almost thirty years ago I wrote, but for one reason and another didn't publish, a few little essays about meetings with interesting contemporaries of mine. One of these essays was about my two first meetings with H. B. Irving—Harry Irving, the elder son of Sir Henry and father of Mr Laurence Irving, whose biography of Sir Henry is assuredly the vividest and best that any actor has ever had.

This little essay I will now read to you.

In the autumn of 1890 I was a freshman at Merton College,

281

Oxford. I was a year younger than most of the other freshmen, and was young even for my age. Except in my very last term at school I had been wearing Eton collars. I was not yet accustomed to collars that stood up. I was a child. Not so Harry Irving.

It was young George Bancroft who presented me to him. He, too, in his way, seemed to me very wonderful. He was so finished and formed—so perfect a little man of the world; a perfect miniature both in face and in costume, of his father, Sir Squire Bancroft. But he did not frighten me. His eyes had the famous twinkle of his mother's, and they had twinkled very kindly on me when he came to call on me and to invite me to breakfast with him on the following Sunday. He was a Brasenose man, was in his third year, and had lodgings in St Giles. 'I'll ask Harry Irving and some other fellows,' he said, in quite a casual tone.

Two or three of the other fellows were already there when I arrived; and two or three others followed. I was presented to them all. They seemed very tall and easy and important, and I thought it impossible that they would remember me if they saw me again. George Bancroft wore a smoking-jacket with quilted facings of blue silk. This summed up for me the possibilities of adult grandeur and emancipation. It was the symbol of all that a Sunday morning at school was *not*. Yet anon it was to be as naught in my eyes— it and the man in it, and all those other men. For anon the door flew open: in, with the paternal forward tilt of the body, came H. B. Irving.

As he crossed the threshold, he said in a deep voice, 'Ha!' He clapped a hand on Bancroft's shoulder, rather in the manner of a very eminent detective arresting a very unimportant thief. Then, with that hand still on that shoulder, he distributed nods and 'Ha!'s' among the company—the company of 'supers'. His gaze alighted on *me*.

'This,' said Bancroft (with the pride of a 'super' who has a line to speak), 'is Mr Beerbohm, of Merton.'

'Ha!' He had a way of looking at one through his pince-nez, less intimidating only than a way he had of looking at one over his pince-nez.

'Ha!' he repeated. And then: 'A brother of Beerbohm Tree, aren't you?'

'A half-brother,' I said faintly.

'Ha!'

It was as though he had said 'That may or may not be an extenuating circumstance. I will consider it.'

We were to have breakfast downstairs. Bancroft led the way. The others instinctively let Irving go out next. I felt I was almost on terms of equality with these others now, and found myself talking quite glibly to one of them on the way down.

Our host was at the head of the table—topographically. But spiritually and truly, and to all intents and purposes, the head of any table at which H. B. Irving seated himself was just where H. B. Irving sat. I do not remember much that he said; he may not even have said much; but his manner was such that anything said by him had at the moment the effect of a Standard Work condensed by him for the occasion. The name of a well-known public man was mentioned by somebody. Irving seemed for a moment to search his memory. 'I once met him at supper,' he said, 'at my father's.' Just that. No more. But it somehow—by some miracle of cadence and glance and eyebrow—implied an adverse and irrevocable judgment. That well-known man had been paraded, inspected, seen through, dismissed: the less said about him the better. And moreover, as I was to find, there always was in H. B. Irving's way of saying 'my father' something which brought to bear on one suddenly and personally the full weight of the Lyceum tradition. True, he always carried that weight around with him, as it were, but it seemed to come down on one with special force whenever 'my father' was mentioned.

It was as 'Young Irving' that he was always spoken of by the undergraduates at large. The adjective seemed rather ill-chosen but it implied no disrespect. As was Old Irving's fame in Great Britain and America, so was Young Irving's in Oxford. In the year before I matriculated he had appeared as King John in Shakespeare's play, and had been highly praised by the many critics who travelled down from London to see him. If not perhaps one of the most eloquent speakers at the Union, he was certainly the most impressive. He had made a special study, too, of Judge Jeffreys, and had read a paper about him to more than one Essay Society. And he was a student of Criminology, and was to practise at the criminal Bar when he 'went down'. Walking up the High, 'Look,' one undergraduate would say to another, 'there goes Young Irving,' and in Hall that evening he would say 'I saw Young Irving in the High today'. Young Irving's rooms were in Radcliffe Square, and it was natural that he often should pass up and down the High on his way to and from them; but the sight of him was never taken as a matter of course. It was always something to have just seen him. And oh—to have just met him at breakfast! I wonder to how many of my fellow freshmen at Merton did I in the course of that memorable Sunday say, as lightly as I could, 'I met Young Irving at breakfast this morning'.

I knew now, after this face-to-face meeting, that the lightness of Bancroft's 'Harry Irving and some other fellows' had been a histrionic assumption. I hoped I was carrying off my own assumption equally well. I tried to make my eyes twinkle in the Bancroft manner. But I think they were yet obviously the eyes of a child who had been frightened.

What a terror to witnesses was lost by Young Irving's abandonment of the Law! True, the days of Sergeant Parry were no more. The tone of the Old Bailey had already been dulcified to that pitch of suavity and ruth which is the key-note of our modern life. Young Irving would have somewhat restored the fine old traditions, showing even from under his stuff-gown the ermine of Judge Jeffreys. Perhaps ere the time came for him to exchange stuff for silk, he would have mellowed. For he did within a few years delightfully mellow; and it may be not really so wonderful as I like to think—not such a sign of later powers developed in myself—that I achieved the habit of calling him 'Harry'. But not at Oxford did the mellowing process begin. And when, one day, I received an invitation to lunch in Radcliffe Square, I quaked as at the services of a writ, and was gratified as by a royal command.

The summons was for the following day. I read it several times. Then I leaned out from my ground-floor window, deeply inhaling. A fellow-freshman was crossing the quadrangle. I greeted him: 'Can you lunch with me tomorrow? Oh no, by-the-by, not tomorrow: tomorrow I've got to lunch with Young Irving. The day *after* tomorrow?'

Within an hour or so, by repetition of this formula, I had accumulated quite a large party for the day after tomorrow. I forget whether it went off well. I remember only the previous day.

It had not struck me that Irving and I might be alone. Else I might hardly have dared to accept. Down went my heart like lead in water when, punctually presenting myself on the threshold of his room, I saw, together with my vision of his back awfully silhouetted against the bow window, covers laid for two. Covers? I knew that I could not hide under my plate.

Probably I uttered a cough, for I remember the suddenness with which the silhouette veered round and said 'Ha!' to me.

I dare say that you, like me, often at important junctures think suddenly of some outrageous thing that you *might* do, and of the appalling results there would be if you did it—results so appalling that for an instant, in your horror, you feel that you actually *have* done the thing. There was for me a gruesome instant in which I felt that I had Ha!'d back at Irving.

The relief of finding that I had not done so seemed to inspire me with a sort of jaunty confidence. I found myself quite articulate indeed, fluent. At school I had been thought clever. 'Has natural abilities of a rare order'—this phrase from a form-master's report came floating into my brain. Why should I not impress myself on Irving today as a man with abilities of a rare order? He seemed to be inclined to draw me out. Let him be astonished with the draft. Let him get more than he bargained for. I thought of David and Goliath. But—what if Goliath had looked at David over his pince-nez as Irving looked at me over his? I felt that what I babbled was in no way remarkable. I felt I had no abilities of *any* order. That form-master had been a fool. So was I. Already, though luncheon had hardly begun, I was seen through, over that pince-nez. I was asked many questions, to which I gave the feeblest and most rambling answers, foreseeing all the while one question which especially I dreaded. Perhaps, thought I, hoping against hope, this question would not be put. But at the end of the meal came a silence which I knew could terminate in only one way. Irving had risen from the table and offered me a cigar. Never having smoked a cigar, I took a cigarette. Irving cut and lit a cigar for himself, motioned me to an arm-chair, flung himself on the sofa, propped his elbow on the back of it, propped his brow on his hand, and over his pince-nez looked at me. 'And what,' he asked, 'are you going to do in after-life?'

'Well,' I said—and the poor monosyllable came out as a poly-syllabic bleat, 'We-e-e-e-ll', after which the other poor words came out in three separate gasps sped by a weak smile—'as a matter of fact I'm—I'm thinking of—being called to the Bar.'

And these words, at the very moment of utterance, became

untrue. I *had*, up to that moment, vaguely destined myself for the Bar. But in expressing to Irving this ambition, I saw the full absurdity of it, I for good and all dropped it before he had time to say (as he did with more than his usual gravity say) 'Ha!' My weak smile, my gasps, the blush burning my brow, had forced this plain moral on me: I was *not* for the Forum. I suppose that in any case I should have discovered this truth for myself fairly soon; but the fact remains that I discovered it then and there by stress of Irving's presence. I did not let him know this. I was too proud to say 'But please, Sir, I've just changed my mind. I'm not for the forum—oh no, Sir! The forum's for you, Sir!' Indeed, I rather resented his power over me; and so glad, presently, was I to be out on the doorstep in Radcliffe Square I not merely could have danced: I did, actually, dance...I was only a child, remember.

I was touched by his typically courteous submission and wrote at once to assure him that, far from being disrespectful to my father's memory, his essay would give to all who remembered my father (and indeed to those who had never heard of him) the same pleasure it had given its subject over the long table at the Garrick Club. A week later my wife and I spent the day with him at the Villino Chiaro and, as it turned out, took our last farewell of him on the vine-shaded patio where we had sat so long after luncheon, listening entranced to his variations on this theme.

INDEX